Symbols in Northern Ireland

To Tom, Ben, Sam and Dan

Symbols in Northern Ireland

Edited by
Anthony D Buckley

The Institute of Irish Studies
The Queen's University of Belfast

First published in 1998
The Institute of Irish Studies
The Queen's University of Belfast

This book has received support from the Cultural Diversity Programme
of the Community Relations Council, which aims to encourage
acceptance and understanding of cultural diversity. The views expressed
do not necessarily reflect those of the NI Community Relations Council.

British Library Cataloguing-in-Publication Data
A catalogue record for this book is available from the British Library.

ISBN 0 85389 692 5

Set in 11 point Times Roman
Printed by W. & G. Baird Ltd, Antrim

Cover design: W. & G. Baird Ltd.

Contents

Contributors

Linda May Ballard BPhil, MPhil is Textiles Curator at the Ulster Folk and Transport Museum, and has lectured and published very widely on many aspects of Ulster's folk life and folk and popular culture and art.

Dominic Bryan MPhil, DPhil is a Research Officer at the Centre for the Study of Conflict at the University of Ulster. He is joint author of two reports on disputed parades in Northern Ireland.

Anthony D Buckley MA, PhD is Curator in Anthropology at the Ulster Folk and Transport Museum. He has written on folk medicine in Nigeria and on ideas, social interaction and identity in Ulster.

Ciro De Rosa PhD has recently concluded a thesis for the degree of Dottorato di Ricerca from the Instituto Universitario Orientale, Napoli on the symbolic practices and ethno-national identities in Northern Ireland.

Neil Jarman PhD has written on parading and visual displays in Northern Ireland as a facet of popular culture. He is working at the Community Development Centre, North Belfast, running a research project on violence in interface areas.

Mary C Kenney PhD has written on ethnic conflict and identity in Northern Ireland, focusing particularly on parades and the politics of neighbour-hoods. She has also undertaken field research on the Afrikaans-speaking 'ultra right' political parties in South Africa.

Michael D McCaughan BA is Head of Transport at the Ulster Folk and Transport Museum. He has written on Irish popular and vernacular culture with special reference to maritime transport. His photography has been exhibited in Ireland, Britain and the United States.

Camille O'Reilly MA, PhD has been investigating aspects of the Irish lan-guage movement in west Belfast since the early 1990s and is now devel-oping more explicitly comparative research which will focus on different language movements in Europe. She currently teaches anthropology at Richmond University, London.

Jack Santino PhD is Professor of Folklore and Popular Culture at Bowling Green State University and Editor of the Journal of American Folklore. He has written extensively on American rituals and celebrations, and is working on the public uses of symbols in Northern Ireland.

Roger Sawyer PhD is an historian who has specialised in two main areas, Ireland and the modern anti-slavery movement, topics which were united in his books about Roger Casement. In 1985 he received the Airey Neave Award for Research into Freedom under National Laws.

Illustrations

The illustrations are reproduced by kind permission of the following: pp. 3, 7, 26, 33, 69, Ulster Folk and Transport Museum (which is now part of the National Museums and Galleries of Northern Ireland); pp. 54, 58, C O'Reilly; p. 90, N Jarman; p. 118, J F R Martin; p. 119, W Middleton; p. 128, J McGilloway, pp. 139, 149, Lagan Lifeboat Visitor's Centre; p. 156, M C Kenney; p. 183, R Duffy.

The cover illustrations are a detail from a White Star publicity booklet, 1911, in the collections of the Ulster Folk and Transport Museum; biker Ian Gourley of Bangor, Co. Down, reproduced by courtesy of the Ulster Folk and Transport Museum and Mr Gourley; and a UFF mural Lord Street, east Belfast, 1997, reproduced by kind permission of Neil Jarman. The back cover illustration (which is referred to on page 88 of the text) is of a mural for the visit of President Clinton, the Falls Road, Belfast, 1995, also courtesy of Neil Jarman.

Introduction

Daring Us to Laugh:
Creativity and Power in Northern Irish Symbols

George Orwell is supposed to have made a joke about Hitler and Stalin. Hitler and Stalin, he said, had something in common. They both had funny moustaches. This was not, he claimed, an accident. On the contrary, he said, Hitler and Stalin were 'daring us to laugh'.

THIS interdisciplinary collection of essays had its origin in an exhibition called *Symbols*[1], put together by Rhonda Paisley in 1994, which displayed some of the symbols found in Northern Ireland. Inevitably, the exhibition included many of the political and religious symbols which have had so much impact in Ulster's troubles. There were banners and sashes and policemen's helmets and holy statues and so forth. However, the exhibition also contained other kinds of symbols whose political impact and local significance was less obvious, from a picture of Jimi Hendrix to a housewife's apron.

The essays in this volume are similarly concerned with the symbols found in Northern Ireland. Some are to do directly or indirectly with the Troubles of Northern Ireland, and with matters relating to ethnic or religious or national identity. Dominic Bryan and Ciro De Rosa look at the vexed question of parades, the one looking at the evocation of meaning in press coverage, the other more directly at the use of parades in the construction of social boundaries. Camille O'Reilly examines the symbolic significance of the Irish language. Neil Jarman discusses murals. And Mary Kenney looks more eclectically at republican symbolism.

Other chapters are much less directly concerned with Ulster's celebrated social division. Thus, Linda Ballard looks at the symbolic costumes of motor-cyclists; Jack Santino examines Hallowe'en customs; Roger Sawyer discusses the symbolic images of womanhood in Irish literature; and Michael McCaughan considers the *Titanic*.

Significantly enough, however, even with the latter essays, it proved difficult to omit matters relating to ethnicity. Ballard's motor-cyclists, for

1

example, are not concerned centrally with sectarian issues, yet their clubs and associations tend to recruit only from one side. Sawyer's viragos are found in a literature which long predates modern conflicts, yet they are ripe to be used as models for modern women engaged, for example, in the politics of feminism or in sectarian strife. And Santino's essay on Hallowe'en, though it is concerned with one of the least sectarian of Ulster's festivals, is nevertheless able to identify important sectarian undercurrents.

Symbolism in Northern Ireland is often a serious business. Many of the symbols discussed in this collection of essays are a focus for passionate loyalties. Some have been the occasion for self-sacrifice or murder. Anyone who approaches the question of symbolism in Ulster soon feels on his neck the hot breath of these passions.

As the *Symbols* exhibition was being constructed, it became obvious to the organisers that many of the symbols on display were powerful and dangerous. In displaying them, one had to employ great care and caution. If the exhibition contained a hint of irony or disrespect, then one felt that some huge foot might come out of the sky and squash the organisers flat.

In this introductory essay, I want to explore some of the reasons why symbols are so powerful and dangerous and why one should treat them with caution: why the organisers of the *Symbols* exhibition, but also politicians and quite ordinary people, are right to be afraid of them.

I want, however, to look at another aspect of symbolism which many of the contributors to this book identify. This is that there is much more to symbolism than just politics and power. Symbols are also a means though which people clarify the world.

Seldom does any symbol have a single meaning. Symbols are therefore a means through which individuals grasp and express new and significant truths about their individual identities and about the world. Symbols, however, may not be taken lightly, since they bring both order and disorder. If they arise out of human creativity and spontaneity, they are also about power. If one were foolish enough to be disrespectful about symbols, then someone could take quite serious offence, the symbol becoming the focus for anger, tears, violence and the exercise of control.

Symbols have a life of their own. They beckon to us, tempting us to treat them with disrespect. Symbols are like Hitler's moustache. They are 'daring us to laugh'.

Symbols and the clarification of the world

The first part of this essay will be concerned not with power, but with the intellectual aspects of symbolism. Looked at like this, the main purpose of a symbol is to throw light on some aspect of the world that would otherwise be neglected or confused. Then I shall consider the other side of symbolism, that which deals with symbolism as a matter of the relations between people, and this involves questions of power.

According to Dan Sperber, a symbol is an object or a piece of knowledge which is in quotes (1975, 99). We see a picture of King William or Cú Chulainn on a wall, and we know that it is quite different from (say) a picture in a passport photograph. In the same way, we know that 'Free Derry Corner' is not 'just another wall' nor the *Titanic* 'just another ship'. We know too that a wedding ring is quite different from (say) a curtain ring. But we also know that, in the right circumstances, a curtain ring can *become* a wedding ring, full of the same meaning as its gold counterpart. The symbolic picture, the symbolic wall, the symbolic ship, the symbolic ring gain their meaning through having been set aside. Symbolic objects have been bracketed off from ordinary objects. They have been highlighted, elevated, put in quotation marks. And so we look at them and know they are symbolic.

More that this, a symbol evokes some other idea beyond itself. A symbol is like coloured glass. We look through it and see the world beyond. But as we look through the glass, our vision of the world is altered. A symbol

Figure 1   *Mural of King William, Donegall Road, Belfast, 1989.* Ulster Folk and Transport Museum.

draws our attention to certain structures, certain patterns in the world. But at the same time, it hides away other structures, other patterns. Any given symbol, therefore, is partial. It reveals a real or a possible pattern in the world, but it also hides away other possible patterns, other realities.

The first thing to say about symbols then is that they clarify some aspect of the world. A symbol draws attention either to the way the world *is* or to the way it should be, or perhaps to both. A symbol defines some segment of the world, so we can see that this strip of events (Goffman 1975) has a recognisable structure (see also Buckley and Kenney 1995, 25ff).

Take times and occasions. Many people in Northern Ireland's past (and of course some people today), want Sunday to be a special day. The problem with having such special days, however, is that they are in constant danger of *not* remaining special. A special day is always in danger of becoming 'just another day'. The only way to keep Sunday special, therefore, is to mark it out symbolically.

So, in the past, certain activities were forbidden. Work especially was forbidden. But also people could not play cards or use a skipping rope or play football. They had to sit quietly and read uplifting books. Just within living memory, elderly Presbyterian farmers used never to shave on a Sunday. Shaving, for them, was a form of work. Instead, they would shave late on Saturday night (see Buckley 1982). Symbolic acts like this were what made Sunday special.

In a different way, Christmas is kept special by filling it up with presents, trees, crackers and drink. Without this symbolism, the distinctiveness of Christmas too would disappear. Every day would be equal.

Days have a tendency towards equality, they tend to become undifferentiated. So when we want to keep them special, we must deck them out with symbolic markers.

Sunday, of course, is already losing its specialness. But the dangers of not using symbolic markers can be found in any standard work on seasonal customs. How many people, for example, took note of last Michaelmas Day? Buchanan tells us that, once upon a time, people might have killed a goose or a lamb and had a small feast at Michaelmas (1962, 34). But with the disappearance of its symbolic markers, Michaelmas has disappeared from all but the diary. The same is true of Chalk Sunday, the second Sunday in Lent. On Chalk Sunday, single people were marked with chalk to signal their failure to get married (Ó Danachair 1964; Danaher 1972. 47–8). Hardly anybody, nowadays, has heard of Chalk Sunday.

And the process occurs in reverse. People continually invent new festivals and new ways of symbolising special occasions. For example, in comparatively recent times, people have started to give Father's Day cards. Even more recently, Catholicism has discovered a new seasonal custom, that of commemorating the dead at Cemetery Sunday.

The point is, however, that special occasions are always in danger of disappearing, in danger of becoming undifferentiated, equal to other occasions, if they are not symbolised.

Symbols and the definition of identity

Importantly, symbols are also used to clarify, to define and give structure to identity, to who a person is. The problem each person faces is that although they may be a Buddhist, or a housewife, or a bus driver or a splendid fellow, these different definitions of a self tend to slide away (Goffman 1959).

Famously, in Northern Ireland there is quite a range of items of information which function as symbolic devices allowing people to tell who is a Catholic and who a Protestant. These include what school you went to, what your name is, what area you live in, and how you say your alphabet, as well as such things as whether you have an interest in certain kinds of music, sport, politics and so forth (Burton 1978, 37ff). Some of these identifying markers have now acquired legal force in, for example, the enforcement of fair employment legislation.

But it is not always clear who *any* person may be at any given moment. We all occupy different social statuses. We all have a gender, a marital status, a social class and perhaps an occupation. But once we get away from these broad categories, our identity is much more subtle.

So we all devote much energy to dramatising who we are. The rites of passage are only the most obvious of these symbolic dramas. Rites of passage allow us to step clearly from one status to another. But on a more casual basis, we engage in symbolic social dramas (Burke 1957; Turner 1982) all the time. We kiss our children, we telephone our mothers, we have coffee with our friends. And we choose not to do these things with other people whom we prefer to keep more distant (Buckley and Kenney 1995, *passim*).

All these little dramas – some of which we call 'rituals' or 'ceremonies' – are symbolic of the broader relationships that we have with these people; they make them clearer. Particularly where a relationship or identity is not grounded in a legal or some other institutional arrangement, there is a danger that, without the symbolic drama, the relationships (and the identities which the relationships define) might disappear altogether.

Thus a man who neglects to greet his friend will soon find that their friendship has sunk into a generalised mass of undifferentiated acquaintanceships. He will find himself demoted so he is one among equals, none of whom is very special. Conversely, if he makes love to very many of his female acquaintances, he will soon discover that the symbolic meaning of his act has become devalued, and that, for him, no one woman is special.

As Don Alhambra remarks to the Gondoliers, 'When every one is some-bodee, then no-one's anybody' (Gilbert 1889, 543).[2]

And of course, if people take part in social dramas in order to define themselves, they must also dress for the part. Acting is all very well, but an actor needs to have props.

Linda Ballard shows how, for Northern Irish bikers, the black jacket (combined with accoutrements such as tattoos, badges or helmets) has quite a complex symbolic content. But more generally, nearly all the things a person owns or purchases can symbolise his or her identity. Hats, houses, clothes, cars: all these things tell us about the person who owns them. We all buy goods knowing that other people will use these objects to find out about us.

It is impossible to be innocent in these matters. Whatever we buy, it allows someone to label us.

One cannot buy a newspaper innocently. If I buy the *Guardian*, you will guess I hold liberal opinions. You may guess I am, perhaps, a social worker, or a teacher, or in one of the creative professions. If I buy the *Sun*, you will make other guesses. Lord Salisbury remarked that the *Daily Mail* was written 'by office boys for office boys'. This is no longer true, but we can nevertheless infer something about someone who reads the *Daily Mail*. Just by carrying a newspaper, I begin to define myself, because I thereby allow you to define me.

In the past, a top hat or a bowler could make a man appear more posh or more respectable than he might otherwise seem to be. Even today, no one buys a hat innocently. A hat will turn someone into a countryman, or a yachtsman, or a best man, or a toff. Or, if he is not careful, as when one misuses any symbol, it can turn somebody into a fraud, or, if he is caught, into a fool.

Symbolising boundaries

It is well known that symbols are found at boundaries. Most obviously these boundaries are physical and to do with territory. In Northern Ireland, murals, graffiti, processions, bonfires are ways of marking off an area as either Protestant or Catholic. Several of the essays in this volume are con-cerned with this potent issue. Camille O'Reilly discusses the use of the Irish language in a nationalist area of Belfast considering especially the use of street signs. Ciro De Rosa looks at the role of processions in defining social and territorial boundaries, an issue touched on by both Dominic Bryan and Mary Kenney. And Neil Jarman examines the spatial signifi-cance of murals.

Territorial boundaries are a matter of much more general importance. Most suburban gardens, for example, have a fence to show that this land is 'ours' and not 'theirs'; and in the inner cities, the Housing Executive now provides neighbourhoods and dwellings with largely symbolic 'defensible spaces' to ward off vandals (Brett 1986, 102).

Sometimes the symbolic definition of boundaries can be quite complex. I once did fieldwork in an area where there were quite a lot of loyalist sectarian graffiti. In fact, the graffiti were only partly to define the area as Protestant. They were mainly intended as a symbolic assault on a respectable middle-class area by working class youths (Buckley and Kenney 1995, 107–8; 204–6; see also Jarman below).

Sometimes, the boundaries marked by symbols are not territorial. There are social boundaries between one status and another. The symbolic dramas called 'rites of passage' (Van Gennep 1960) are concerned with moving across some conceptualised social boundary. Ceremonies at birth, marriage and death, but also first communion, confirmation, adult baptism, and degree ceremonies all have this character.

The activities of many brotherhoods (societies with secrets) found in Northern Ireland – Freemasons, Orangemen or Buffaloes for example – consist quite centrally in initiating their members through different degrees

Figure 2   *Patrick Sarsfield, Hibernian procession, Draperstown, 1989.* Ulster Folk and Transport Museum.

of membership by means of often highly symbolic rituals. And in the past, other brotherhoods, such as the Hibernians, National Foresters or Knights of St Columbanus had directly comparable initiation rituals, with transition from one status to another across an elaborate symbolic boundary (Buckley and Anderson 1988).

Seasonal customs often contain the idea of transition. New Year is the most obvious of these. Again, Buchanan has suggested that the four quarter days of Hallowe'en, St Brigid's Day, May Day and Lammas once marked changes in the Irish agricultural seasons (Buchanan 1962, 1963). In all cases, their function of these days as boundary-markers has virtually disappeared. Where the festivals still exist, as with Christmas or Hallowe'en, they have a different significance (see Santino below).

Symbols and narrative

In Ireland, many quite important symbols are associated with narrative, and especially with myth and history.[3] We see this even in advertising. An important advertising technique is to place the product in the framework of a story. The hope is that the prospective customer will see himself or herself as similar to one of the characters in the narrative and therefore buy the product.

Take the advertising of beer. Tennents lager, for example, is comparatively cheap. Its advertisements for many years, in Northern Ireland and elsewhere, showed it being consumed by members of a lively, intelligent, fun-loving family of working-class people. These were the sort of decent, honourable folk that many people might hope to resemble. The advertisers undoubtedly hoped that their working-class customers would use Tennents beer symbolically to label themselves as lively, sensible, fun-loving family members. Tennents lager could, therefore, become one of the quasi-theatrical props that sustained this identity.

Carlsberg lager, however, is quite different. It is, indeed, 'probably the finest' beer you can buy. Its advertisements for several years in Northern Ireland showed that this fact is well-known by well-dressed, well-educated young Englishmen who travel first class on trains, and who solve impressively cryptic crosswords. The beer is also shown as the chosen drink of a senior Church of England cleric, who also knows that this is 'probably' the best beer.

Carlsberg, therefore, is the beer of the old fogy. It is also the beer of the young fogy. It is the beer for the intelligent and knowledgeable; for the man at home in the higher reaches of society; and for one who can imagine himself similar to a member of the English upper-middle-class.[4]

Many symbols often belong in this way first of all in a narrative. Sometimes, as in the beer advertisements, the narrative associated with a symbol is a fictional story. Quite commonly, however, the symbol points to 'true' stories, to events that are supposed actually to have happened. In other words, symbols are often items taken out of a myth or a history.

A good example of a symbol taken out of an historical narrative is the picture, well-known in Northern Ireland, of King William crossing the Boyne (a picture whose presence echoes around several of the essays in this book). On its own, this picture does not signify a great deal. Its importance lies in the way the picture draws attention to a narrative. It is not the symbol so much as the historical narrative which is relevant to present realities. The symbol evokes the narrative, and it is the narrative which has significance for the present.

An even better example is the cross. The symbolism of the cross is entirely due to its place in the story of the crucifixion. It is the events of the crucifixion (rather than the cross itself) which have significance for people in the present. The symbol of the cross has significance only insofar as it evokes the narrative.

A final example of this kind of symbolism is found in the collarette emblems of the Orange and Black Institutions (Buckley and Kenney 1995, ch. 11). Each emblem of the Black Institution, members told me, signifies the fact that the wearer has been initiated into a particular degree of that institution. A badge showing a pair of scales, for example, shows that its wearer has been through the rituals of the Link and Chain degree. A slingshot emblem will show he has been through the Royal White degree. And so forth.

On its own, a symbol on a Black collar has some significance, but this significance is limited. It is a badge of membership of a degree, and little more. The balance or the slingshot, do not, in themselves relate to the concerns of everyday life.

When one discovers, however, that each badge is associated with a Bible story, the symbolic significance blossoms. The balance (associated with the Link and Chain degree) refers to a text in the story of Belshazzar's feast: 'Thou art weighed in the balances, and art found wanting' (Daniel 5, 27). The slingshot (found in the Royal White degree) features in the story of David and Goliath (1 Samuel 17). Each of the degree ceremonies involves recounting – even sometimes partially enacting – the Bible story to which the emblem points. Armed with this knowledge, therefore, one can look at the Bible story and ponder what the narrative might signify to people in the present.

It is easy to draw a strong metaphorical link between the Bible stories to which Black Institution emblems and rituals refer. To oversimplify the matter, the Ancient Israelites and Jews in these Bible stories are confronted with opponents – usually, peoples whose religion they do not share. The symbol therefore encourages the Blackman to see himself as a Daniel amidst the might of Babylon, or as a David facing a Goliath. As such the historical situations of the Bible can be seen as similar to those of Ulster Protestants in the present day (Buckley and Kenney 1995, ch. 11).

Structure and anti-structure

I have suggested that the function of a symbol is to highlight a particular definition of the way the world is, and often symbolism does this with little difficulty since the meaning of a symbol can be very clear. But this is not the whole story.

The realities to which symbols point can sometimes be very fragile. First, as I shall show, the meaning of a given symbol can be highly equivocal. And second, given the fact that every symbol only symbolises a partial truth about the world, there are plenty of alternative symbols which have alternative meanings. Every conjured-up world is pregnant with its opposite.

Almost all of the essays in this collection lay particular emphasis on the creativity, the borrowing and the innovation involved in symbolism. Kenney's article makes this point most strongly. She argues that the symbolic articulations of republicanism draw upon ideas and images from all over the world. In one particularly good example, she tells of how a visit of Native Americans provided a source of symbols first for republicans, and then for loyalists. The republicans could readily identify with the Native Americans since they each believed themselves to have been invaded. But loyalists too sought images of themselves which defined them as the 'natives' of Ulster whose territory has been invaded and not as invading 'settlers'.

The same emphasis on creativity is found in the other essays. For example, Bryan looks at the conscious manipulation of the symbolic meanings of the Twelfth of July by press and participants alike. Sawyer describes the creative use of feminine images drawn from Irish literature. For McCaughan, the *Titanic* is a complex symbol, available to define the *hubris*, vulnerability and folly in countless real life situations. And Santino looks at the variety of different meanings found in Hallowe'en customs, a fluidity which allows a potentially sectarian set of symbols to be used to symbolise a non-sectarian harmony.

Kenney argues below that the torrent of different symbolic images and meanings available in Northern Ireland arises out of the fragmented nature of post-modern society. Certainly it is the case that developments in the late twentieth century have made this complexity more obvious. However, it seems likely that the ability to choose between images, and to choose between different meanings for the same image, is something which seems to be inherent in the practice of symbolism itself.

I have said, somewhat glibly, that to drink one kind of beer can help define a person as an educated upholder of upper-middle-class values, an old fogy or a young fogy. Or that to drink another beer can assist another person define themselves as a fun-loving exemplar of a working-class family. I have also suggested that to carry one newspaper defines someone as a liberal, while to carry another defines them as a businessman. I have further suggested that a Blackman who wears a slingshot emblem on his collarette, may suppose himself to be a David opposed to the Philistines. The problem which arises, however, is that any given symbol may symbolise any number of things.

When Simon Charsley (1987) began to study the symbolism of weddings in the British Isles, he assumed that, for example, the wedding cake was a fairly straightforward symbol. It was clear enough what it symbolised. But when he took the trouble to ask a range of different people what it symbolised *for them*, he found a wide range of disagreements. To some people, it signified virginity; to others, it signified male domination of women; to others it signified the sexual act. There seemed to be an astonishing array of different meanings for the wedding cake.

More obviously, a lot of mainstream art is like this. Paintings, operas, dramas and sculptures are, in Turner's words, 'polysemic' or 'multivocal' (Turner 1969, 41–2). They are, as Sperber said, put 'in quotes' (Sperber 1975, 99), set aside so the audience or customer feels disposed to find meaning in them. It is not, however, always very clear what meaning the artist intended to convey. The possible meanings of any given work of art are, of course, limited, but they are also sufficiently wide to allow each person to discover his or her own meaning. The art work can become, therefore, a sort of mirror for the observer's own prejudices and fantasies.

Because symbols point to a particular view of the world, there is a tendency for groups of people to use symbols as a focus for their allegiance. The symbol – a flag or an anthem, or a religious symbol – expresses their unity. It suggests that they have something in common. But this idea is often a misconception.

Take, for example, religion. If several people attend a particular congregation, they will, effectively, gather around a set of symbolic actions and objects, acquiescing in the value of those symbols. The symbolism may suggest that everybody agrees in the significance of these symbols. If, however, an investigator were to look, so to speak, 'backstage' (Goffman 1959) and ask the individuals in the congregation what they *actually* think or believe – or what the different symbols mean to them – one will find their opinions differ quite sharply.

I have myself interviewed the members of different congregations, but in almost any congregation, there will be different views. The bigger churches, for example, are all divided broadly between conservatives, who cling to the traditions of their church, and liberals, who are more willing to test doctrine against experience and the 'common sense' of the day.

Thus some Catholics long to return to the Tridentine Mass, while others fiercely support the reforms of the second Vatican Council; there are also charismatic Catholics and even born-again, Bible-believing Catholics. Yet all turn up to the same liturgies and ceremonies affirming a unity which scarcely exists apart from the liturgy.

And there are divisions within the Protestant churches too. Some Presbyterians, for example, insist on being baptised by total immersion; most do not; some insist on being born again; others are more sceptical, and so forth. Yet somehow, all share in the same ceremonies, and listen to the same sermons.

In fact, in most organisations, individuals acquiesce in the symbolic forms they share with others, while they tacitly disagree with each other about what the symbols signify. Almost any symbol will evoke a wide range of possible meanings. And this allows symbolism to explore the recesses of our imaginations, discovering new truths about the world.

There is, in this, a contrary impulse from the one I identified at first. I said that the main function of the symbol was to clarify or define a state of affairs that otherwise would remain unclear or undefined.

This second function of the symbol is to provide alternative visions, to subvert such given states of understanding. Symbols, on the one hand, can reduce real life to a cliché. But, on the other, they can also help us overcome clichéd, predigested versions of the world, so we may grasp the world in all its immediacy and complexity.

Symbols and the search for the real

If a prime function of a symbol is to point to realities beyond it, there is also a tendency for all symbols to become clichés, to cease to point to the real world.

This idea has been explored by Rudolf Otto. Echoing in some ways Max Weber, Otto claimed that that the religious impulse tended to become 'rationalised'. Otto said that we experience the divine directly as a half-horrific, half-attractive sense of awe, a *mysterium tremendum et fascinans*, a 'burning bush' kind of experience. To confront such an experience – to avoid being burned by it – we use reason, theory, symbolism. But in the process, we can let the rational, the symbolic, get in the way of the raw *Numen* (Otto 1959).

This aspect of symbolism is not especially confined to religion. We are all full of formulas which, when they were conceived, enabled somebody somewhere to grasp a reality in all its freshness, but which have become old and stale. 'Window of opportunity'; 'doing your own thing'; 'small is beautiful': these phrases once resonated with excitement, but are now dead and ready to be buried in the dictionary.

There is, therefore, in many spheres of life, a passion for the new. One reason that fashions in clothing change so fast is so they may express the same old things in a new and fresh way. Rebellious youth, sparkling femininity, pompous authority – all of these are much the same as they always were. But in each generation, even each year, we give them fresh symbolic expression. We need to stop the old idea getting stale. There is, therefore, a tendency to rebel against the symbol. There is an urge constantly to look through the symbol in search of the reality beyond.

This search for the real goes in different directions. One tendency is to proliferate symbols. Catholicism, over the centuries, has tended to accumulate symbols, to pile symbol upon symbol. The Church has had, therefore, all sorts of backwaters and eddies off its mainstream, many of them represented in orders and societies and fraternities. In these nooks and crannies, there are doctrines, disciplines, symbolic structures. Through them, each individual can discover a new and vital truth which for him is not tired and worn, but which speaks to him directly.

The same pattern is also found in Protestantism. Here the tendency has been to schism, with different religious tendencies being represented in separate, often warring institutions. Religious movements, therefore, come and they go. When I did my own fieldwork into religion in Ulster, Pentecostalism and charisma were all the rage. Despite the arrival of the Toronto Blessing, I sense that these are already becoming tired. Perhaps some other more vital form will come along to replace it.

Another tendency has been to mistrust symbols completely. This ancient view, which flowered in the Protestant Reformation, emphasises the fact that symbols are not the reality itself but only point to reality. The problem here, as Mary Douglas (1966) pointed out, is that the absence of symbolic forms is itself a symbolic means of pointing to reality. As with any other symbol, the symbolic practice of 'doing without symbols' can also become dry and clichéd.

This is indeed a universal tendency. In different ways, all societies have individuals who specialise in cutting through the symbolic clichés. Such individuals bring us face-to-face with those realities of life which a particular set of symbols is in danger of hiding. They do so usually by means of other symbols.

Sometimes this is done by serious means, sometimes by comic. Japanese Zen Buddhists (who, incidentally, have a foothold in Ireland) are renowned for using symbolic sayings and actions to evoke the unstructured nature of the world and the mind. Zen discovers that thought and action arise out of emptiness. So its symbols seem strange and paradoxical. 'What is the sound of one hand?' Buddhism is 'that tree in the garden'. And, 'in

the beginning not a thing is'. The aim in these cases is 'to shift one's attention from the abstract to the concrete, from the symbolic self to one's true
nature' (Watts 1975, 146). Asian or American shamans, for example, find
a symbolism in their visions, trances and dreams, evoking new interpretations of the world. Pentecostalists in Belfast sometimes do much the same
(Buckley and Kenney 1995, 129ff). But clowns and comedians also have
this role. Every school, every workplace, probably everywhere in the
world, has its comedians casting doubt on that institution's dominant symbols.

The main point, however, is that there are two uses of symbolism. One
is conservative. It expresses a structured definition of some part of the
world. The other is subversive. It subverts those symbols which have
become ossified and clichéd. It grasps the world afresh, presenting new,
vital aspects of the world, undreamed of in existing philosophy.

The politics of symbolism

I want now to relate this discussion of symbolism to politics. My suggestion is that it is the very fluidity of symbolism that links its intellectual and
creative aspects to questions of power. For against the fluidity, it is social
control that sustains a symbol and its significance.

The nub of the question is this. Symbolism is mainly used to give definition to a slice of reality. However, left to itself, symbolism can be
remarkably flexible. As Cohen puts it, 'Symbols do not carry meaning
inherently. They give us the capacity to make meaning' (1987, 16).

There are so many symbols from which one can choose; each symbol
can be interpreted differently; a symbol can become ossified and can fail
this year to evoke a reality which it evoked last year; and the realities to
which any symbol refers are themselves subject to change. And above all,
each social group and each individual is likely to shape reality in a different way, bending the symbolism to their particular desires.

It follows that the question of which symbols will define any given situation will largely be determined by the practical question of which people
and whose interests predominate. Symbolism, therefore, is closely related
to politics.

I once went to a huge art conference in Dublin, and at the end, we all
went to a reception. I arrived, and found myself in an endless queue of people. We all shuffled forward. There, at the door, stood a small figure. He
hardly moved. He grasped my hand and squeezed it. Then, looking straight
through me, like a waxwork, he said: 'So glad you could come'. And then
he grabbed some other hand. It was the then Taoiseach of Ireland, Mr
Charles Haughey.

Without thinking, I turned to the man standing next to me. 'You would think he would have something more important to do,' I said. 'You'd think he'd be governing the country.' Later, I thought better of it. Politics is like much else in social life. A central feature of it consists in performing ceremonies. I felt that perhaps Mr Haughey's advisors had made a mistake in getting him to shake hands with 400 delegates to an art conference. Nevertheless, the principle holds good. Governing the country consists to a remarkable extent in *dramatising* the fact that you govern the country. It consists of a succession of ceremonial acts.

Anthropologists are familiar with this concept from studying other countries. The great Meyer Fortes wrote of the Tallensi of Northern Ghana. The Tallensi social order he found to consist almost entirely of sacrificial rituals. Their kinship, their politics, their system of justice all came together around rituals attended by representatives of lineages and clans. All disputes had to be settled before the rituals could take place. So in a very real way, the rituals both dramatised and created the fact that all was well in the society at large (Fortes 1945).

Symbols, therefore, cannot be taken lightly. They show that a state of affairs is the case. But sometimes too, they provide a focus for the *enforcement* of that state of affairs.

Every world, I suggested, is pregnant with its opposite. It is continually being challenged or opposed by other symbols or other interpretations expressing other visions of the world. And, as those who live in Northern Ireland know well, a conflict of symbols is not just a clash of ideas and intellects. It is not just a matter of human creativity questioning old assumptions (though this is, of course, important). There are often times when the practical ideas of one person or one group actively threaten the practical ideas of another. In such a case, one person's symbolism can bring the vital world of another person crashing down. It is because symbols represent the genuine political interests of real people that they so often have their force.

Teenage children, for example, may challenge the authority of their parents and impose some social order of their own. So they do this symbolically. They put music on the radio which differs from the sort their parents enjoy; they decorate their room or leave it untidy; they wear distinctive clothes; they become vegetarian. I once knew a Communist whose daughter became a Seventh Day Adventist. And by so doing, teenagers demur at the authority of their parents.

Employers want to dramatise that they are have control over their workforce. Unfortunately for them, people have a tendency to become equal, undifferentiated. Bosses can, therefore, get sucked into an easy-going community of equals. To avoid this, the boss may decide to eat separately, perhaps with the typists who are no threat; he may decide to have a distinctive office with a modern oil painting; to have a separate toilet. All of these things – and more – have symbolic value. They maintain or transform a social order.

Language is regulated in all sorts of contexts to make symbolic statements. Individuals sometimes insist that others use particular words (and avoid others) when referring to their ethnic or other group. Sometimes, the words to be avoided are unambiguously offensive (such as 'nigger', 'poof'). Notoriously, however, when people at large have altered their vocabulary to accommodate such groups, the group in question will change the rules. Thus people of African descent have at different times opposed the use of epithets such as 'black' or 'coloured' to describe their race, and at other times, they have insisted on these same words. For example, too, the word 'handicapped' has been successively replaced by 'disabled people' and 'people with disabilities'.

In Northern Ireland, where questions of territory are a preoccupation, the symbolic regulation of language attaches itself less to the names of the ethnic groups and more to the names of geographical features. Famously, some nationalists are offended by 'Londonderry' and 'Ulster' while some unionists see 'Derry' or 'the north of Ireland' as an affront.

Whether one approves or disapproves of this kind of thing seems to depend on one's sympathy (or lack of it) for the group in question. In all such cases, the regulation symbolically dramatises that someone has the power or the right (a particular form of power) to insist that others take account of their sensitivities.

Symbolism also has a place in more devious forms of power-play. Scheper Hughes (1979a; 1979b), for example, writes of abstruse kinds of cruelty in rural Irish families, involving the bewildering manipulation of confused symbolic messages. She claims that this kind of activity can induce schizophrenia in its victims.[5] Though the connection with schizophrenia may be doubted, Scheper Hughes is undoubtedly right to claim that the 'double binds' involved in such symbol-laden interactions are related to the acquisition and dramatisation of power.

In these contexts, and one can think of many others, it is not the symbols alone which are relevant. When one uses a symbol in this way to define (or disrupt a definition of) a state of affairs, it is only because, politically – through superior physical strength or social support, or just through guile or skill – one can get away with it.

So one comes back to Orwell and to Hitler's moustache. Symbols do very many things, and I have emphasised the creative and destructive element in symbolism. In a political context, however, all symbols are like Hitler's moustache. They are daring us to laugh. Symbols proclaim that a state of affairs exists, but only if nobody challenges the symbol – only if nobody laughs.

Several of the essays here (O'Reilly, De Rosa, Kenney, Jarman, Bryan)

deal directly or indirectly with a major issue in Ulster, the symbolic definition of local territory. When somebody puts up a mural or graffito in
Northern Ireland, the picture remains there as a challenge. In principle at
least, another person can come along and deface it, or put up an another
mural to represent another vision of reality (see especially Jarman below).
The mural is effectively daring other people to laugh.

The dare is in part directed against the young men of the other ethnic
group. However, as I found in my own fieldwork, there may be opposition
from other residents, older, more respectable people who do not always
like graffiti or murals (Buckley and Kenney 1975, 107–9). Whether the
mural remains is a matter of power. The question at issue is: who, in any
given street, has the power to put up and sustain a mural, or to deface it and
wipe it away? The existence or non-existence of the mural is a symbol of
who is in control, who can get away with what.

Life, however, does not have to be like this. When faced with the symbols of other people, one need not have only the simple option of defiance
or capitulation, scornful laughter or fear. Other possibilities have always
been available to people in Northern Ireland.

In the mid-1970s, when the Troubles were at their peak, I visited a rural
area of County Down which I called the Upper Tullagh (Buckley 1982).
Here, many Catholics and Protestants were making a very real attempt, as
they put it, 'to get on well' together.[6] Part of this pattern was a deliberate
attempt, by people on both sides, to show open respect for at least some of
the other side's symbols. I heard strange stories of Catholics raising money
to rescue the flute band associated with the local Orange Hall; of a town
gala whose organising committee was selected deliberately from both
Catholics and Protestants; and of individuals rather self-consciously supporting the fund-raising events of churches across the divide. And indeed,
despite major hiccups, one of the good things that has happened in the last
quarter of a century has been a growing recognition of the importance of
showing respect for other peoples' symbols.

Conclusion

I want, however, to end on a note of caution. Symbols are important to
everybody. Intellectually, symbols allow people to explore and discover
reality. Politically, they are a means of defining one's position, testing
one's strength against opponents, and perhaps establishing a social order.
Despite this, one should not overestimate their importance.

Writers since ancient times have urged that a symbol should not be mistaken for the reality it represents. The finger which points at the moon is not
the same as the moon. The fancy tail is not the same as the peacock. Symbols
of all sorts do have importance. But they should not be mistaken for what

they represent. This is true in religion. It is certainly true in politics.

There is a tendency, however, in Northern Ireland to regard the conflict as totally about what is called 'culture', but what really should be called 'symbolism'. The two sides in the conflict, for example, are misleadingly called 'two cultures' and they are said to be 'culturally divided'. I have heard quite intelligent people say that if only we could sort out the cultural problem, then the troubles would go away. This is, of course, not the case.

First of all, the social division in Northern Ireland is not, fundamentally, a matter of cultural difference. There are cultural differences, of course, between the two sides but these differences only symbolise more fundamental divisions. Much more fundamental to the Troubles has been the failure of Catholics and Protestants to interact in certain crucial respects.

The fact that Catholics and Protestants do not intermarry is central. It divides society from top to bottom. All of one's parents, grandparents, children, grandchildren; the brothers and sisters of all of *these* people; the spouses of all of *these* people; and all the relatives of all of the spouses of all of these people: all belong to the same segment of society as oneself. The family is still the basis for society in Northern Ireland. Since family life is segregated by ethnicity, so too is the whole of society.

Add to this the residential and territorial segregation, and segregation in schools, churches, clubs and workplaces, and one discovers the mountainous nature of the social division.

This colossal division in society is, of course, given symbolic expression in names, alphabets, theology, 'cultural heritage' and the rest, but the division cannot be reduced to the symbolism.

In the same way, the political conflict has a much more substantial basis than just the symbolism of that conflict. One may paint murals, walk in processions, sing party songs, burn flags and so forth. But the conflict is not about any of that. More substantially it is about the ways that Protestants and Catholics live together, given that they are so divided.

My point is this. The social division is expressed through symbols. So too are the political aspirations of the two sides. One must not, however, mistake the word for the object, the pointing finger for the moon, the symbol for the underlying reality.

Much can be achieved through symbolism. Symbolism can stake out a position against the opposition and laughter of one's critics. It can present a vision of how society ought to be. Symbolism is also creative and flexible: old symbols can gain new meanings; new symbols can emerge to meet new circumstances. Symbolism can express old divisions and it can also proclaim (as did the *Symbols* exhibition) that Catholics and Protestants should have equal value.

Symbols, however, cannot achieve everything. Fine symbols alone butter no parsnips. Symbols succeed only when they highlight social realities with sound political foundations. There is a need, therefore, permanently to end the violence, to break down social barriers, to end segregation and discrimination, to mix up the two sides in the hurley-burley of family life, to create the substance of a decent caring society. Only then will the symbolism of peace reflect the reality. Only then will the people who despise the symbolism of peace be disposed not to laugh.

Notes

1. The exhibition was created under the auspices of the Cultural Traditions Group of the Community Relations Council. Since its launch, the exhibition has travelled to many parts of Northern Ireland and beyond.
2. The remark concerns social class, the snobbish don deploring a ruler's enthusiasm for social equality:
   > On every side Field Marshals gleamed,
   > Small beer were Lords-Lieutenant deemed,
   > With Admirals the ocean teemed
   > All round his wide dominions.
3. Turner (1969) points out that symbolism is not universally associated with narrative.
4. Deserving attention in the Carlsberg advertisements is the word 'probably'. 'Probably' is a word used by scholars and other professionals when they want to cover themselves against criticism. One only uses the word in this way if one's opinions carry some weight. By describing a beer as 'probably the best beer' the speaker turns himself into an expert. The phrase alone is, therefore, enough to give the speaker an identity. He becomes a man of discernment, an old or a young fogy.
5. In this, she follows the ideas of Bateson and his colleagues (Bateson et al 1956) Haley 1959a; 1959b). Typical forms of this kind of activity include the inconsistent offering and withholding of symbolic tokens of affection, while denying that this is in fact what one is doing. See also Berne (1964; 1975) for a rather different view. Whatever might be its connection to mental illness, this general approach to communication has immense theoretical strength (see Goffman 1975; Buckley and Kenney 1995 ch. 9).
6. This, indeed, was a recurring theme in anthropological community studies in other parts of Ulster (eg Bufwack 1982; Harris 1972; Leyton 1975; 1976).

References

Bateson, G, J Haley, D D Jackson and J H Weakland, 1956 'Towards a theory of schizophrenia'. *Behavioural Science* 1, 4.

Berne, E, 1964 *Games people play.* New York, Grove Press.

Berne, E, 1975 *What do you say after you say hello?* London, Corgi.

Brett, C E B, 1986 *Housing a divided society.* Dublin, Institute of Public Administration.

Buchanan, R H, 1962 'Calendar customs: Part 1, New Year's Day to Michaelmas'. *Ulster Folklife* 8, 61–79.

Buchanan, R H, 1963 'Calendar customs: Part 2, Harvest to Christmas'. *Ulster Folklife* 9, 61–79.

Buckley, A D, 1982 *A gentle people: a study of a peaceful community in Ulster.* Cultra, Ulster Folk and Transport Museum.

Buckley, A D and T K Anderson, 1988 *Brotherhoods in Ireland.* Cultra, Ulster Folk and Transport Museum.

Buckley, A D and M C Kenney, 1995 *Negotiating identity: rhetoric, metaphor and social drama in Northern Ireland.* Washington D C, Smithsonian Institution.

Bufwack, M S, 1982 *Village without violence: an examination of a Northern Irish community.* Cambridge Mass, Shenkman.

Burke, K, 1957 *The philosophy of literary form: studies in symbolic action.* New York, Vintage.

Burton, F, 1978 *The politics of legitimacy: struggles in a Belfast community.* London, Routledge and Kegan Paul.

Charsley, S, 1987 'Interpretation and custom: the case of the wedding cake'. *Man* (NS) 22 93–110.

Cohen, A P, 1987 *Whalsay: symbol, segment and boundary in a Shetland island community.* Manchester, Manchester University Press.

Ó Danachair, C, 1964 'Chalk Sunday'. *North Munster Antiquarian Journal* 11, 123–6.

Danaher, K, 1972 *The year in Ireland.* Cork and Dublin, Mercier Press.

Douglas, M M, 1966 *Purity and danger: an analysis of concepts of pollution and taboo.* London, Routledge and Kegan Paul.

Fortes, M, 1945 *The dynamics of clanship among the Tallensi: being the first part of an analysis of the social structure of a trans-Volta tribe.* Oxford, Oxford University Press.

Gilbert, W S 1889 'The Gondoliers, or The King of Barataria'. In W S Gilbert 1983 *The Savoy operas: the complete Gilbert and Sullivan operas originally produced in the years 1875–1896.* London, Macmillan 1983.

Goffman, E, 1959 The presentation of self in everyday life. Garden City, New York, Doubleday, Anchor.

Goffman, E, 1975 *Frame analysis.* Harmondsworth, Penguin Books.

Haley, J, 1959a 'An interactional description of schizophrenia'. *Psychiatry,* 22, 321–2.

Haley, J, 1959b 'The family of the schizophrenic: a model system'. *Journal of nervous and mental diseases* 129, 357–74.

Harris, R, 1972 *Prejudice and tolerance in Ulster: a study of neighbours and 'strangers' in a border community.* Manchester, Manchester University Press.

Leyton, E, 1975 *The one blood.* Institute of Social and Economic Research, Memorial University of Newfoundland.

Leyton E, 1976 'Opposition and integration in Ulster'. *Man* (NS) 9, 185–98.

Otto, R, 1959 *The idea of the Holy.* Trans. J W Harvey. Harmondsworth, Penguin Books.

Scheper Hughes, N, 1979a 'Breeding breaks out in the eye of the cat: sex roles, birth order and the Irish double bind'. *Journal of Comparative Family Studies* 10, 207–26.

Scheper Hughes, N, 1979b *Saints, scholars and schizophrenics: mental illness in rural Ireland.* Berkeley, Los Angeles, University of California Press.

Sperber, D, 1975 *Rethinking symbolism.* Trans. Alice C Morton. Cambridge, Cambridge University Press.

Turner, V W, 1969 *The ritual process: structure and anti-structure.* London Routledge and Kegan Paul.

Turner, V W, 1982 *From ritual to theatre: the human seriousness of play.* New York, Performing Arts Publications.

Van Gennep, A, 1960 *The rites of passage.* Trans. M B Vizedom and G L Caffee. London, Routledge and Kegan Paul.

Watts, A, 1975 *The way of Zen.* Harmondsworth, Pelican.

'Ireland's Very Own Jurassic Park': The Mass Media, Orange Parades and the Discourse on Tradition

DOMINIC BRYAN

THE summer of 1995 was proof, if proof were ever needed, of the importance of demonstrations and parades within the political culture of the north of Ireland. With both loyalist and republican paramilitary groups observing cease-fires the focus of politics again switched to the streets, with some sections of the world's media eagerly awaiting a repeat of the communal clashes of the late 1960s and early 1970s. Attention first turned to the Ormeau Road in south Belfast, where members of loyalist orders attempted to assert the 'right to march' on a number of different occasions in the spring and summer. Then in Portadown, County Armagh, Orangemen were involved in a three-day 'siege' while waiting to be allowed to march down the predominantly Roman Catholic and nationalist area around the Garvaghy Road after a church service early in July. A month later, Derry took centre stage with the Apprentice Boys of Derry seeking, successfully, to re-introduce the 'tradition' of marching along the walls of the city to mark its relief from the siege in 1689. Derry's walls overlook the Catholic Bogside, and many people date the start of 'the troubles' to riots following this parade back in August 1969. Punctuating these loyalist occasions were moves by republicans to assert their own right to march. A major rally into Belfast city centre to commemorate the introduction of internment was attacked by a gang of young loyalists and in Lurgan a number of parades into the town were halted by the police because of counter-demonstrations organised by various loyalist groups.

This paper will examine the way that various arms of the media cover Orange parades. In the first section, I will give a brief description of the parades that take place around the Twelfth of July. In particular, I will point to the way these forms of symbolic expression reflect contemporary politics. This, despite the insistence by many of the participants that the events are 'traditional'. Indeed, the basis upon which the Orange Order claims a right to parade is its continued use of that route over a significant period of time. The withdrawal of this right is understood as an attack on the historical roots of the Protestant community. The rest of the paper will be taken up with an examination of the way newspapers and broadcasters depict the parades. I will argue that their coverage, rather than focusing upon the contemporary aspects of the parades, instead reinforces the idea that the present behaviour of political actors is fundamentally governed by a history, that the media, to a great extent, also understands the parades simply as 'tradition'.

The ways in which communities understand the past, and the processes by which 'a history' of that past is constructed, has in recent years particularly concentrated the minds of anthropologists and historians. Eric Hobsbawm most notably discussed 'invented tradition' as 'a set of practices, normally governed by overtly or tacitly accepted rules and of a ritual or symbolic nature, which seek to inculcate certain values and norms of behaviour by repetition, which automatically implies continuity with the past' (Hobsbawm and Ranger 1983, 1). For the purposes of this paper, it is important to note that 'tradition' and a continuity with a past are seen as legitimisation for a political position by the political communities, as opposed to ideas of 'innovation' or change (Smith 1982).

It is not altogether surprising that the loyalist community should claim the 'right to march' based on the legitimacy of having 'traditionally' marched a particular route. The hegemonic position of that community, particularly during the Stormont years from 1921 to 1972, has allowed a relative domination of public spaces by groups such as the Orange Order. I will suggest ways in which parts of the mass media reassert this ideological position by stressing the longevity of events through the uncritical use of categories such as 'tradition', 'heritage', 'pageant' and 'community'. What is a little more surprising is the way those areas of the media less sympathetic to unionism fail to critically oppose this position and indeed in many ways reinforce it. This, I will speculate, is because of the inherent link between any nationalist position, be it Irish, Ulster, British or otherwise, and an idea of a legitimate past. As such, an attack on the veracity of the historical legitimisation of symbols logically undermines much nationalist rhetoric. Consequently, the major changes that have taken place in these ritual occasions over the years if largely ignored in favour of an image of people 'trapped in history' postulating an unchanging continuity with the past.

The role of symbolic expression, of ritual, in the dynamic politics of Northern Ireland cannot be underestimated (Jarman 1992, Bryson and McCartney 1994, Buckley and Kenney 1995). While it is economic and power structures which provide the social environment within which political activity takes place, it is through displays of symbols such as flags, banners, and anthems, that the majority of people comprehend and 'imagine' the political community in which they live (Anderson 1983). The release, by the British and Irish governments, of the *Framework*

Document, in February 1994, despite being perceived by most unionists as having a nationalist agenda, failed to bring people on to the streets. However, the halting of an Orange church parade in Portadown proved an altogether more potent symbolic moment allowing diverse unionist groupings to coalesce. It is therefore important to attempt to understand how the meaning of these events is controlled and how this reflects on the 'imagined' communities in Northern Ireland.

The Twelfth as ritual

Among all the commemorative events in Northern Ireland, none has quite such a galvanising effect on communal politics as the Twelfth of July. It is on that day that thousands of Orangemen take to the streets, accompanied by a variety of types of bands, and carrying flags and banners symbolising a British, Protestant 'heritage'. Spectators watch and cheer as Orange lodges parade images that constantly hark back to the past, chief among them being the picture of William III, Prince of Orange, astride a white horse at the Battle of the Boyne in the process of defeating Catholic King James in 1690. Accompanying these images is the sound of the bands playing tunes recalling past glories such as *The Boyne Water, Dolly's Brae* and, most played of all, *The Sash.*

> It is old but it is beautiful, and its colours they are fine,
> It was worn at Derry, Aughrim, Enniskillen and the Boyne.
> My father wore it as a youth in bygone days of yore,
> And on the Twelfth I love to wear the sash my father wore.

However, it is also around the Twelfth that many Roman Catholics and some Protestants, inconvenienced, alienated and threatened by the parades, feel hemmed into their particular streets, and make plans to avoid travelling through Northern Ireland, or if possible to escape over the border to Donegal or Dublin. Many plan a holiday abroad in July so that they can be away over the Twelfth.

The Twelfth is only part of a cycle of rites which takes place each year. From March onwards there are a number of occasions when different loyalist groups parade. As July approaches bunting is hung between houses in many loyalist, working-class areas. Kerbstones are painted in the red, white and blue of the Union flag and in many towns Orange arches are constructed across the road. Local parades to church services take place and in the two weeks before the Twelfth most districts have a large local parade sometimes known as a mini-Twelfth. On the Eleventh night bonfires are lit with the flag of the Republic of Ireland or an effigy of the Pope often put to the flames. In some areas, large drums known as Lambeg drums beat out a rhythm while in others a disco might be held. On the day following the Twelfth there is a large parade in Scarva organised by the Royal Black Preceptory, an organisation closely related to the Orange Order. At this event there is a 'Sham Fight' where William III ritually defeats King James. Around 12 August attention is focused upon Derry where another loyalist organisation, the Apprentice Boys of Derry, commemorates the relief of the city from a siege King James had put it under prior to his battle with King William. The final major parades take place on the last Saturday of August. Known as 'the last Saturday' they are also run by the Royal Black Preceptory and are generally deemed to mark the end of what is collectively referred to as the 'marching season'. In all there are now around 2,500 parades held by loyalist organisations annually compared to around 250 parades organised by Irish nationalist and republican groups.

The parades which take place on the Twelfth of July are ritual occasions demanding certain standards of behaviour that have the effect of bracketing off that behaviour from 'everyday' actions. They have a formality within which symbols are grammatically linked and dramatically displayed. Each Orangeman, wearing a collarette with his lodge number upon it, takes up a place with his lodge. That lodge has a Worshipful Master, a

Figure 3   *Eleventh night bonfire, Donegall Road, Belfast.* Ulster Folk and Transport Museum.

Secretary and Treasurer (as indicated by their sash) who often walk at the front of the lodge. At the head of the lodge is the banner bearing the name and number of the lodge as well as images helping to signify the particular history of that lodge. As such, one side of the banner may have a picture of William III astride a white horse while the other side could depict anything from the foundation of the lodge, for instance a train or ship for those with a particular industrial heritage, to popular deceased Past Masters, or popular deceased unionist, royal or military figures. The lodge will 'march' or walk in columns and at the head will have a marshal and 'Tylers' carrying ornamental swords or pikes which appear to stand in symbolic defence of the lodge. A spectator crossing the road and breaking the ranks of a lodge, or even walking between two lodges that are in close proximity to each other, is likely to be roughly shown back to the side of the road they came from. There is a strong sense of integrity to the parade which is broken at a spectator's peril.

Lodges are themselves formed into districts which march together headed by district officials such as the District Master, Secretary, Treasurer and Chaplain. Before them is carried a bannerette with the district number upon it as well as a crown placed above an open Bible indicating loyalty to the throne and the centrality to the Protestant faith of scriptural teaching. The district lodges are themselves formed into county lodges whose officials march at the head of the parade. Upon the Orange collarettes they wear initials indicating their place within the order's hierarchy. All Orangemen wear relatively smart attire with officials, elderly members, and a few lodges, such as those with military connections, wearing very smart dark suits, bowler hats and white gloves.

Although there is an ordered integrity to the parade, the behaviour of individual Orangemen and lodges can vary quite widely and is to a certain extent indicative of diverse understandings of the nature of the event. At one extreme are those Orangemen, often district and county officials or those with military connections, who 'march'. There is a dignity and regularity to their behaviour which may even preclude waving at spectators. However, many of the Orangemen, albeit in regular files, 'walk'. They will watch for people they know along the route and may even fall out of line to talk to friends or members of their family. And at the other extreme some Orangemen may dance or weave down the road shouting as they go or singing *The Sash*. This last, more carnivalesque behaviour is perhaps more common at the end of the day, among younger members of the Order, and can also be related to the consumption of alcohol. Drinking is frowned upon by many, and some of the lodges carry the title of 'abstinence' or 'temperance'. Nevertheless, many Orangemen, particularly in Belfast, drink quite heavily on the Twelfth and although there are rules governing such behaviour it is not difficult to spot them being broken.

Orangemen themselves are only part of the event. Each lodge normally hires some musical accompaniment. In the last century that might have consisted only of 'a drumming party' – a fife (small flute) and one or two large drums, now known as Lambeg drums – or very 'rough' flute bands. From the 1870s onwards, as parades came to be seen as increasingly more respectable, more organised bands formed. Some of the silver, flute, accordion or 'kilty' (bagpipe) bands were funded by factory owners, the local Conservative Club or the Orange lodge themselves. Since the late 1960s, and most noticeably in urban areas, there have developed flute bands known as 'blood-and-thunder' or 'kick the Pope' which are largely separate from the Order and are predominantly not made up of Orangemen. These bands have proved so popular that they can contain up to 60 members and in some cases they may even have a waiting list to join. They have their own internal structure which includes having a band captain or master, and often raise money by holding their own local parades or even by effectively running drinking clubs at band halls. Since the size and success of a Twelfth parade is to some extent incumbent upon the musical accompaniment, and more 'respectable' bands have become expensive and fewer in number, Orange lodges have hired the blood-and-thunder bands in greater numbers, sometimes reluctantly but sometimes with relish.

What makes the involvement of the blood-and-thunder bands so significant is the role they have played in the recent developments at Twelfth parades at a number of venues. In the early 1970s their main input was to introduce a larger number of more overtly sectarian tunes, played with a swagger rarely shown by other types of band. This rougher, less 'respectable', style may well have been borrowed from the bands that take part in the Twelfth in Scotland and visit Northern Ireland in great number. The bands are also dominated by young males, and their macho bravado attracts young teenage girls who follow 'their' band often carrying with them large amounts of alcoholic refreshment. This can in itself promote a different atmosphere within the event. However, the blood-and-thunder bands have themselves developed. Most particularly they have in the main abandoned the simple uniform of a v-neck jumper, shirt and black trousers for elaborate colourful military-style uniforms drawing inspiration from as far in the past as the Protestant Volunteer movement of the 1780s. Even more significantly, uniforms and instruments, particularly the main bass drum, carry insignia which relate to loyalist paramilitary groups both past and present, particularly the Ulster Volunteer Force (UVF) and Young Citizens Volunteers (YCV), but also less often the Ulster Defence Association (UDA). Further, within the last 15 years, these bands have also started carrying flags of their own in front of them, independently of the Orange lodge they are with. District and county Orange lodges have regularly carried significant flags, most often the Orange Standard or flags of the United Kingdom, and single lodges may carry a Union flag, but the blood-and-thunder bands have introduced a whole new symbolic dimension. They regularly carry UVF and YCV flags and sometimes their own band flags or that of the Red Hand Commandos, a wing of the present UVF paramilitary group. Such has been the development of these symbolic displays that some bands, and occasionally lodges, have carried flags indicating support for Ulster Independence or, in the 1970s, the Ulster Vanguard movement. This is in marked contrast to the central principle of the Orange Order, that Ulster should remain within the United Kingdom, and to the Orange Order's orderal relationship with the Ulster Unionist Party. The Orange Order, albeit somewhat half-heartedly, introduced rules to try and control the type of flags displayed and the behaviour of the bands.

Many of these developments are of course closely connected with contemporary political and economic changes. That period which is commonly called the troubles also dates back to the late 1960s with the modern UVF becoming active in 1966 and the UDA in the early 1970s. As such while a symbolic link can be made between the Orange Order and the old UVF (which was formed in 1912, predominantly from Orange lodges, to fight against the third Home Rule Bill) the majority of symbols now displayed carry altogether more modern, and for many, highly ominous connotations (Bryan et al 1995).

Seeking to understand the Twelfth of July we are faced with the paradox that probably exists in some way within most ritual events. Its symbolic structure, its formalised and repetitive nature, and its link to a calendar of historical events, all help serve to legitimise it as 'tradition' that in some way exists outside time, and for all time. Its political authority derives from its 'timelessness' and is linked to the identity of those involved. Effectively those taking part are only following in the footsteps of their Williamite 'forefathers' and in doing so providing an apparent continuity to the Protestant community. However, the event exists in the present. It can be shown to be dynamic, altering over time, influenced by changing political interests. To that extent each of the rituals is unique (Bryan and Tonkin 1996). Dealing with the theoretical and methodological problem of continuity and change in ritual has produced some stimulating academic discussions (e.g., Smith 1982; Hobsbawm and Ranger 1983; Bloch 1986).

What I would now like to go on to consider is the way in which this paradox is played out within the coverage of the Twelfth in the mass media. Cannadine, in his study of the coronation of Queen Elizabeth II, alludes to the vital role played by newspapers, television and radio in framing the meaning of such an event (Cannadine 1983, 159). The power to impose particular understandings exists in a far more diverse realm than just among those directly participating in, or witnessing, the parades. Indeed, it is significant to note that the coverage given to the Twelfth by newspapers, and latterly by the broadcast media, has been, and still is, a constant concern in the higher echelons of the Orange Order.

The Twelfth and the mass media

Coverage of the celebrations of the Battle of the Boyne can be traced right back to 1738 when one of the earliest editions of the *Belfast News Letter* reported the marking of the occasion in Dublin. The Orange Order was founded in 1795 and from that point on the Belfast-based newspapers the *News Letter* and the *Northern Whig* provide reports of parades from various parts of the north of Ireland. The conservative politics of the *News Letter* make it generally supportive of these events, which were at this time, in the main, relatively small and localised. As soon as the parades produced sectarian clashes, disturbing the status quo, the newspaper's support quickly waned.

> When intelligence reaches London, how will the subject be taken up, and what severe animadversions will it give rise to against this town, which has long been the theme of eulogium, alike distinguished by its internal peace, its opulence and its industry. All these high and honourable qualities are thus thrown into the shade by an idle parade, having rekindled those animosities and heartburnings which should have forever sunk into oblivion. (*Belfast News Letter* 13 July 1813)

This 'idle parade' had sparked the first major sectarian riot in Belfast. The more politically liberal *Northern Whig* was, to begin with, not so approving of these events although it did make interesting attempts to reinterpret the Battle of the Boyne commemorations in ways it believed had existed prior to the formation of the Orange Order. On 8 July 1824 it appealed to the spirit of the earlier celebrations by the Volunteers of Ireland in the 1770s and 1780s and suggested that the Orangemen's loyalty 'was conditional, not permanent'. Indeed, as the middle part of the nineteenth century progressed, the relatively limited political influence of the Orange Order, together with its regular involvement in sectarian clashes, meant parades were banned, and even the normally supportive *News Letter* could not always be relied upon.

> In these days of education and enlightenment, Protestantism and loyalty have discovered better modes of asserting themselves, than by wearing sashes and walking to the music of fife and drum. (*Belfast News Letter* 3 July 1846)

Much of this changed in the 1870s as the threat to the Union grew and many more of the upper classes joined the Orange Order as a bulwark against Irish nationalism. The growth of the railways allowed easy travel making the parades much larger events. The widening of the franchise made it worthwhile for Members of Parliament to come and talk to their electorate as they rested in 'the field' which forms the mid-point of a parade. Consequently the *News Letter* started to produce pages of reports, particularly of the political speeches taking place at the field. Each year the *News Letter* told its readers that the parades were bigger than the last and the Twelfth began to move closer to the centre of Protestant and unionist identity, its success read as a sign of political virility. The parades had become 'respectable'.

The Twelfth as pageant

Newspapers

The reporting of all political speeches in full took place in the *News Letter* right through to the 1950s. With the introduction of a local parliament in Northern Ireland in 1921, and given that nearly all Ulster Unionist MPs were Orangemen, the Twelfth speeches were made by senior politicians. As such, the Twelfth was at once both an event of state, a restatement of Ulster Unionist Party power, and also a 'traditional' day of pageant for many Protestants. Each year the success of Northern Ireland as a 'state' is reported in terms of the claimed annually increasing numbers at the parades. The editorial of the *News Letter* every Twelfth links political themes of the speeches to the Battle of the Boyne and other moments in Orange history. It is interesting that even on occasions when the events contain divisive moments, such as heckling of one of the speakers or perhaps some stone-throwing near a nationalist area passed by the parade, these incidents are reported separately from the main body of the reports on the day. The unity and peaceful integrity of the day is maintained.

The general development of printing technology since the First World War has allowed the major unionist newspapers, first the *Belfast Telegraph* and then the *News Letter*, to develop their coverage of the Twelfth pictorially. Together with the reports, an increasing number of pictures start to appear framed with particular headlines. This montage of images is used by both newspapers to this day. To begin with, photographs had to be of rather static images such as Orange decorations, a lodge standing outside its hall, or of the politicians on the platform at the speeches. However, other activities within the parade were soon becoming part of the montages: long lines of Orangemen heading through Belfast, pictures of senior members of the Order in their carriage, a Lambeg drummer and people lining the street.

What makes this style of reporting so interesting is that it is consistently maintained after the mid-1960s despite ferment developing around the parades. Typically in the 1970s these two newspapers produced a pull-out supplement showing a happy carnivalesque day, old men and young babies, women dancing in their Union flag skirts, impressed overseas visitors, pretty girls from an accordion band seated in the field, an Orangeman resting his feet, a group having a picnic, and occasionally a flute band.

Back in 1972 the *Belfast Telegraph* produced a 12-page supplement with pictures of Orangemen braving the rain, Lambeg drums and plenty of smiling faces. Each page leads with a headline: 'Never mind if it rains'; 'Lambegs catch the ear ... and it's quite a sensation'; 'A step through the tunnel'; 'Off they go at a brisk pace'; 'No-go is not an obstacle'; 'The Somme remembered'; and 'Thousands go on parade'. In 1978 we find, 'Impressive pageantry ... and also in Portadown'; 'A spectacular show ... and it's country style'; 'Happy marchers ... and the sun shines on'; and 'An anniversary prelude ... to a familiar sound'. In 1980, 'I'd walk a million miles'; 'A day to enjoy and remember' and in 1981, 'All the ceremony of the big day'; 'Spectators show their own style'; and 'A time to enjoy ... for all ages'.

By the 1990s the *Belfast Telegraph* no longer produces a special supplement but the headlines are just the same. In 1992: 'Sprightly spring in the step ... for a summer spectacular'. In 1993: 'Doing it in style'; and the rather bizarre 'Big slappers are hard to beat'. In 1994: 'Young and old step out on parade'.

The *News Letter* provides us with similar themes, in a special pull-out edition even if it is not as big on corny headlines. For instance, 1992 saw 'A piping hot extravaganza' and 'Night of flags and fun'. The local newspapers in unionist areas follow a similar style. Take for example the *Larne and East Antrim Times* 1980: 'Preserving Twelfth heritage, young and old share'. In 1981: 'A happy day for all'; 'A smart turnout'. In 1982: 'Pageantry on parade'; 'Brethren and bands relax'. In 1984: 'All decked out to celebrate'. In 1987: 'Glorious Twelfth'.

The main theme articulated in this pictorial form, and reinforced by the headlines, appears to be to show as little sign of division as possible. The overwhelming discourse is one of a community taking part in a 'traditional' occasion as they have through the generations. In 1972 the *Belfast Telegraph* did have a picture of marchers heading towards a road block under 'No-go is not an obstacle' and also pictures the controversial Tunnel area in Portadown although no protesters were in sight. We have people 'taking things in their stride', 'enjoying a well earned rest' and 'doing it in style'. The *News Letter* gives us 'the spirit of the Twelfth' (13 July 1993) and 'traditional tunes of the flutes' (14 July 1992). The *Ballymena Guardian* has 'Family day out in Cullybacky', while the *Larne and East Antrim Times* also produces the same sort of material.

What is perhaps more significant is what is not shown. In all the supplements I have seen there is not one picture of anyone drinking alcohol or any suggestion that part of the fun might involve intoxication. Of even more interest, despite the recent proliferation of paramilitary symbols on

Figure 4   *The Twelfth of July, Saintfield, 1989.* Ulster Folk and Transport Museum.

flags, bannerettes, uniforms and drums carried by bandsmen there are almost no pictures with even a hint of such regalia. I can find only two occasions when any such symbols appear anywhere in the pictures. This situation is particularly noticeable in Belfast where the blood-and-thunder bands with their many references to the UVF, YCV and even the Red Hand Commando now dominate the parade.

Major disturbances at parades, as there were in Portadown in 1985 and 1986, are kept to the 'news' section of the paper and not allowed to adulterate the 'traditional' community occasion reported in other parts of paper. So marked is this separation, that at times the heckling of a speaker is reported on the front page, but, in the special Twelfth supplement section, that same speech is reported as if nothing happened. This apparent division between the reporting of the events and the reporting of the 'news' surrounding the events is sustained in broadcasting.

Broadcasting

During the late 1930s the BBC managed to side-step pressure to broadcast radio commentary of the Twelfth, claiming the political nature of the event would lay it open to criticism of partiality. This refusal was despite attempts by Northern Ireland cabinet ministers to force the issue (Cathcart 1984, 88–9). The first recorded programme of the Twelfth was made in 1952 and the Twelfth was shown on a television newsreel the following year. The first live television broadcast from the Belfast parade occurred in 1958 and in 1961 a highlights programme was shown in the evening. In 1964 even the Republic of Ireland broadcasting company RTE covered the Twelfth, and in 1965 the BBC extended its coverage outside Belfast. During the period up until the mid-1960s coverage appeared to be relatively unproblematic. The *News Letter* is fulsome in its praise for the broadcasts. In 1968, the BBC introduced *Orange Folk*, a radio programme full of Orange tunes to be broadcast on the evening of the Twelfth. A similar programme, *Green Folk*, was shown on the evening of the 15 August after the Lady Day parades by the Ancient Order of Hibernians (Cathcart 1984, 207).

The civil unrest into which Northern Ireland slipped in 1969 was closely connected to both Civil Rights and Loyalist marches. Orange and Apprentice Boys' parades started appearing in a new light on news and documentary programmes. Interestingly, it seems that the way the broadcasters dealt with this was not dissimilar to the way the *News Letter* and *Belfast Telegraph* dealt with it. Coverage and highlights of the parades were seen as separate from incidents that took place in and around the parades. Nevertheless, despite the continued patronage given to the Twelfth by broadcasters, their relationship with the Orange Order over news and documentary coverage became more fraught. The situation deteriorated even further in 1975 on the showing of a drama called 'Just Another Saturday' which gave the depiction of a threatening and drunken Orange parade in Glasgow. This drama has been re-shown twice since then, much to the renewed ire of the Orange Order.

Some news coverage also continues to upset the Orange Order. During the platform speeches at the Twelfth in 1994 a couple of speakers complained about an interview on a BBC morning radio show with a young lad from the Donegall Pass area who apparently had said that the Twelfth was all about getting drunk, having a good time, and throwing stones at Catholics.

> It is deplorable that the radio station concerned actually used that report and I trust the people will realise that what was said by that young man does not reflect the view of the Orange Order, or the Protestant people of the Province. (John McCrea, the Twelfth platform 1994)

In 1986 the BBC decided not to have live coverage. One can only guess at the actual reasons for this decision, but in 1985 there had been major disturbances surrounding parades in Portadown and this probably gave the BBC the excuse it had been looking for. This coverage was replaced with extensive mid-day news reports and an extensive highlights package shown in the late evening. A similar package is shown on UTV. While the news reports, not surprisingly, cover 'incidents,' occurring where marches take routes through nationalist areas, the highlights package provides us with images, a commentary, and interviews that in many ways replicate the aforementioned newspaper coverage.

A quick review of recent programmes reveals the overwhelming stress upon the historical nature of parades. This is not only done by the continual use of the word 'tradition' – and it is used a lot – but also by the way the subject-matter is framed. There are continual references to past events – the Battle of the Boyne, the Battle of the Diamond, the Battle of the Somme, or the two world wars. There are also continual references to 'the generations' taking part, as commentators seem to go out of their way to find the youngest and oldest participants in the parade. As we are told by the BBC commentators during an interview with two members of the Banbridge District in 1993: '... there may be 60-odd years between them but they joined the Order for the same reason – tradition'. There are lots of background histories to lodges, banners, and bannerettes as well as stories of founding members of the Orange Order itself. Also there are plenty of interviews with older members of the Orange Order, often some who have their 'long service' medals. A sample of the commentary on the BBC programme looking at a Ballinderry parade should suffice.

The road to Ballinderry in County Antrim.

At the head of the parade the officers from host district Ballinderry No.3, accompanied by the Orange Order's Imperial Grand Master, James Molyneaux. At the front a bannerette older than any of the marchers. A gift from a local Church of Ireland rector to Ballinderry No.148 in 1883.

Six other districts joined the march. Derriaghy, Lisburn, Hillsborough, Aghalee, Glenavy, and Magheragal. At one-and-a-half miles this was a mere stroll compared to the old days. It is recorded then on the 12 July 1849 the lodges of the area marched via Glenavy and Crumlin to Antrim and back, a round trip of some 40 miles.

The history of the Orange Order here goes back a long way ... [*interview with the District Master who tells us how lodges used to meet by the light of the moon*].

For one of today's marchers, a certain brother . . . from Ballinderry, it was a double celebration, his birthday. Born on the Twelfth 33 years ago his parents called him William. Among the youngest at the parade two-year-old . . . from Lisburn, watching out for her father . . . of Flower Hill lodge.

At the field the main speaker was James Molyneaux, who accused the Irish Foreign Minister, Dick Spring, of firing an Exocet at the prospects of new political talks, by suggesting joint authority for the province. And Mr Molyneaux predicted news of moves towards better local democracy [*interview with Molyneaux*].

It is interesting that despite the introduction of modern party politics into the programme, through an interview with the then leader of the Ulster Unionist Party, other political aspects to the parades are conspicuous by their absence.

The discourse of tradition is departed from when older Orangemen suggest that things are not what they used to be. For example, a District Master in Fermanagh, interviewed on the 1993 highlights programme, suggests that the county lodges better represent the Orange Order than the city parade, which he believed sometimes brought the organisation into disrepute. However, even this is in some senses a call for a return to the past, the way it used to be. The overwhelming image is one of continuity and historical stability.

Also noticeable among the shots of happy smiling faces and prominent unionist politicians is the absence of paramilitary symbols. In fact, there is a general concentration on the Orangemen rather than the bands, and on the 'respectable' bands rather than the 'blood-and-thunder' variety. Neither are there any shots of alcohol being consumed or of the consequent behaviour. This type of television coverage is therefore very similar to the newspaper coverage discussed earlier.

Significantly, given the 'ongoing' peace process, in 1995 the BBC agreed to show the Twelfth live again. This threw up some interesting problems because without the editor's cutting room it is less easy to mould an image. The BBC commentator mentioned both the problems with part of the parade on the Ormeau Road and the demonstration, at the front of the parade, by the fringe loyalist parties demanding the release of political prisoners. Nevertheless, the commentary, using Orangeman Clifford Smyth as co-host, was replete with historical references. The recent developments in the bands were mentioned, but the paramilitary insignia, when shown on camera, were completely ignored. When one recently dead paramilitary member was shown on a bannerette, Clifford Smyth failed to mention who it was, and simply described the lodge as having a 'militant nature'. Any discussion of the UVF or YCV took place in terms of their 1912 existence and not their contemporary manifestation. As such, although it was forced to reveal some of the more contemporary aspects of the parade the coverage nevertheless continually reverted to the historical model.

The Twelfth as sectarian demonstration

Newspapers

An alternative image of the Twelfth which upsets the Orange Order so much is not hard to find. Nationalist newspapers in Northern Ireland, national newspapers in Britain and the Republic of Ireland, television news items and particularly documentaries tend to use more aggressive, threatening and sectarian images of the parades.

Not surprisingly the Irish newspapers, reflecting nationalist politics, concentrate on those occasions where parades through nationalist areas cause concern – recently in the Ormeau Road and Ainsworth Avenue areas of Belfast, and on the Garvaghy Road in Portadown. A more general image is also built up which stresses a sectarian, territorial view of the event – Unionism banging the old drum. Dick Grogan in the *Irish Times* provides us with some amazing images from a re-routed mini-Twelfth on the Ormeau Road.

> Each drummer in turn almost literally spitting venom, risks a hernia as he redoubled his deafening pounding and gyrated like a tom cat undergoing castration without an anaesthetic.

> The camp followers with their cans of lager and bags of wine, followed reluctantly in the wake of the mini-parade. (*Irish Times* 10 July 1994)

Suzanne Breen gives a similar vivid image.

> Young women teetered in mini-skirts and dangerously high heels, clutching glasses of cola into which they poured vodka and Bacardi. The tattooed, t-shirted young men preferred cheap cider, cheap wine and bottles of beer. Grizzly old men with worn bumpy hands sat on folding chairs along the route. This was their high point of the year. (*Irish Times* 13 July 1993)

Brenda Anderson in the *Irish News* (13 July 1993) sets up the image of the folk festival and compares it with the feelings of Catholics as they are hemmed into their streets. There is also a tendency for critics to use zoomorphic imagery, depicting Orangemen as displaying the territoriality of animals (Bryan 1995).

In spite of overt opposition to them, in one sense the image presented of the parades does not deviate from the discourse of the unionist newspapers – the discourse of tradition. Not only does the language used by journalists continually refer to the past, but the papers produce potted histories of the Orange Order to remind us of that link with the past. In 1992 the *Irish News* had Andrew Boyd provide us with a history lesson (11 July 1994) on what actually happened at the Battle of the Diamond. The editorial of that edition informs us that the Orange Order is an organisation which was founded in the aftermath of an anti-Catholic pogrom and throughout its history has been associated with sectarianism in its crudest form. Just two days later the same paper provides us with another history, this time by Denis Lehane, which takes us back to the Battle of the Boyne. The following year it covers the parades down the Ormeau Road with a piece headed 'Marchers to stick with tradition' that tells us that the Ballynafeigh District was in fact re-routing its mini-Twelfth away from the lower Ormeau Road while retaining its route on the Twelfth (1 July 1994).

Andersonstown News uses the frequently-repeated idea that somehow people are living in the past.

> It is only when the Orange Order stops its triumphalism and tries to bring its members into the 20th century, should it be trusted to march wherever it likes without let or hindrance. (*Andersonstown News* 3 July 1993)

Sinn Féin's Alex Maskey is not afraid to frame his observations around the theme of 'tradition'.

> There will always be – there must always be – respect and goodwill for those who wish to celebrate the Twelfth and salute their heritage. (*Sunday World* July 1993)

The *Irish Times*, over a Dick Grogan article, produced the headline 'Tub thumping with traditional refrains' (13 July 1993). Gerry Moriarty describes the Lambeg drums in Portadown in historical terms.

> The din they beat up was truly loud and threatening. One would have feared such a sound at Derry, Aughrim, Enniskillen and the Boyne. If King James had better drums he might have knocked King William off his white horse. (*Irish Times* 13 July 1993)

The fact that these drums only date back to Belfast in the 1850s need not ruin the image. *Andersonstown News* surely achieves the best headline with 'Ireland's own Jurassic Park' (17 July 1993). The Orangemen are part of a zoo for the pre-historic, living in the present but revealing the past.

In 1994 the *Irish News* printed an article by Brian Lennon which delved into the past to try and understand the parades (7 July 1994) James Downey in the *Irish Independent* pointed out that one '... may deplore the triumphalism and sectarianism, but the Orange songs are part of our musical heritage' (12 July 1994). The *Irish News* provided us with a three-page special on the Twelfth concentrating on the Ormeau Road and the political speeches from the platform. However its editorial again returned to the theme of history.

> Organisations which do not change with the times quickly become irrelevant ... The Order is wedded by a sectarian vision of a world which has passed it by, and it is obsessed by an inward looking political philosophy. (*Irish News* 13 July 1994)

Broadcasting

It is important to note that documentary television coverage of parades regularly uses them to stand either for the whole Protestant community or for loyalism in general. Along with wall murals they are the most accessible image for a medium that demands pictorial representations (Jarman 1996). The accuracy of such representations appears almost irrelevant. In 1994 a Channel 4 documentary *Dispatches*, commenting on links between the British National Party and the UDA symbolised the political group by showing an Apprentice Boy parade in Derry and a Twelfth parade in Belfast. The parades provide a convenient backdrop with which to comment on any number of aspects of Protestantism, unionism, and loyalism in Northern Ireland.

The image of the parades that documentary and news programme makers are looking for are, in some senses, very different to the images discussed earlier. A fine example of this was the 1993 BBC series on nationalism from Michael Ignatieff in which the Protestant community of Northern Ireland was covered, *Blood and Belonging*. Comparing this programme's image of the Twelfth to the highlights type programme, we find a far more ominous depiction. The commentary is in many ways sympathetic, but the images of the Eleventh Night and the Twelfth are disturbing and sometimes almost manic. For instance, we are shown paramilitary murals in the background as an effigy of the Pope is led to an Eleventh Night bonfire. As well as talking to Orangemen Ignatieff interviews young lads painting the kerbstones red, white and blue, obtaining from them a bitterness towards their Roman Catholic neighbours. However, Ignatieff also indulges in a discourse linking the past with the present.

> The bonfire is ready. On top flies the Irish tricolour awaiting the flames. An effigy of the Pope is carried to the top of the funeral pyre. [Group of lads singing: 'We are the Billy Boys ... we're up to our necks in fenian blood, surrender or you'll die ...]
>
> At midnight the bonfire ignites, the Twelfth is finally here. When the enemy flag goes up the crowd roars its approval. As it was with Serbs and Croats so it is with loyalists and republicans, the hatred of brothers runs deeper than the hatred of strangers. We've known this since Cain slew Abel.

An old preacher warns that Roman Catholics are 'breeding like rats' and girls marching with the blood-and-thunder bands are shown dancing in slow motion – presenting them as vaguely hysterical. Indeed, the filming tempts one to wonder if those on the parade are going so slowly they are being left behind.

> Monday 12 July
>
> There is a form of belonging here more ritualised than any I've seen on my trav-

els. I feel like an archaeologist discovering layer after layer of forgotten British history [UVF bannerette pictured]. As an expatriate I've always been envious of belonging, to have roots, know your history, have a sense of destiny. When cosmopolitans talk blithely about moving beyond nationalism, they underestimate the desire, the need to belong.

But there is also something sad here, the people wave their flags and bang their drums but deep down they fear that time is running out. They fear the day when Catholics become a majority in Northern Ireland and Protestants cease to be masters in their own home. They fear the day the British government decides enough is enough and pulls out.

And what happens to a nationalism cut off from the mainland. It ceases to be a claim that must be honoured. It becomes a caricature that can be disowned. That's the tragedy of loyalism. It won't be because they lack loyalty but because they were too loyal, loyal to a past the British left behind. ('Blood and Belonging' BBC 2, 16 December 1993)

The contrast between this image of the Twelfth with the highlights programme discussed earlier is in many senses stark. Nevertheless one theme is contained in both – that of historical continuity. Never is there any suggestion that a modern, changing, developing event is being witnessed. The overall effect of using the parades as a shorthand for the Protestant community is to allow journalists to indulge in the idea that people are trapped in their history.

Conclusions

In the brief description of the Twelfth parades that I started with, I tried to indicate ways in which the events could be seen as reflecting present economic and political conditions. They are active political rituals contested by a variety of political groups, classes and denominational interests. Part of the symbolic power of these ritual occasions is that they appear to offer a legitimisation from the past. This image of stasis is crucial to its ideological strength. Apparent repetitions within the event, the integrity of the parade, the use of social space and the link to an annual set of chronological events – the closing of the gates of Derry, the relief of Derry, the landing of William at Carrickfergus, the Battle of the Somme, the Battle of the Boyne, to name the more prominent – almost gives an appearance to the parades as existing 'out of time' (cf Tonkin 1988, Bryan and Tonkin 1996). The introduction of new symbolic material reflecting ongoing political change can only take place within limits. As such, UVF flags with their link to an Orange history have become common yet UDA flags are rare and frowned upon by the arbiters of the parade, the Orange Order. The Orange Order itself serves to act as a conservative gate-keeper taking care that its own political interests are served through the Twelfth. Nevertheless, its power has been greatly limited, particularly since the mid-1960s, and the ability of other interest groups, such as the bands and young spectators, to appropriate the event and impose understandings – legitimated by a past – has grown.

The media discourse about the ritual acts to disguise the changes taking place. The journalists provide us with vivid descriptions, occasional political insights, frequent factual inaccuracies, and a continuing discourse of tradition. What they rarely do is offer insights into the way rituals work over time, and change over time. In general there are two different perceptions of the Twelfth of July to be found. One as a pageant, an occasion for all the family, a festival. The other of territorial marking, of drunken behaviour, of sectarianism. But both images accept the historical, traditional, foundation of the event. They see it as something rooted in the past, not in the present, as reflecting a continuity in social relationships. As such the media are playing an important role in sustaining an image of the ritual, indeed helping it to work ideologically.

That those arms of the media that serve unionist politics take this line is hardly surprising. That the BBC, with its claim of 'neutrality', of serving the community, and maintaining the status quo, therefore reflects this, is also not particularly surprising. By making a demarcation between 'news and current affairs' and coverage of an annual event, it is effectively able to produce a view of the Twelfth unadulterated by the present.

Perhaps more surprising is that Irish nationalist views of the event, for all their criticism of the Twelfth, rarely deviate from a claim of historical continuity. However, this may not be as paradoxical as it at first appears. Irish nationalism, as with all national identities, is largely based upon ideas of a continuity with a past. What is more, the way in which that past is understood is inseparable to an opposition to what is British and Orange. To undertake a critique of 'the Orange' in terms of questioning a continuity with the past is to lay bare the possibilities of a critique of Irish nationalism itself. To attempt to wrestle the weapon of historical legitimisation from your opponent may involve being relieved of it yourself, demanding a complete re-think of political identity.

Bibliography

Anderson, B, 1986 *Imagined communities: reflections on the origins and spread of nationalism.* London, Verso.

Bloch, M, 1986 *From blessing to violence.* Cambridge, Cambridge University Press.

Bryan, D, 1995 'Orangutango' *Fortnight,* July/Aug No. 341.

Bryan, D, S Dunn and T G Fraser, 1995 *Political rituals: loyalist parades in Portadown.* Coleraine, Centre for the Study of Conflict, University of Ulster.

Bryan, D and J E A Tonkin, 1996 'Political ritual: temporality and tradition' In (ed.) A Boholm *Political ritual.* Institute for Advanced Studies in Social Anthropology, University of Gothenburg, 14–36.

Bryson, L and C McCartney, 1994 *Clashing symbols: a report on the use of flags, anthems and other national symbols in Northern Ireland.* Belfast, Institute of Irish Studies, Queen's University of Belfast.

Buckley, A D and M C Kenney, 1995 *Negotiating identity: rhetoric, metaphor and social drama in Northern Ireland.*

Washington D C: Smithsonian Institution Press.

Cannadine, D, 1983 'The context, performance and meaning of ritual: the British monarchy and the "invention of tradition", c.1820–1977'. In (eds) E Hobsbawm and T Ranger, 1983 *The invention of tradition.* Cambridge, Cambridge University Press.

Cathcart, R, 1984 *The most contrary region: The BBC in Northern Ireland 1924–1984.* Belfast, Blackstaff.

Hobsbawm E, 1983 'The invention of tradition'. In (eds) E Hobsbawm and T Ranger *The invention of tradition.* Cambridge, Cambridge University Press.

Jarman, N, 1992 'Troubled images: the iconography of loyalism'. *Critique of Anthropology* 12, 133–65.

Jarman, N, 1996 'Violent men violent land, dramatising the troubles and the landscape of Ulster'. *Journal of Material Culture.* 1, 39–61.

Smith, M E, 1982 'The Process of Sociocultural Continuity'. *Current Anthropology* 23, 127–42.

Tonkin, J E A, 1988 'Cunning mysteries'. In (ed.) S Kasfir *West African masks and cultural systems.* (Sciences humaines, 126), Terveuren, Musée Royale de l'Afrique, 241–52.

The Irish Language as Symbol: Visual Representations of Irish in Northern Ireland

OVER the past decade or two interest in the Irish language in Northern Ireland has increased, particularly within the nationalist community. Irish language play groups and schools have mushroomed all over the North, especially in west Belfast, and the number of Irish classes for adults has also grown. The 1991 census included a question about the Irish language for the first time since 1921, with 37,253 people claiming to have some knowledge of the language in the Belfast urban area alone (WBEF 1993).

With the rise in interest in the language has come an increase in its visibility. Irish street names have been erected in some nationalist areas, many murals and painted slogans include words of Irish, and in west Belfast numerous shops have put up bilingual signs. As with so many things of symbolic significance in Northern Ireland, interpretations of this phenomenon vary. Many are pleased to see an increase in the use of Irish, viewing it as a valuable part of Irish identity or an important part of the cultural heritage of the island as a whole. Others see negative connotations in the visible use of Irish, or view it as a threat.

In fact, such a variety of interpretation is one of the key characteristics of symbols (Turner 1967), and it is part of what makes them so powerful. Put simply, a symbol is something which stands for or represents something else. Things start to get more complicated, however, when we try to interpret precisely what is being represented or communicated by a particular symbol. Although the form is shared, multiple meanings can be read from it. As Cohen points out, 'symbols do not carry meaning inherently. They give us the capacity to make meaning' (1987, 16). Virtually anything can be considered a symbol, although clearly some are more potent and emotionally charged than others. Everyone familiar with our own culture, for example, knows that in the context of the Highway Code, a red light is a symbol to stop. In most circumstances such a symbol is unlikely to excite much emotion. Other symbols, for example the cross or a national flag, are more complex and also more likely to invoke a powerful response. In the context of Northern Ireland, the Irish language has become a powerful symbol, and its use in public places has given rise to some strong reactions.

The use and interpretation of symbols is almost invariably an integral part of the political process and can have significant political consequences, as is clearly the case with the Irish language in Northern Ireland. Harrison suggests that 'competition for power, wealth, prestige, legitimacy or other political resources seems always to be accompanied by conflict over important symbols' (1995, 255), what he calls 'symbolic conflict'. He argues that symbolic conflict takes four different forms – valuation contests, proprietary contests, innovation contests and expansionary contests – because there are essentially four different ways in which a political symbol can be used.

We need not go into all four types of symbolic conflict here, but what Harrison calls proprietary contests are of particular significance to this discussion. Groups, he says, often claim proprietary rights in their symbols. Any dispute over these rights, over ownership or control of an important collective symbol, is a proprietary contest. The need to establish legitimacy can lead to struggle to reinvest the same collective symbolic form with different meanings (Harrison 1992, 236). Clearly, there is a struggle within the nationalist community in Northern Ireland – and to some extent between nationalists, unionists, and the British government – for the right to define the meaning and political significance of the Irish language. Part of that struggle is, quite literally, written on the walls.

The debate over signs in Irish

Examples of the debate surrounding the use of Irish in high profile situations abound, but just a few cases should illustrate the point. Signs in Irish have stirred up controversy for years in the Students' Union building of The Queen's University of Belfast. In 1977 the University's *Cumann Gaelach* (Irish Society) proposed that Irish be used alongside English in official Students' Union communications and in the Students' Union building. After a long debate, the motion was passed at a general meeting. Nothing was done about it, however, and in 1980 another similar motion was passed. In 1983 bilingual Irish/English signs were put up, and the post of Cultural Affairs Officer was created to implement the bilingual policy wherever possible. *An Cumann Gaelach* saw this as a way of promoting Irish and encouraging people to take an interest in the language. Unionist student organisations saw it differently. They condemned the decision then and continue to do so to this day. They argue that the Students' Union is nationalist controlled and therefore not representative, and that the signs in Irish are sectarian and contribute to the feeling of alienation felt by unionist students at Queen's.

Issues concerning the Irish language have spurred considerable conflict in an already beleaguered Belfast City Council, from arguments over the use of Irish in the Council chamber to debates over proposals to introduce bilingual headed notepaper. One event which is of particular relevance to this discussion involved the hanging of a banner reading '*Guíonn Glenand Nollaig Shona Daoibh*' (Glenand wishes you a Happy Christmas) from the Andersonstown Leisure Centre in December 1988. Glenand Youth Training Programme (YTP) put up the banner and other Christmas decorations, as they had done for a number of years previously. However, at the Leisure Services Committee meeting of the Belfast City Council on 13 December, unionist councillors banned the hanging of the banner because it was in Irish. Councillor Robin Newton of the Democratic Unionist Party (DUP) called the proposal to erect the banner 'disgraceful' (*Andersonstown News* 17 December 1988).

After permission to hang the sign was refused to Glenand YTP, a number of Irish language activists decided to erect their own banner reading '*Nollaig Shona*' (Happy Christmas) to protest the decision. This sparked off a heated debate at the Council's next monthly meeting in January. Shankill Councillor Elizabeth Seawright proposed that the Leisure Centre be shut down until the sign was removed, but the proposal was ruled out of order. During the meeting a unionist councillor told a Sinn Féin councillor to '*póg mo thóin*' (literally, 'kiss my backside'), alarms were set off to interrupt speakers, and unionist councillors walked out of the council chambers during the debate (*Andersonstown News* 7 January 1989).

Belfast City Council is not alone when it comes to heated debates on the Irish language. Fermanagh Council has a bilingual policy which is often the subject of controversy. In September 1989, during a meeting of the council, unionist spokesman Roy Coulter declared that Irish was a 'Mickey Mouse' language which '99.9 per cent of people cannot understand and do not want to understand' (*Andersonstown News* 23 September 1989).

Another controversy has arisen recently over efforts to rename the Victoria Barracks flats in the New Lodge area of north Belfast. Residents campaigned for many months to have the names of the high-rise blocks of flats changed. Named after British war heroes and battle victories like Churchill, Dill, Alexander and Templar, the mainly nationalist residents believe that the names do not reflect the culture and traditions of the area. While a previous campaign in the 1970s was unsuccessful, the Northern Ireland Housing Executive recently agreed to allow the changes as long as the local community was consulted. The Rename Our Flats Committee conducted a survey of residents to decide on names, and these were submitted to the Housing Executive for approval. What was initially heralded as a new era of improved relations between Irish campaigners and government agencies turned sour when the Housing Executive refused the names chosen by residents on the grounds that their 'computers only accept the English language'[1] (*Andersonstown News* 23 September 1995). The refusal was met with some surprise, and it was pointed out that any computer that could accept the English alphabet could accept words in Irish. The Housing Executive eventually backed down, and the flats were renamed.

Incidents like those described above clearly demonstrate not only the widely differing views of the Irish language espoused by different people in Northern Ireland, but also the deep passion with which these views are held. '*Nollaig Shona*', a relatively innocuous holiday greeting for one group from the nationalist community, is seen as a serious political issue by other nationalists, and is viewed as a 'disgrace' by a group of unionists. Yet the configuration of meanings with which the Irish language is imbued is by no means static, as is evidenced by the ceremonial use of Irish by unionists in the past. When Queen Victoria visited Belfast a banner reading '*Céad Míle Fáilte*' ('A Hundred Thousand Welcomes') was erected in her honour, and the mayoral chain of Belfast is inscribed with the mottoes '*Lámh Dhearg Abú*' ('Red Hand Forever') and '*Erin go Brágh*' ('Ireland Forever'). The motto of the Royal Irish Rangers (recently merged with the Ulster Defence Regiment to form the Royal Irish Regiment) was also in Irish – '*Fág an Bealach*' ('Get out of the way'). For much of the nineteenth century Irish was not so closely associated with nationalist Irish identity, and its meanings were clearly somewhat different than they are today. In Harrison's terms, nationalists appear to have 'won' the proprietary contest over Irish, at least in relation to past unionist interpretations of the language, but the struggle for control continues within the nationalist community.

For the vast majority of people in the region that was to become Northern Ireland, Irish ceased to be spoken as a language of everyday communication long before partition. By that time it had become imbued with symbolic importance strongly associated with Irish nationalism. The story of how this came about is a long one and cannot be recounted here (see, for example, MacDonagh 1983, ch. 7; Ó hUallacháin 1994; and Hindley 1990). Suffice it to say that in spite of the involvement of Protestant and Catholic alike in revival efforts from the mid-nineteenth century onwards, the language became associated with a particular kind of Irishness typified by the newly formed Irish Free State. Bilingual road signs in Irish and English throughout the South were, and still are, a highly visible indication of the importance of Irish as a symbol of Irish identity.

It is significant that the only piece of legislation explicitly against the use of Irish in Northern Ireland prohibited its use in street signs (in an amendment to the Public Health and Local Government Act 1949). It was passed after nationalist councils in Newry and Omagh erected Irish-language street signs in parts of the towns in 1948. During the debate which preceded the vote prohibiting the use of Irish in street signs, future Prime Minister Brian Faulkner stated that the naming of streets by certain local authorities in County Down, 'in a language which is not our language', should not be allowed (Maguire 1991, 11).

Ironically, the continued existence of this law on the statute books seems to have encouraged the erection of street signs in Irish, particularly in more recent years. In 1979 a west Belfast branch of the Gaelic League announced that a campaign to have street signs erected in Irish was being launched, beginning with streets in the Lenadoon and Glen Road area. In 1981, Irish street signs were put up in the Twinbrook estate on the outskirts of west Belfast, along with a sign at the entrance of the estate reading '*Fáilte go Cill Uaighe*' ('Welcome to Twinbrook'). One of the organisers is quoted in the *Andersonstown News* (24 January 1981) as saying: 'We have some beautiful names in this estate when translated into Irish, and Irish is the common heritage of all the people here, no matter what religion or political persuasion.' In 1983 Irish street signs were erected in Ballymurphy[2] and Sinn Féin became involved in the campaign for Irish street names by carrying out door-to-door surveys in most areas of west Belfast. The Irish language organisation *Glór na nGael* also became involved in erecting Irish street names, and called on the British government to repeal the 1949 law prohibiting them.

The involvement of Sinn Féin in this campaign, even though they were only one organisation among many who were involved over the years, sparked an interesting debate in the letters pages of the *Andersonstown News* between February and March 1983. Over the years many articles about Irish street signs and place names have appeared in the *Andersonstown News*, all of which were supportive of the campaign and in agreement with the erection of Irish street signs in principle. This is not surprising, considering that the paper has been owned and operated by a number of well-known Belfast Irish speakers since the 1970s.[3] In the 19 February 1983 edition of the paper, a letter appeared in *Mála Poist*, the section for letters to the editor. Signed 'Turf Resident', it claimed that Sinn Féin and *Conradh na Gaeilge* (the Gaelic League) received support for the survey on Irish street names only because, called on 'in the dark of night', people were afraid to disagree with Sinn Féin. If you refuse to agree with the campaign, the writer states, 'you can expect trouble later on'. The writer goes on to say that it is all part of a plot – first the Irish names go up, then the English ones will come down, and finally the Irish version will be replaced with 'a well-known if not well-loved Provo name'.

Four letters appeared in the following week's issue in response – one from a Turf Lodge resident, another from a Turf Lodge resident who participated in the survey, one from a local Sinn Féin *cumann* (the smallest level of party organisation based on the neighbourhood), and one from the Sinn Féin Cultural Department written in both Irish and English. The first letter writer denies that anyone was called on in the dark of night, the survey being carried out during daylight hours. He also says that no one who refused to sign the petition has been harassed. The second writer who took part in the canvassing says no intimidation took place at the time of the survey, and that four weeks later no one who refused to sign the petition has come forward with accusations of intimidation. He also rubbishes what he calls the 'sinister plot' to put up Provo street names as nonsense. Predictably, the two Sinn Féin members also deny the claims made by 'Turf Resident'.

A final letter on the matter appeared in the 12 March 1983 issue. Signed 'An Irishman,' the writer dismisses 'Turf Resident' as a person either suffering from severe paranoia, or someone who is out to spread propaganda against Republicans. Assuming 'Turf Resident' is female, he writes: 'To alleviate her distress, she should try adopting some convictions and self-respect. If she feels at home with nationalists, she should be true to her Irish heart and delight in any Irish revival.'

Aside from being a rather colourful exchange, these letters are informative on a number of points. The views expressed by 'Turf Resident' would probably be considered by most to be somewhat exaggerated, particularly the assertion that erection of Irish street names is part of a wider plot to eventually change the names to those of well-known IRA members. However, the letter does reflect the belief held by a significant number of people from outside the area, as well as by some nationalists, that the Irish-language revival (or at least the erection of Irish language street signs) is intimately linked with republicanism. In this case, the writer sees it as a full-blown conspiracy. As has become apparent, there is a fair amount of republican involvement in the language, and high profile campaigns such as the one to erect street names in Irish has helped to foster this image. The letters also show to a certain extent the differences in attitudes held towards the Irish language, even within an area considered to be very supportive of Irish. Most significantly, though, the letter from 'Turf Resident' is one of the very few negative reactions to the Irish language to be voiced publicly by a nationalist in my experience as a researcher. It is significant as well that this person's negative feelings seem to have as much to do with a low opinion of Sinn Féin as they do with the Irish language itself.

Since the 1980s the trend towards erecting Irish street names has gathered momentum, and Irish signs have been erected in many nationalist areas both inside and outside Belfast. For example, bilingual road signs were erected on the main approach roads to Coalisland in 1993, and Newry and Mourne District Council's bilingual policy allows both English and

Irish to be included on district welcome signs. In spite of the illegality of this according to the above legislation, no action was taken against any of the various groups or councils who participated over the years. The lack of official legal action against the signs has not stopped some people from taking the law into their own hands, and a few signs have been defaced. For example, a bilingual welcome sign erected on the road between Newcastle and Annalong, leading to a predominantly unionist area, has been defaced and knocked over[4] on a number of occasions. In the end, Newry and Mourne District Council agreed it would probably be best not to put Irish on the new sign in that area.

In December 1992, Sir Patrick Mayhew declared the government's intention to remove the ban on street names in Irish. No action was taken at that time, however. In 1994 the Northern Ireland Office again promised the repeal of the legislation prohibiting street signs in Irish. Finally, in February 1995 the Local Government (Miscellaneous Provisions) (NI) Order 1995 was approved by the House of Lords, allowing street signs to be erected in both Irish and English.

Since then, controversy has again broken out over the use of bilingual signs, this time in Derry, where the City Council is held by the nationalist SDLP (Social Democratic and Labour Party). A new city council building is graced with a ten-foot granite nameplate bearing the name 'Derry City Council' in both English and Irish. The debate in this case is particularly interesting because of the changes which are taking place in the nature of the arguments both for and against Irish being used in signs.

An article in the *Irish News* reports DUP alderman Gregory Campbell's protest that the sign was a 'double insult' to unionists. It was bad enough that the Council insists on using 'Derry' instead of 'Londonderry' in its title, but 'just in case we didn't get the message the council's name in Irish is at the bottom' (*Irish News* 22 August 1995). His argument against this use of Irish is twofold. First, he says it does nothing to bridge the divide between people to use language that is insulting to unionists, and second, he argues that it will have a negative effect on the council's efforts to employ more Protestants. The DUP has generally not been supportive of equal opportunities legislation in the past, which makes this second argument an interesting new addition to their arsenal of verbal weaponry.

Arguments in support of the other side have altered somewhat as well. After ridiculing Campbell's protests by calling them 'a bit hilarious', Derry mayor John Kerr argues that the bilingual policy regarding the new building was approved in advance in the full council, and that no proposal was made against it. SDLP councillor Pat Devine backs this up with a number of other arguments. First, he frames the bilingual use of Irish and English in the European context as showing 'respect for languages'. More interesting, perhaps, is his second argument, that the council has a strong link with a council in the Scottish Western Isles. Apparently, members of this unnamed Scottish council have attempted to explain the pride they have in their own language to Democratic Unionist and Ulster Unionist councillors in Derry. Devine goes on to say that 'their Scots-Gaelic takes priority in speeches, on council literature and on road signs. That is the kind of pride in language we should be aspiring to and taking language out of petty political differences' (*Irish News* 22 August 1995). Devine's arguments are not particularly novel – they have been used by campaigners for the financial support of Irish-language education, for example, for some time. It is more uncommon, however, for them to be used in the context of the debate over street signs.

The nature of symbols

This debate is indicative of the widely different meaning attributed to the language by different sections of the community in Northern Ireland. As with any symbol, there is no fixed relationship between signifier and signified, between the Irish language and the ideas and concepts which it represents. The meaning of the same symbol can and does vary over time and space. Symbolic meaning tends also to be polysemic – the Irish language signifies a multitude of beliefs and concepts, some differing from each other only subtly, some differing quite dramatically. The anthropologist Victor Turner (1967) has highlighted the capacity of symbols to 'condense' complex sentiments and beliefs into a kind of shorthand. The very value and importance of symbols lies in this characteristic ability to convey multiple meanings, varying according to context and the circumstances of the interpreter, and especially in the ability to convey meaning which is difficult or even impossible to express with words.

Complicating the matter still further is the difference between the interpretations intended by those using or displaying the symbol, and those who observe the display. As Bryson and McCartney (1994) point out, it is important to try to understand both the interpretation of those who use the symbol and those who observe it – both the intention and the impact – especially in the context of Northern Ireland, where the gulf between these interpretations can be wide indeed. Perhaps no one in Northern Ireland needs to be reminded of Turner's other point about the competence of symbols – their capacity to stimulate people's emotions.

Harrison (1992), in a discussion about ritual which also offers some valuable insights into symbols, argues that ritual constitutes a special class of intellectual property which can be compared with the concept of property found in gift economies. Property in this sense differs from the way we tend to conceive of property in our own society. In a gift economy, goods are personified, symbolising their owners' identities, rather than being objectified, as in a commodity mode of exchange (Harrison 1992, 234). If we look at symbols in this way, as intellectual property which is the personification of it's owners' identities, we obtain a different perspective on the struggle to impute and interpret symbolic meaning. The Irish language, for example, becomes more than just a symbol of Irish identity, merely standing for or representing a certain type of Irishness – it becomes the symbolic personification of the Irish people. This might go some way towards explaining the emotional intensity associated with some symbols noted by Turner.

The depth and complexity of symbols means that any attempt at interpretation is likely to be somewhat crude and over-generalised. Cohen (1987) points out that symbolism can be experienced with such diversity that attempts to impute generalised meanings to symbols is almost futile. The meanings of symbols are by nature difficult to translate into words. Cohen writes that 'much of what symbols "mean" or express may be beyond or behind consciousness' and that their meaning is therefore difficult to describe '...either because these meanings are so inchoate as to be inexpressible, or because their value depends upon their being left unstated' (1987, 12). While I will try to do justice to the nuances of meaning symbolised by the Irish language, it is important to remember that the examples I have chosen are not exhaustive of possible interpretations, and that they may inevitably lean in the direction of over-generalisation.

Marking the boundaries

The erection of Irish street signs has sometimes been viewed as little more than an exercise in sectarian boundary marking. Like curb painting, it has been seen as a way of indicating to the outsider that they are now entering territory clearly staked out as belonging to nationalists (or to unionists, in the case of red, white and blue curb-stones). Burton (1978) discusses the phenomenon of 'telling' in Northern Ireland, the way people attempt to distinguish between Protestants and Catholics in individual encounters with strangers. In a similar sense, curb painting and street signs may help people 'tell' which area they are in, the absence of such markings suggesting 'neutral territory' in some instances. No doubt there is an element of this sort of boundary marking intended by at least some of those involved in putting up signs in at least some areas. Such an image is perhaps reinforced by the abrupt change from English only signs to bilingual signs when the border with the Republic is crossed. However, this is far from a complete picture.

In an area such as the Lower Ormeau Road in south Belfast, this type of interpretation is more easily arrived at. A small nationalist community consisting of a handful of short streets running between the Lagan River and the Ormeau Road, the street signs on the corners of buildings fronting the Ormeau Road are visible to the driver or pedestrian going in or out of this main thoroughfare to the city centre. Small enough to be easily over-looked, nevertheless the signs mark out the boundary of the tiny enclave – Irish street signs are absent from streets on the far side of the Ormeau Bridge over the Lagan, and from the opposite side of the Ormeau Road on streets which lead into the mixed University area.

In the Falls Road area of west Belfast, however, the majority of street signs, shop signs, slogans and murals containing words in Irish are well inside the accepted boundaries of the area. None are visible without sig-nificant penetration of the boundaries, and none are visible to the casual passer-by. Jarman has made a similar observation with regard to loyalist murals and physical signs of allegiance, noting that by the time one is aware of these signs, one has already crossed the boundaries (1992, 149). Marking the boundaries, then, is more than simply a matter of sectarian-ism or the physical division of territory. Boundaries also have a symbolic element. When we talk about the boundaries between ethnic groups, for example, we are talking about more than just frontiers – we are also talk-ing about identity and culture. The pliability of meaning invested into the Irish language as a symbol makes it an effective means of marking out the boundary of identity (Cohen 1987). This involves not only a process of communication with those defined as outside the boundary, but also a process of internal dialogue within the nationalist community.

Irish signs and murals as internal dialogue

An imaginary walk from the city centre up the Falls Road might help enlighten us as to the many meanings and interpretations which can be extrapolated from the increasingly visible presence of the Irish language in this area.

Leaving the city centre from Castle Street, there are already indications of what lies ahead. Inside the security gates which still surround the city centre of Belfast, there is a solicitors office in Castle Street with the name painted in the windows in both Irish and English. Since it is on the first floor, most people are unlikely to notice it. Once outside the gates the green bilingual signs of the West Belfast Taxi Association rank on King Street are clearly visible. From there we walk a fair distance into the heart of the Falls Road before the Irish language again makes an appearance.

Over the M1 motorway, up Divis Street and on to the Falls Road itself, the first sign of Irish is a black on white slogan painted in simple letters. It reads '*Fiche bliain ar aghaidh chun bua*', along with its English transla-tion, '20 years onward to victory', on the wall[5] across the street from the recently built Twin Spires shopping centre. The slogan has been there for years, and is partially obscured by scorch marks. For detractors from the language and for some of its supporters as well, the republican sentiments expressed in this slogan are a cause for anger and resentment. For loyalists, it provides proof that Irish is a 'Provie' language, perhaps inherently republican, and that Irish speakers are by default republican sympathisers. For unionists, it is likely to confirm their worst suspicions about the motivations of Irish language campaigners. For some Irish speakers, it represents an attempt by Sinn Féin to jump on the bandwagon and to score political points from their support of the language, regardless of any long-term damage the association of Irish with republicanism might do. For republicans, on the other hand, it is a powerful symbol of liberation and cultural identity. Even those who do not know what the words actually mean may have a strong reaction to the symbolic message the slogan communicates to its readers.

A short way up the road is the Sinn Féin advice centre. The shop next door has its name written in Irish in bold letters, with an English translation which takes up only a small fraction of the sign. Running along the top of the building are two murals painted on board. One belongs to the group campaigning for the release of Republican prisoners, *Saoirse* (meaning Freedom). It contains two messages, one in English and one in Irish which thanks supporters of the prisoners of war (*'Dea-Mhéin Dár dTacaithe Go Leir, ó na cimí cogaidh'*).[6]

A close association has developed between republican prisoners and the Irish language, especially since the hunger strike in 1981. Learning Irish while in prison or interned has almost become a tradition. Irish was used and taught in some of the cages of Long Kesh during internment in the 1970s, and it became increasingly visible in banners and slogans during the hunger strikes. The now infamous republican slogan *Tiocfáidh ár lá*, a rather ungrammatical translation from the English 'Our day will come', is a well-known example.[7]

While many prisoners became less involved with the Irish language upon their release, their interest tends to have a knock-on effect on their families and friends. This becomes clear when you consider the relatively high proportion of republican prisoners' children who have attended *Bunscoil Phobal Feirste* since they started admitting children from English speaking families (cf. Maguire 1991, 133–4). The effects on children, friends and relatives means that interest spreads not only in republican circles, but among people of different political persuasions and no politics at all.

On the other hand, it is important not to overemphasise the effect ex-prisoners have had. Other Irish language enthusiasts involved in the schools and the Shaw's Road *Gaeltacht*, for example, have had an equal if not considerably greater effect. At the same time, the influence of republi-

Figure 5   *'Our day will come', Whiterock Road, Belfast, 1991.* C O'Reilly.

can ex-prisoners cannot be ignored, not only because of the importance of their contribution, but because republican influence on the Irish language revival has been disproportionately visible in the form of murals, banners, slogans, and high profile political activity by Sinn Féin councillors in places like Belfast City Council.

Returning to our walk up the Falls Road, the bilingual sign of the Dunlewey Centre (*Ionad Dhún Lúiche*) contrasts with the republican murals next door because of its apolitical ordinariness. Rather than being flanked by republican murals, the Dunlewey Centre sign stands next to a Belfast Institute of Further and Higher Education sign and a Worknet sign. Bilingual street signs first come into view in this part of the Lower Falls as well, although most street signs are in English only.

Heading towards the junction with the Grosvenor Road, we see more shop signs with words in Irish – a newsagent, and a barber shop. Flyposted on a nearby wall is a series of Sinn Féin posters written entirely in Irish calling for '*cothromas do chách*' (equality for everyone). Passing the Royal Victoria Hospital there is a stretch of the road without much of interest to the Irish language spotter. However, just past the Royal Hospital is *Glór na nGael*, an organisation which has been primarily concerned with Irish medium nursery schools. They were also one of the main organisations involved in erecting Irish street signs. At one point they were campaigning to encourage shopkeepers in the area to put up bilingual signs. The result is an increase in the number of shops with Irish in the sign over the door, as well as some shops which use Irish on labels and notices inside. For example, one off-licence has a bilingual Irish/English sign near the till notifying the public that they do not sell alcohol to people under the age of 18, and a few shops sport *fáilte* and *slán* signs on their doors.

The idea of this campaign and others like it was to get people interested in the language by increasing its visibility. It had little to do with politics in the narrower sense of the term, nor with marking the boundary between Catholics and Protestants. As a strategy it is meant to work against the tendency for things to be 'out of sight and out of mind'.

Another aspect of the campaign was an attempt to convince shopkeepers that it was worth their while to cater for the Irish speaking community in west Belfast, however small it might be. This, in turn, has to be understood in the context of a wider strategy to bring Irish out of the classroom (and in some instances the home) into all spheres of life, both public and private. Part of the downfall of Irish, it is believed, was that it was not seen as a language of commerce or of the cities. To counter its rural, backward, or even 'quaint' image, it is important for it to be possible to say all things and to carry out all types of activity through the medium of Irish. Trivial as the use of Irish in a shop sign might seem, it is seen to be a small aspect of a much deeper and more complex set of beliefs about the language itself, about community, and about how Irish society should ideally be.

A few hundred yards up the road from *Glór na nGael* is the *Cultúrlann*, an Irish language cultural centre which houses a cafe and Irish language bookstore, the offices of the newspaper *Lá*, and the Irish language secondary school, *Meánscoil Feirste*. The outside of the building carries a myriad of signs – An *Caife Glas* written on a large green coffeepot, *Cultúrlann McAdam – Ó Fiaich* written in decorated Celtic script, and the sign for *Meánscoil Feirste* beneath it. Across the road is another barber shop where the proprietor uses the Irish form of his name on the sign,[8] and a few doors down is a relatively new bilingual chemist's shop sign. As we walk up the road, there are more street signs in Irish above their English equivalents. At the top of the Donegall Road there is a 7-Eleven convenience store whose large plastic signs are entirely in Irish (with the exception of the shop name itself).

The erection of this 7-Eleven sign in 1991 was hailed in the local press as a big boost to the Irish language. West Belfast Irish language activist Gearóid Ó Cairealláin, now president of the Gaelic League, was quoted as saying: 'It is a visible sign of the respect people here have for their native tongue and visitors particularly appreciate this' (*Andersonstown News* 5

January 1991). According to the same article, 40 businesses in west Belfast displayed signs in Irish outside their premises in 1991.

If we were to take a detour here and head up the Whiterock Road, many more street and shop signs in Irish would appear, including the signs for a local resource centre, a fancy goods store, and a hardware store. Looping around to the Monagh Bypass there is an Italian restaurant with a bilingual painted sign and menu headings in Irish, English and Italian. Andersonstown has a particularly high density of signs in Irish – the Falls Community Council (Comhairle Phobail na bhFál) , Casement Park GAA grounds (Páirc Mhic Ásmaint), the *Andersonstown News* offices (*Nuachtán an Phobail*), and another chemist's shop.

Street and shop signs, however, are only part of the picture. Increasingly, Irish is being incorporated into murals and graffiti as well. Nationalists and republicans did not traditionally paint murals, as was common in the unionist and loyalist traditions.[9] According to Bill Rolston (1992), the emergence of nationalist murals dates from the hunger strike period in 1981, and developed out of graffiti in support of the prisoners' campaign for political status in the late 1970s. Simple graffiti became increasingly ornate, with pictures of coffins, flags and the letter 'H' symbolising the H-blocks prison where the blanket protest and the hunger strike occurred (Rolston 1992, iii-iv). Hundreds of murals were painted in 1981 as part of the campaign to support the hunger strikers, with themes centring on the hunger strike itself and the IRA's military campaign. As Sinn Féin became increasingly involved in electoral politics in the period following the hunger strike, election murals were painted. From there a whole range of themes began to appear, including military action, protest against repression, prison conditions, Britain's hold on Ireland, historical figures and events, solidarity with political struggles around the world, mythology, and celtic imagery (Rolston 1992, iv-v).

From the very beginning Irish was used in graffiti and a small number of murals. Graffiti dating from the summer of 1978 includes '*Beidh ár lá linn*' (Our day will come) and '*Sasain amach*' (English out) (*Andersonstown* News 15 July 1978). A simple mural dating from 1981, not much more than an illuminated piece of graffiti really, reads '*Tiocfáidh an lá nuair beidh Éire saoir arís*'.[10] (The day will come when Ireland will be free again). It is written in simple block lettering on a black background, and painted around it are a large letter 'H', the flag of *Fianna Éireann*, and a coffin with the letter H written on it (Rolston 1992, 25).

It is significant, I think, that there is no English translation or other words in English with this mural, considering that the great majority of people in west Belfast, then and now, do not speak Irish. In the context of the historical events of the time and because of the juxtaposition with other symbols, it is not essential to understand the words in order to understand the message. However, if the non-Irish speaking viewer did want to understand the words, it is likely they would have to seek out someone with at least a minimal knowledge of Irish to ask for a translation. From the perspective of some Irish language activists, this can be seen as a positive thing because it encourages a passive viewer to become a more active participant, perhaps also helping to spark an interest in learning the language, but at least helping to raise people's awareness of Irish.

There is another aspect to the importance of the use of Irish in murals such as these. Being able to understand the words transforms the observer from being a metaphorical outsider into an insider, making them a part of something larger, and drawing them into the circle of those who understand. This element of belonging is partially engendered by the fact that so few understand Irish, making it exclusive by nature at least in this context. It is also encouraged by the folklore surrounding the use of Irish by republicans in prison.

Phrases or individual words in Irish are more common in murals than complete sentences like the one discussed above. References to Easter (*Cáisc*) and the 1916 Easter Rising (*Éirí Amach na Casca*) are often made in Irish, for example in graffiti at the parade assembly point on Beechmount Avenue and on a mural in Ballymurphy, west Belfast. Frequently occurring words and phrases include '*saoirse*' (freedom), '*i ndil chuimhne*' (in loving memory), and '*a fuair bás ar son na hÉireann*' (who died for Ireland). Honour roles of the names of the hunger strikers or those killed in action from a particular neighbourhood are quite often accompanied by one or both of the last two phrases. Increasingly, people's names are also written in Irish, for example the names of the eight IRA men killed in an ambush in Loughgall in 1987 as commemorated on an ornate mural featuring an IRA honour guard of six volunteers, a Celtic cross, an Easter lily, and shields of the four provinces of Ireland (Rolston 1992, 56).

The words to the Irish poem '*Mise Éire*' (I am Ireland), written by Patrick Pearse, have appeared on a number of different murals. One such mural in Derry (circa 1985, Rolston 1992, 44), is accompanied by a mythological-looking female Celtic warrior, Celtic artwork, standing stones, one of the spiral inscribed stones from New Grange, and a sunburst. Another from Belfast (circa 1988, Rolston 1992, 58) pictures a dying *Cú Chulainn* surrounded by portraits of the seven signatories of the Proclamation of Independence (1916). The latest appeared in Armagh in 1991, showing a *Cú Chulainn* similar to the one in Belfast, a map of Ireland showing the four provinces, and symbols such as an Irish wolf hound, harp and Celtic knotwork (Rolston 1995, 28).

More recently, the slogan '*Slán abhaile*' (literally 'safe home,' used like the English 'good-bye') has appeared in a number of murals, the most well-known of which is probably the copy of the Robert Ballagh poster painted on a gable end in Ardoyne, north Belfast (circa 1994). It depicts the backs of English soldiers walking down a road signposted 'England', with an arrow pointing in the direction they are walking. Above their heads is a banner reading '*Slán Abhaile*' with festive-looking green, white and orange balloons on either side. The caption on the bottom is another recent slogan, '25 years – time to go'. The '*slán abhaile*' idea has been picked up and used elsewhere, for example a mural (circa 1995) painted on a gable end facing the Whiterock Road, west Belfast. Similar to the Ballagh design, it depicts a front view of an armed British soldier with the Whiterock Road painted in the background and a banner above his head reading '*slán abhaile*'. The caption below reads '*Fág Ár Sráideanna*' (leave our streets). '*Slán*' was also painted on the walls of RUC stations the night the IRA ceasefire came into effect (Rolston 1995, 43).

Irish also features in less overtly political murals, like the three painted especially for the Ardoyne *Fleadh Cheoil* (Ardoyne Music Festival) in the summer of 1994. Two of these have Irish captions. One depicts a number of youths playing hurling and camogie. The English caption above reads 'Gaelic Games Part of Our Heritage'. A saying in Irish is painted below,

Figure 6   '*Safe home*' to the army, Ardoyne, Belfast, 1995. C O'Reilly.

'*Is treise d'chas na oiliúint*' (Instinct is stronger than upbringing). The other mural depicts the mythological queen of the *Tuatha dé Danann* sitting by the water and releasing a white dove. In the background is a megalithic tomb situated in green countryside. The caption in Irish below it reads '*Meon an phobail a thógáil tríd an chultúr*' (To build the spirit of the community through culture). This caption is particularly interesting, because it reflects the belief that an awareness of one's own culture and language has a consciousness raising effect. The learning of the language and the participation in Irish culture through music, dance and sport is often seen as a means to raise spirits, build solidarity, and increase people's political awareness. Through the Irish language, it is felt, the Irish people can come to know who they really are and reclaim their true identity and heritage. For some, this includes their political independence from Britain.

Concluding remarks

A tour around the Falls Road and other nationalist areas such as this might give a false impression of the politics of the Irish language, because so much of what is visually represented is associated with a particular type of nationalism or republicanism. This is in part due to the nature of republican politics. Their tactics tend to be more grassroots, and there is a strong tendency to use what might be termed 'street politics', such as demonstrations, flyposting, political graffiti and murals. All of this increases the visibility of both the Irish language and republican issues, and as a consequence increases the connections that some people make between them, simply because the two are juxtaposed in a highly visible and symbolically powerful way.

If this was taken as the whole picture, however, it would be quite a distorted one. Even within the nationalist community there is a great variety of opinion regarding the meaning and importance of the Irish language, and the appropriate relationship between the language and politics in Northern Ireland, not to mention the increasing numbers of people from the unionist community who are taking an interest in Irish.[11] Tucked away off the main roads are the schools, and behind their Irish language signs – *Bunscoil Phobal Feirste* (Belfast Community Primary School), *Gaelscoil na bhFál* (Falls Irish School), *Scoil na Fuiseoige* (School of the Lark), *Bunscoil an tSléibhe Dhuibh* (Black Mountain Primary School), to name just those in west Belfast – lie many different stories of long years of hard work and struggle against the odds, which took place outside of the limelight and for the most part away from public view. The people involved hold a wide range of political beliefs, but all have in common their love for the Irish language and their desire to see it thrive. The anthropologist Clifford Geertz wrote that '...man is an animal suspended in webs of significance he himself has spun ...' (1975, 5), the webs he refers to being human culture. Our culture is largely built from symbols, and our behaviour is based very much on our interpretations of symbolic communication. Everything, according to Cohen, 'may be grist to the mill of symbolism' (1985, 19).

Visual representations of Irish are more than simple boundary markers, or political slogans, or art. Examined carefully, they offer insights into the politics of identity and power both within the nationalist community, and between nationalists, unionists, and the state. At one level, support for the Irish language can be seen as an expression of unity and a sense of identity among nationalists, its increasingly prominent place in signs and murals a display of solidarity. On another level, activities surrounding the Irish language can reveal contested power relations within the nationalist community as well (Harrison 1992).

The fact that the same symbol can mean different things to different people means that certain interpretations of the meaning of Irish can drive a wedge between unionists and nationalists, while at the same time the power of Irish as a symbol can gloss over differences in interpretation and help to unite nationalists with widely varying political points of view. In this sense, Irish in Northern Ireland is a symbol which both unifies and divides. Irish is generally seen in such a positive light in the nationalist community that it often succeeds in uniting a broad spectrum of opinion in a political context where few things are capable of accomplishing this. At the same time, there are those who seek to reinterpret the meaning of Irish in such a way that it might unite all the people of Northern Ireland under the banner of a common heritage. Whether they will be able to accomplish this remains to be seen, but the broad range of meaning associated with the language over time and today offers some hope for the future.

Notes

1. A New Lodge campaigner apparently retorted, 'that may come as some surprise to the many Maeves and Grainnes who work for the Executive or who live in Housing Executive accommodation'. The names put forward to the Housing Executive are drawn from Irish mythology: Teach Grainne, Teach Cú Chulainn, Teach na bhFiann, Teach Meabha, Teach Oisín, Teach Eithne, and Teach Fionn.
2. Currently there are nothing but Irish street signs in Ballymurphy. The English versions were painted over or removed long ago, reportedly to confuse patrolling British soldiers and the RUC. It is also pretty hard on visitors to the area who may be unfamiliar with the circular layout of the streets.
3. This makes *Andersonstown News* a particularly interesting source of information about the Irish language revival over the years, including the changes in attitudes towards the language and ongoing debates about politics and beliefs associated with Irish.

4. According to one report, the sign was mowed down by a JCB digger on at least one occasion.
5. This wall has been knocked down recently.
6. These two board murals were recently removed and replaced with a mural painted directly onto the building. It depicts a white dove on a blue background, with a rainbow coloured banner stretching horizontally across it.
7. A mural in Strabane, County Tyrone portrays this slogan in the shape of an armalite rifle with an Irish tricolour as background (Rolston 1995: 21).
8. There is a growing trend towards the use of Irish given names, and the use of the Irish version of both first and last names which is also significant. The conscious decision to use the Irish version of one's name, or in some cases to even have it legally changed, is seen by many as an important political act on behalf of the Irish language.
9. For interesting discussions on loyalist murals and banners, see Jarman (1992, 1993).
10. Grammar and spelling mistakes are copied from the original. It should read 'Tiocfáidh an lá nuair a bheidh Éire saor arís'.
11. Irish classes were recently held in Glencairn, a working-class Protestant estate in west Belfast, and a small number of classes can be found in Protestant and neutral areas of Belfast and other parts of Northern Ireland. The *Ultach* Trust is an organisation largely funded by the British government which makes special efforts to nurture this interest as part of their official policy.

References

Bryson, L and C McCartney, 1994 *Clashing symbols: a report on the use of flags, anthems and other national symbols in Northern Ireland.* Belfast, Institute of Irish Studies, Queen's University of Belfast.

Burton, F, 1978 *The politics of legitimacy: struggles in a Belfast community.* London, Routledge and Kegan Paul.

Cohen, A P, 1985 *The symbolic construction of community.* London, Tavistock.

Cohen, A P, 1987 *Whalsay: symbol, segment and boundary in a Shetland island community.* Manchester, Manchester University Press.

Geertz, C, 1975 'Thick description: toward an interpretive theory of culture'. In (ed.) C. Geertz, 1975 *The interpretation of cultures,* London, Hutchinson.

Harrison, S, 1992 'Ritual as intellectual property'. *Man* (NS) 27, 225–44.

Harrison, S, 1995 'Four types of symbolic conflict'. *Journal of the Royal Anthropological Institute* (NS) 1, 255–73.

Hindley, R, 1990 *The death of the Irish language.* London, Routledge.

Jarman, N, 1992 'Troubled Images'. *Critique of Anthropology* 12, 133–65.

Jarman, N, 1993 'Intersecting Belfast'. In B Bender (ed.), *Landscape: politics and perspectives.* Oxford, Berg, 107–38.

MacDonagh, O, 1983 *States of mind: A study of the Anglo-Irish conflict 1780–1980.* London, Allen and Unwin.

Maguire, G, 1991 *Our own language: an Irish Initiative.* Clevedon, Multilingual Matters.

Ó Cuív, B (ed.), 1969 *A view of the Irish language.* Dublin, The Stationery Office.

Ó hUalacháin C, 1994 *The Irish and Irish: a sociolinguistic analysis of the relationship between a people and their language.* Dublin, Irish Franciscan Provincial Office.

Rolston, B, 1991 *Politics and painting: murals and conflict in Northern Ireland.* London, Associated University Presses.

Rolston, B, 1992 *Drawing support: murals in the north of Ireland.* Belfast, Beyond the Pale Publications.

Rolston, B, 1995 *Drawing support 2: murals of war and peace.* Belfast, Beyond the Pale Publications.

Turner, V W, 1967 *The forest of symbols.* Ithaca, Cornell University Press.

WBEF, 1993 *Briefing paper no 1: the 1991 census results.* Belfast, West Belfast Economic Forum.

Light Up The Sky: Hallowe'en Bonfires and Cultural Hegemony in Northern Ireland[1]

JACK SANTINO

L ARGE-SCALE, fire-based public events are a staple feature of traditional celebratory life in Northern Ireland. Bonfires are indeed connected to a large variety of different festivals and celebrations (Gailey 1977; cf. Newall 1972). For example, bonfires associated with the victory of William of Orange at the Battle of the Boyne are burned in July, and bonfires are used by various members of the population to mark diverse events such as the anniversaries of the relief of Derry, the enactment of the internment laws, and the feast of the Assumption of the Blessed Virgin Mary. Effigies of unpopular people or representations of unpopular ideas are frequently immolated ritually on these bonfires. Effigies are also set afire on their own, distinct from bonfires *per se*. The annual burning of Lundy in Derry in December is one such occasion; a festive event that involves parades, bands, and public drinking, but which is centred around the dramatic burning of the 15-foot figure.

Along with the above-named events, bonfires are very much a part of Hallowe'en as well, as are fireworks. There is, I believe, a thread of connections that links bonfires, effigy burnings, fireworks, and other fire customs that allows us to look at them within the same analytical framework (see for instance Cressy 1989, 88). This thread is frequently recognised by the Northern Irish people themselves. Effigies, as mentioned, might be burnt on bonfires or might be the basis of their own public fires. While neither bonfires nor fireworks displays are always part of Hallowe'en festivities (the bonfire tradition is highly localised, within both rural and urban areas), the ways in which these customs are enacted imply that people recognise at least a metonymic relationship between the two. For instance, family fireworks displays are often constructed next to Hallowe'en bonfires. The relationship can be seen also as metaphoric: I have on several occasions overheard people identify the sparks flying heavenward from the fire as the probable inspiration for manufactured fireworks. Sometimes boys load the bonfires with bangers for the thrill of hearing them explode as the fire roars, thus joining the two traditions into one. Michael

63

McCaughan told me in 1991 that one of his outstanding Hallowe'en memories concerned getting bulrushes and soaking them in paraffin to make large torches, 'theoretically to light the bonfires,' he said, 'but we quite liked the torches'. Fire is a constant of traditional life in Northern Ireland, and it is specifically an important component of Hallowe'en.

Nevertheless, bonfires are not always a part of Hallowe'en proceedings. Like other customs, the tradition varies from place to place and region to region (see Gailey 1977). However, even when bonfires are present at Hallowe'en festivities, I found that the interpretations of their meaning varied immensely. Likewise, fireworks displays in back or front gardens were also interpreted in varying and often conflicting ways. While many Hallowe'en customs vary from locality to locality, what I find more interesting are the varying interpretations of the same custom, or as in this case what I will approach as a bundle of related customs (see Charsley 1987, Handelman 1990). The relationships of these customs has to do in part with the particular history and ethnic settlement of Ulster.

In this article I am interested in the multiple interpretations of Hallowe'en customs having to do with fireworks and fire displays, in the context of the interrelationships of ethnic groups in Northern Ireland. By ethnic group here I am referring to Roman Catholics and Protestants generally without noting the very real cultural differences among Protestant denominations (for religious groups as ethnic groups, see Buckley and Kenney 1995). Generally it is said that members of these various Protestant denominations, such as Church of Ireland, Presbyterian, and Free Presbyterian, are united in their wish to retain the union with Great Britain rather than join the Republic of Ireland; that is, they are unionists rather than nationalists despite other differences of identity such as Scottish or English national background. It is precisely along the unionist-nationalist split that we find different uses and significant differences of interpretation of Hallowe'en customs having to do with fire and explosives.

We will need to consider two problems: the question of the relationship of Guy Fawkes to Hallowe'en in Northern Ireland; and the allegedly apolitical nature of Hallowe'en. Throughout my field research in Ulster I was repeatedly told that as a social event, Hallowe'en is a festival blessedly free of sectarianism. Hallowe'en in Northern Ireland seems to be almost universally considered a non-political event, perhaps the only large-scale social event that can make such a claim in this troubled place.[2] Meanwhile, I was told by highly reputable scholars that Guy Fawkes Night was not celebrated in Northern Ireland and meant nothing to the people here. Yet, not only is Guy Fawkes Night celebrated publicly by some people in such towns as Kilkeel in the Mourne Mountains, it also serves as a model for some people by which to interpret certain Hallowe'en customs. We shall return to this point below.

Family fireworks

What is typical of Hallowe'en (also known as Hallow Eve, or Halleve, among other names) in Northern Ireland is not so typical of Hallowe'en anywhere else. Not that there can be any such thing as a typical Hallowe'en, of course, even in a relatively small area such as the six counties of Ulster that comprise Northern Ireland. In fact there is enormous variation in customs, beliefs, and practices associated with Hallowe'en throughout this geographical area, but within these there are higher level thematic similarities. For instance, the foods prepared and consumed at Hallowe'en vary from locale to locale, but are generally comprised of fruits, grains, and earthy vegetables such as turnips and potatoes. Likewise, the many divinatory beliefs and customs associated with Hallowe'en are similar. Whether it's a button in the barm brack (a bread or cake prepared for Hallowe'en and other special occasions) or a ring in the apple tart, the intent is to divine, playfully, the future course of one's life. Both foodways and games frequently revolve around divination; examples are too many to mention here, but these seem to focus on aspects of the life-cycle: will one marry? Have children? Live alone? Die an untimely death? Become wealthy? Again we see the thematic continuities of divinatory customs that vary in the details of their components.

To me as an American the most distinctive feature of the Northern Irish Hallowe'en celebration is the presence of fireworks, the uses of which range from an essentially adolescent boys' culture surrounding bangers and squibs to family back garden (or back yard) displays to large-scale public events. As a visitor to Northern Ireland I was surprised to find that rockets, Catherine wheels, and Roman candles (Anthony D Buckley has directed my attention to the apparent anti-papist names of some of these fireworks) are so much associated with the Hallowe'en festival in Northern Ireland that images of them are used iconographically in advertising posters. For instance, in one store window posters advertising Thornton's chocolates, exploding rockets take their place as Hallowe'en icons alongside ghosts and bats, while on the poster for *October Song*, a drama partly about youthful memories, burnt-out fireworks are depicted prominently among the imagery. And the front cover of a Hallowe'en food supplement to the *Belfast Telegraph* features fireworks cascading from the night sky.

As an outsider to Northern Ireland, I was aware that fireworks were in some way exploded during the season, but it was not until I saw the use of these images in advertising that I realised the extent to which fireworks occupy a central place symbolically and emotionally in Hallowe'en. Symbolically, they can fully stand for Hallowe'en and are used as emblems of it. Emotionally, I have noticed that the sensual aspects of back garden fireworks trigger nostalgic childhood memories of that evening.

In 1991, for example, I attended a family Hallowe'en celebration that had both a bonfire and a back garden display. The fireworks dated to the late 1960s, and were brought to the party by a police officer. A woman had found them in her attic, and in view of the ban on explosives that was imposed in the early 1970s, she brought them to the local police station. The police divided them up among themselves and each took them to his or her own respective festivities. This is not uncommon; I know of other instances where police have brought confiscated fireworks to Hallowe'en parties they have attended. I was impressed that I was able to witness the actual fireworks that would have been exploded prior to the ban. Also, however, I noticed that the participants who viewed the display commented nostalgically on the smell of the expended fireworks. To a person, people mentioned how the distinctive smell of smoke and gunpowder brought them back to their childhood memories of Hallowe'en. Not the spectacular visuals, not the noise, but the smell. These other sensory experiences of sight and sound are undoubtedly important as well, but the frequently undervalued olfactory sense was of primary importance here. I think it is no mistake that the *October Song* poster depicts rockets that already have been exploded as an image that summons nostalgia.

Since 1971 fireworks have been banned as explosives for personal or family use.[3] Official municipal fireworks displays, usually held on a weekend evening close to Hallowe'en are the only legal use of fireworks, but in reality they have been widely available, particularly since the mid-1980s, and widely used by private citizens. As 31 October approaches, they are openly hawked on the streets of Belfast and other cities and newspaper accounts have reported apparent increases in the private uses of fireworks in recent years. Certainly I witnessed a great many in Bangor in 1991 (see for instance the *Belfast Telegraph*, 1 November 1991, 'Bangor Boom: Law Broken as Ulster Skies set Alight,' p.1).

In the United States there is no connection at all of either official or family fireworks to Hallowe'en symbolically or iconographically. In some regions, such as in the Appalachian mountains, adolescent males may light firecrackers at that time of year as part of a general sense of youthful pranking, but fireworks are not associated with Hallowe'en in any nostalgic or emotional way. Instead, personal (but not familial) fireworks – legal or illegal, depending in which state you happen to live, are very much a part of the American Independence Day, the Fourth of July. There is no equivalent to the family displays, but children play with firecrackers (the equivalent of squibs and bangers) all summer long, while municipally-sponsored firework displays are perhaps the most dramatic and pronounced of Independence Day traditions. The photograph referred to above on the Hallowe'en food supplement could be used on an American July Fourth announcement. In England, of course, fireworks are a part of Guy Fawkes

Night. In fact, the relationship of the British Guy Fawkes Night to Northern Ireland's Hallowe'en is central to both the presence and semiotics of fireworks in Ulster's Hallowe'en.

Fireworks displays and bonfires are associated with both. Guy Fawkes Night, 5 November, is known also in England as Bonfire Night. Within the past 40 years Hallowe'en was called Bonfire Night in parts of Northern Ireland, but that term now applies almost universally to the Eleventh Night: the eve of the Twelfth of July commemoration of the victory of King William of Orange over James II at the Battle of the Boyne in 1690. This victory insured the British throne for Protestantism, and is viewed as an almost mythic event by Ulster Protestants, one which is indirectly responsible for the existence of the predominantly Protestant British state known as Northern Ireland. In effect, the largest public celebration of the year (with its Eleventh Night bonfires) celebrates the victory of Protestantism over Roman Catholicism.

Bonfires are generally used in other highly politicised contexts as well. In republican areas of Belfast, bonfires are lit on 8 August, the eve of the anniversary of the 1971 establishment of the policy of the internment laws under which people could be detained by police without actually having to be charged with a crime. The Apprentice Boys, an organisation similar to the Orange Order, have a parade in commemoration of the Relief of Derry from the forces of King James on or around 12 August; here too, the evening before the demonstration is marked with bonfires. In all of these cases and others, effigies, flags, and emblems representing the enemy or traitors to the cause are burned on the fires regardless of which 'side' of the unionist-nationalist split one is on (see Buckley and Kenney 1995).

When I asked people in Northern Ireland about Hallowe'en I noticed a sensitivity, a reluctance on the part of most of them people to discuss bonfires, including the allegedly apolitical Hallowe'en bonfires, not just the Eleventh Night fires. The parades on the Twelfth of July a Roman Catholic might watch and enjoy, especially as a youngster. The bonfires the night before were different – rowdy, often overtly sectarian, dangerous. Thus the bonfires of Hallowe'en have become stigmatised by their association with Bonfire Night on 11 July and the other, politicised bonfires. Yet my asking questions about the topic of bonfires, even Hallowe'en bonfires raised suspicions. This is because the very concept of the bonfire has been politicised, due to the centrality of the custom to the celebration of the Twelfth of July; Roman Catholics celebrate bonfire night in August, both on the eve of the Assumption, 15 August, and more recently, on the eve of the anniversary of the imposition of the internment policy, 8 August. These summer night bonfire night celebrations, both Catholic and Protestant, are clearly and manifestly political and often overtly sectarian events.

On the other hand, I was repeatedly told Hallowe'en is non-sectarian, the only such festival of this magnitude that is notably apolitical. In fact, Hallowe'en in Northern Ireland may represent an ideal state in which sectarian-based identity is not foregrounded but actually put aside, and it provides an occasion when otherwise clashing traditions co-exist peaceably. No one who lives in Northern Ireland or who has ever been there is not interested in seeing progress in the political stalemate that, until recently, the small country seemed doomed to endure indefinitely.

The first hint I had concerning a relationship between Guy Fawkes Night and Hallowe'en in Northern Ireland came at the end of an invited public presentation I made to a group of gentlemen associated with Bangor Abbey. During the questions following my talk, which dealt with my research on Hallowe'en in Northern Ireland, I repeated my interest in the back garden firework tradition, which was so different from my experiences in the United States. In the back of the room a man raised his hand. 'Jack,' he said, 'we have fireworks here because we celebrate Guy Fawkes Night on 31 October'. I was taken aback by this very direct statement, a statement that in effect claimed 31 October for the British by declaring it a kind of local variant of the British Guy Fawkes Night commemoration. The gentleman in question, Mr Ferris Dennison, repeated his assertion with great authority and assurance. I asked if he meant that 31 October was literally celebrated as Guy Fawkes Night, marked with the British customs of making of Guys (effigies), children asking for pennies, and so forth. He insisted it was. At this point, some men in the room agreed with him about the Guys, while others stated that they, at least, had never seen Guys in evidence on 31 October. The fact that both Hallowe'en and Guy Fawkes Night share the custom of exploding fireworks allows an identification to be made between the two celebrations. Also, the begging of pennies for the Guy is identified in the transcript below with the Northern Irish Hallowe'en rhyming tradition in which, for several weeks prior to Hallowe'en, youngsters go from home to home either reciting a traditional rhyme or otherwise performing, usually in return for money, fruit or nuts. The most commonly used Hallowe'en rhyme today is one derived from the mumming traditions found elsewhere in Ireland during the Christmas season: 'Hallowe'en is coming and the geese are getting fat/ Please put a penny in the old man's hat/ If you haven't got a penny, then a ha'penny will do/ If you haven't got a ha'penny then God bless you/ and your old man too'. The following is a transcription of some of that interchange:

Ferris Dennison: Over here we simplify it. We just celebrate Guy Fawkes on Hallowe'en. We have the fireworks here at Hallowe'en as opposed to celebrating at the proper time. We celebrate it at the end of the month. Over in England and in America you celebrate it on the 5 November, is it?

Jack Santino: No. We don't celebrate it in America at all. Do you have it here? I'm confused. Do you have 5 November in Northern Ireland?

FD: We have it at the end of October. We have Guy Fawkes Night on 31 October: Bonfire Night. We have Guy Fawkes Night every night. [This is a reference to the explosives used by the IRA and other paramilitary groups]. Go back and tell your friends in America we celebrate every night. More of them would be coming here. We celebrate the fact that Guy Fawkes didn't blow up the Houses of Parliament. Hallowe'en gives us an excuse to celebrate Guy Fawkes Night. An excuse to have fireworks. The children of course go round to homes and asking for a penny for the Guy. If you give them too much the word goes round.

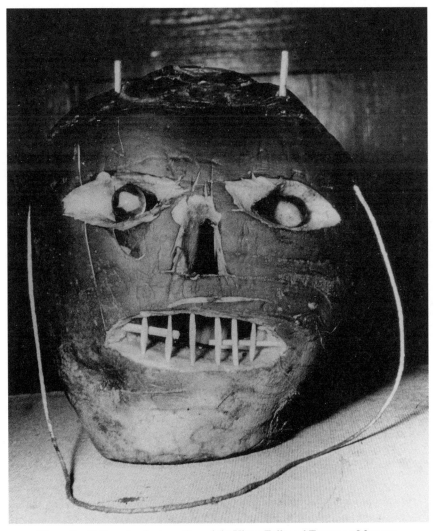

Figure 7 *Hallowe'en lantern.* Copyright Ulster Folk and Transport Museum.

JS: Do they actually ask for a penny for the Guy?

FD: Yes. 'If you haven't got a penny.' There's a number of alternatives. 'If you haven't got a ha'penny.'

JS: But they don't actually say 'a penny for the Guy', do they?

Another voice: Yes.

JS: Do they have a Guy?

Voice: No.

Jim Muller: The Irish people brought Hallowe'en to America, the English people brought Guy Fawkes here.

I would run into similar situations frequently throughout my research. Whenever I made public presentations to various groups – local history societies, women's clubs, men's clubs, etc. I asked about any Guy Fawkes Night–Hallowe'en connection. Invariably the answers ranged from people saying they knew of no such connection and in fact thought of the two celebrations as very different, to individuals who did relate them or even equate them as Mr Dennison had. One man in Bangor specifically told me he used to make Guys for Hallowe'en and took them around to people's homes for money.

Philip Robinson, a cultural geographer and Head of Collections at the Ulster Folk and Transport Museum, told me of an incident in his childhood in which he and his friends used a Guy while Hallowe'en rhyming. His testimony reflects his childhood perceptions of social class, economic status, and ethnic identity with regard to housing patterns in a rural area north of Belfast:

PR: I think there was a thing, you know, where these new people – in a sense – the outsiders, were fair game, you know, for pranks because they had this sort of distance and also you were less likely to get identified and so on. There were all sorts of reasons why you'd be more likely to play pranks on them. Ah, I also remember – an interesting thing – about these new houses, the bungalows they were. We tried to gear – because they were fertile ground for rhyming – we tried to gear what we did obviously. We were sort of market-conscious, and I remember one occasion we had the sort of sense that these people – I mean our simple minds, middle class, couldn't distinguish between what was meant by 'middle class' and what was meant by 'English', for example. These people weren't English, but we somehow thought the people were English. And I remember on one occasion we deliberately made a Guy Fawkes to take round with us. I think I had seen this in a comic of a – of somebody pulling in one of these buggies or children's – what we called guiders – a little sort of four-wheeled, ah ...

JS: A cart?

PR: A cart or wagon, yeah, that's the sort of thing. But I'd seen it in a comic with a Guy, spelt wrong in a comic, and assumed that this was a way of how they did it in England – how they Hallowe'en rhymed in England. That's what

I thought – that's what I assumed. So, we made one of these things – in fact we did but we didn't. We got one of the smallest boys, we turned his coat inside out and stuffed straw inside his cuffs – we put his hands right up and made him into a Guy. We made him like a scarecrow and sat him on this thing so that we wouldn't have to carry him. Sat him on the guider and took him – wheeled him – to the front door of these bungalows. And I would never have dreamt of doing that but this, looking back on it now – and don't try to analyse it – but looking back on it now, I think what we were trying to do was give these people what they wanted or what we thought they might've wanted, or what we thought they might have expected.

JS: What happened?

PR: Well, I think we went to one door (*laughing*). And we, unfortunately the door we went to was one place we were chased from and the Guy had to get up and run, leaving the kids behind him. So it was a very unsuccessful visit. And it was – it was just a sort of trial, and it didn't work.

Robinson's humorous anecdote clearly relates an unusual incident and reflects more the influence of the media, in that he was aware of the British custom through magazine and newspaper reports, than it does the accretion of two separate traditions. However, other men were more insistent that the making of Guys was in fact something they had first hand experience with and regularly did in their youth, sometimes for the 5 November (thus challenging the scholars who said that Guy Fawkes day meant nothing in Northern Ireland), or, more interestingly, for Hallowe'en.

Guy Fawkes Night is celebrated as an entirely discrete event from Hallowe'en in some places in Northern Ireland. For instance, I interviewed a family who lived in the Mourne Mountains relatively near Kilkeel. Present were Mrs McConnell, grandmother, Sharon, her granddaughter (a woman in her 30s) and John, a 19-year-old, her great-grandson and Sharon's nephew. I asked if effigies were ever burnt on the local Hallowe'en bonfires (as they are in some places, which I will discuss below). 'No,' John responded. 'That's more for Guy Fawkes.'

Sharon: Guy Fawkes Night would've been the night for doing that, not Hallowe'en.

JS: Would they have done Guy Fawkes Night here?

Sharon and Mrs McC simultaneously: Yes.

Mrs McC: Well they had something dressed up like, what would you call the man?

Sharon: The Guy?

Mrs McC: The Guy, Guy Fawkes, they had one made up like that and take him way up to some field where it wouldn't cause harm and get it all alight there.

Sharon: Sometimes though in recent days instead of seeing a Guy Fawkes being burnt you'll see an effigy of Margaret Thatcher's head, you know, a mask of her.

JS: Where would you have seen it?

Sharon: I would've seen that on television, just from across the water.

JS: But is Guy Fawkes celebrated here in Kilkeel?

Mrs McC: Yes, yes. They'll have a parade through the streets first, and then they'll go to whatever field it was that was for the fire.

JS: Was it a community or town bonfire?

Mrs McC: Well, a lot of country boys do it as well.

Sharon: I remember being at one, I'm sure it's nearly ten years ago it was, when I remember. In Kilkeel and, you know, people with chip vans would come up and sell their chips. But I do remember that that night was also an excuse to maybe, to play tricks on Roman Catholic folk, and I remember a slurry tank, that's like with manure, being taken out in the road because they know that some Roman Catholics were going to be there, they were going to spray them with slurry.

JS: What is slurry?

Sharon: Pig manure.

JS: So they are really close to each other. You might have a bonfire for Hallowe'en then five, six days later you'd have an official one for Guy Fawkes Night.

Sharon: That would be a bigger thing, much bigger thing.

JS: And there could be mischief again.

Sharon: Mm-hmm.

JS: Although, aimed specifically at the Roman Catholics. Would there likely be mischief straight through, like a week of children playing tricks?

Sharon: Yes.

Mrs McC: Well what day is Guy Fawkes? There's just a few days between each.

JS: Did you feel that they were two different events altogether, though? Or did you feel that they were sort of alike?

Mrs McC: No, just different. Different.

Sharon: I thought they were different.

This point needs to be made: many if not most people deny the connection of Hallowe'en and Guy Fawkes Night vigorously, as does the family quoted at length above. The testimony of the McConnell family instead demonstrates not only that Guy Fawkes Night is indeed celebrated, formally and officially, in Northern Ireland, but also that it is the vehicle for sectarian pranks that strike outsiders (and presumably the victims) as quite ugly. Likewise, Philip Robinson's recollections indicate class-based childhood perceptions of the world, especially insofar as he interpreted middle-class Northern Irish people as being English. In other words, even though Guy Fawkes Night figures in one way or another in the lives of the different informants quoted so far, according to their testimonies it reflects very different aspects of their lives and has very different meanings to each of them.

There are still other linkages between the two festivals. Both the terms 'Lundy' and 'Guy' have become synonymous with 'effigy'. The term 'Guy' probably predates the actual Gunpowder Plot and derives from 'guyser,' referring to someone in disguise. 'Lundy' as a generic term dates directly to the Siege of Derry and the subsequent traditional burning of this unpopular (among unionists) figure.

Several residents of the Greyabbey area told me that they burnt effigies on the Hallowe'en bonfires, usually of the 'traitor Lundy', governor of Derry at the time of the Jacobean siege. Lundy had attempted to come to terms with the troops who had a stranglehold on the city but was prevented from doing so by a band of apprentice boys. In Derry, these events are commemorated twice a year, in December and in August. In December, an effigy of Lundy is publicly set aflame, following a day of band parades. This day, the Saturday closest to 16 December, is known as Lundy Day and is at least in part the occasion for the public display of anti-Catholicism. That Lundys should be burnt on Hallowe'en elsewhere adds a political and sectarian dimension to the festival in those instances, and is a direct contradiction of the supposed non-political, non-sectarian nature of the celebration. Archive materials in the Ulster Folk and Transport Museum indicate that Lundys were burnt as part of Hallowe'en festivities in Belfast and Fermanagh in years past, and I recorded the testimony below in 1992 in Greyabbey:

T McKee: I'm Teddy 'Bear' McKee from the holy city of Portavogie. There's not a pub in it!

JS: Did you burn a Lundy here?

T McKee: Only in fun. But that's years ago. I'm sure it's years ago. I'll tell you. Hallowe'en went out here when the fireworks went out (*general agreement*). Aye, the squib, that was it. We used put them in keyholes, in the keyhole and lighting them.

JS: Did you light bonfires out in the back?

T McKee: Yeah.

JS: Did you have a dummy you would burn?

T McKee: Yeah. Lundy, we called it. Lundy. Aye that's right. Hallowe'en night.

JS: Did it have anything to do with Guy Fawkes?

Other voices: No, no.

JS: When did you stop doing that?

Other voices: When the fireworks went, all that went. That'd be '69.

One voice: Fireworks were banned.

JS: Were they burning Lundy up until then?

Same voice: No. I don't think so. The war – after the war. They stopped for the war (*general agreement*).

T McKee: The fifties. They called it a Guy. They wouldn't have bothered now to make the Guy. They wouldn't have time, you see. Before the days of television there was more time in the house. Oh aye, there was nothing else to do. The thing was, you were always knocking doors. Bang bang. Kick the door, you see, and run. And it was no good unless they chased you.

JS: Where did you have the bonfire?

Previous voice: I've seen them in the square over here, and I've seen them burned up on the top of the street too.

JS: What time?

T McKee: Just after it got dark, just early evening. Because everybody else would go back to their own house to play ducking for apples, and games, stuff like that. Oh, just a few of the boys would get together and say: 'C'mon and we'll make a Lundy'. You get an old coat and a pair of trousers and you get some straw and you stuffed it with straw. In those days, you see, you went together with a gang of boys and you feel everything. You just all went about together. You played football together, you did this and that together. And therefore, if there was anything happening you were all in on it. But maybe somebody had more room at his place or his back yard. So you'd say we'll built it up in so and so's yard, so he went and got the straw. You build it before Hallowe'en night. It was brought out on Hallowe'en night and placed somewhere. Maybe depending on where it's placed, maybe if it was built on top of the street you didn't come any further than the top of the street, maybe it was brought down here to the square, and we set it alight.

Another voice: Did you bring it straight to the bonfire or did you parade up and down?

T McKee: No, you just brought it straight to the bonfire. You'd start – with that type of thing its dark at that time. Of course the gang was all together. And then it took a week or so to collect the wood for the fire.

Second voice: Ah no, I don't think.

Third voice: No, Teddy, there would have been tar bars about somewhere.

T McKee: Tar bars. Remember those? Wooden bars.

Second voice: Wooden bars burned well. You'd have got maybe some tyres. There was no wood involved because some of it just burned up in a half an hour.

T McKee: You would put squibs in it.

Second voice: Oh, you would put squibs in them.

T McKee: The fingers, put squibs in the fingers. Put'em in the ends of the sleeve, you see? Then they went off, the bangers went off – you'd put the bangers in a bottle, an empty bottle, that took off up into the air. You'd use squibs and jumping jacks, they'd be jumping around your feet, you know.

Other voice: I remember jumping jacks on a thread, with a safety pin. You stuck it on your coat (*great laughter*). Stick it on your coat and light it.

Second voice: And the there was the Catherine wheel. You'd set them onto a piece of wood or something. Do you have fireworks in America?

T McKee: No, no but you see that's – fireworks is Guy Fawkes. I wonder what they had before Guy Fawkes. They probably had Hallowe'en before Guy Fawkes.

Other voice: Normally, yes. But we never had Guy Fawkes. It depends when fireworks were introduced in this country. Maybe we had more of a Scottish connection on the coast here. See, Guy Fawkes didn't mean anything to us at all.

T McKee: No. Fireworks aren't banned. Explosive substances are banned. See, somebody was caught one day with 100 pounds of explosives. They said it wasn't – it was fireworks!

Second voice: That's right (laughter). So they have to ban it all now. It's a shame, you know, but I know a lot of fishermen brought them in. It's amazing how many fireworks were exploded just around our place on Hallowe'en.

T McKee: Here, yes. Even in the new towns now.

Second voice: You couldn't hear a firework on Guy Fawkes, the 5 November, here. Its only here for Hallowe'en.

T McKee: But you see Guy Fawkes wasn't actually burnt. Was he not hung?

Second voice: Well I know they've got bonfires now in England.

T McKee: No, I mean that was his sentence. Was he hung? Or was he burnt at the stake?

Voice: He was burnt at the stake, I'm sure.

T McKee: I'm just wondering, I don't know about that, because I presume that Hallowe'en had a bonfire maybe before Guy Fawkes time and then –

Second voice: Was there not rhyming at Hallowe'en?

T McKee: Yes, of course, we used to beg with a dummy. Took it around in a wheelbarrow. A Guy, penny for the Guy.

Second voice: Guy Fawkes never burned. There's no Guy at all. Just stuck a false face on, its a penny for the Guy, and there's no, maybe a door or something. Just a way of begging. We never knew anything about Guy Fawkes (*emphatically*).

JS: You still said 'penny for the Guy'.

Voices: No, no, not in our town. Not in our town. Lundy has no collection.

JS: You did do the burning of a dummy and you called it a Lundy?

Voice: Lundy.

Woman's voice: With Lundy you see you maybe got a tub of paraffin or something and you just threw it in and you lit Lundy and away he went. You maybe had a time or something, you didn't, you never sung a song or anything. Somebody just went up to the fire, their fireworks lit off, squibs and that and then everybody on the way back home we knew at every house there was a party, ducking for apples.

JS: Did you have to guard it?

T McKee: You just lit it. Ten years ago you could've left the Twelfth bonfire with nobody near. But there's this attitude now you have to destroy things so they would set it on fire before the day.

Other voice: Same thing, if you got stuck in a boat in Greyabbey you could have left a boat upside down and left it for two or three days. You couldn't leave it for an hour now. They'd have it on the bonfire! [laughter] Even if we burnt one on the Twelfth of July, it was still called a Guy. It wasn't until we were quite a bit older when we realised it was Lundy. See to us here a bonfire's not right unless it has a dummy on it or a Guy.

The testimony above is typical in its internal contradictions. People are simultaneously reminiscing about building dummies and asking 'a penny for the Guy', which is a Guy Fawkes tradition, while others are insisting there are no Guy Fawkes customs in Northern Ireland, at least not in their town, or experience. For instance, when I interviewed Ferris Dennison, whom I quoted earlier, on another occasion in his home with his wife present, he was less insistent that Guy Fawkes Night was celebrated on 31 October in Northern Ireland. This was due entirely to the presence of his wife, who disagreed sharply with him on this point.

FD: I guess Guy Fawkes Night, during the night time you have the fireworks. We refer to it as Guy Fawkes Day or Guy Fawkes Night. We don't just say Guy Fawkes. It's an overlap between the Hallowe'en which is at the end of October and Guy Fawkes and we're peculiar in Northern Ireland because we really link the two together to a certain extent. Well, there's fireworks associated with it.

JS: Where are you from?

FD: Belfast.

JS: All your life?

FD: Uh huh.

JS: Where are you from?

Mrs D: Co Cavan.

JS: No, I was just curious frankly in talking about Guy Fawkes Night, it is essentially an English holiday. Do you have an English background? No, no English background at all. Do you think you can tell me why these overlapped?

FD: Well, at Hallowe'en you have ducking for apples, you have nuts, and you dress up and for a while beforehand you go around house with a Guy and the Guy is Guy Fawkes and you have fireworks the night of Hallowe'en, just like Guy Fawkes Night, which is Guy Fawkes Night and therefore it's Guy Fawkes Night and that's what I say therefore there is a certain linkage.

Mr Dennison's wife insisted that the two were separate events, and, at least in her presence, Ferris did not disagree. Initially he had been making a claim for a kind of British authenticity to the Northern Irish 31 October celebration. People might call it Hallowe'en, he implied, but the use of fireworks proved that this was really the Guy Fawkes Night celebration, albeit a few days early. An interaction I had with a city official from Derry sheds some light on this dynamic. I had been in Derry for the burning of the Lundy in December and had arranged an interview with this official regarding Derry's famous city-wide fancy dress Hallowe'en festival. We met outside, after the day's parade had ended but before the lighting of the effigy at twilight. The city was alive with band members and tourists wandering the streets and packing the bars. We had been talking about Hallowe'en for some time, and the individual repeatedly attributed the success of the Hallowe'en event to the fact that it was all-inclusive. Everyone could and did come, all ages, all backgrounds. Only once had there been any trouble, I was told, when some soldiers drove into the crowd and some people threw rocks at them. 'They (the soldiers) shouldn't have been there,' the official said, with some vehemence. This should have indicated to me that the crowd was predominantly Roman Catholic, but what was said next was more revealing. Distracted by some noise made by Lundy Day revellers, the official explained the events surrounding us to me. 'That's fine. It's all right. It's a tradition for the other side, you know. Lundy Day is theirs. Hallowe'en is ours.' This despite the official stance of inclusiveness.

Hallowe'en, due to its presumed Celtic origins – it is generally said to be the festival of Samhain, Christianised and in modern dress – falls into the cultural property claimed by Roman Catholics. Guy Fawkes Night is clearly British and often anti-Papist, anti-Catholic. On one level, people see and experience Hallowe'en as non-sectarian, but in many instances, there is a struggle of definition as to whose cultural property it really is, to which 'side' it belongs, who's hegemony it falls under. Ferris Dennison makes a claim for Hallowe'en as British by redefining it as Guy Fawkes Night. The Derry official, while asserting the openness of Hallowe'en, confided to me personally that it really belonged to one group.

I have tried to demonstrate that the relationships between Guy Fawkes Night and Hallowe'en in Northern Ireland are several and complex. The fireworks tradition is widely thought to be a unique adaptation of a British custom associated with an early November celebration to the Irish 31 October festival. Both Guy Fawkes and Hallowe'en have bonfires associated with them and are, or have been, known as Bonfire Night. Despite the assertions of some scholars and many residents, Guy Fawkes Night is celebrated by some people in certain localities in Northern Ireland. Even in places where the residents deny any connection between the two events, we have seen the burning of effigies on Hallowe'en bonfires, a custom that parallels the more politicised Guy Fawkes Night, and introduces political elements to a festival renown for its absence of politics. Finally we have seen instances where individuals directly claimed the day for their 'side'. According to one man, Hallowe'en in Northern Ireland is in actuality Guy Fawkes Night, while to a city official in Derry, Hallowe'en properly belongs to the Roman Catholic tradition.

And yet, in the face of all this, people maintain that Hallowe'en is non-political and non-sectarian. I do not doubt that they are right. What I think is important about all this and what I have tried to show is that Hallowe'en is not neutral: it contains symbolism that has the *potential* to be read in divisive sectarian terms, and on some occasions is. There are in fact multiple readings of these symbolic forms. What is important is that usually these readings are not put forth as the only correct way to interpret the symbols. They are not used to validate one's personal political, cultural, or ethnic allegiance or identity although the potential exists for doing just that. Hallowe'en could be another site of conflict (on all levels) but it is not. The opposite is the case. People universally relish it as a great family event. It is frequently referred to as the Irish Christmas (Buchanan 1963), a jolly and peaceful occasion, a haven of non-sectarian sentiment. But if one scratches the surface, one finds potentially conflicting, oppositional readings which could lead to political strife. However, people choose not to assert specific conflictual or sectarian interpretations, nor attempt to impose them on others. Hallowe'en allows for a peaceful coexistence of these interpretations and for the interpreters as well.

Perhaps the terrorist killings on 31 October 1993 in Greysteel should be mentioned as well in this context. The paramilitaries shouted 'trick or treat', a foreign, American phrase, as they murdered 13 pubgoers (both Protestant and Roman Catholic; the gunmen were loyalist, and the act was the culmination of a particularly bloody October). One might speculate as to why the terrorists should choose a foreign phrase, although it certainly fits the circumstances better, in terms of both time and semantic meaning, than does 'Hallowe'en is coming and the geese are getting fat'. Actually, although under the circumstances it seems almost frivolous to say, the use of the phrase points to the growing internationalism of the day. For the purposes of this article, it is enough to point out that, horrific as it was, this event has not stigmatised Hallowe'en in Northern Ireland. It remains a day that is felt to be free of the sectarianism that has otherwise troubled the annual calendar of ritual, festival, and celebration.

What is finally most important about the sectarian or non-sectarian nature of Hallowe'en is that the potential for conflict is only rarely realised. One large-scale public Hallowe'en demonstration in Derry resulted in fighting, largely because British soldiers drove into the liminal, play space of the festivities, thus violating its ludic nature. As we have seen, Hallowe'en in Northern Ireland includes a good deal of symbolic forms and customary activities that can be interpreted in a variety of ways according to one's personal background and predilections, but which are not contested. The symbols in question, whether they be objects or actions, are like all symbols multivocal and polysemic. Hallowe'en symbols are ambiguous enough to allow multiple readings that stretch across both sides of the unionist-nationalist debate, unlike the burning of Lundy, a public fire on 8 August in west Belfast, most of the gable-end paintings, or a parade of the Orange Order. These may all be read differently, but they are semantically limited as far as political allegiance and sentiment are concerned.

My impression is that people find a haven in Hallowe'en. There seems to be almost an unspoken agreement that allows Hallowe'en to remain a rich celebration but one free from sectarianism. I have written elsewhere that in the United States Hallowe'en mediates oppositions or dichotomies having to do with nature and culture, transitional seasons, and life and death (Santino 1982, 1994). In Northern Ireland dichotomies having to do with indoor-outdoor, and male-female are also addressed. It is interesting to think that Hallowe'en is capable of reconciling within its liminal time perhaps the greatest social division in Northern Ireland as well. Certainly before the cease-fire of 1994, Hallowe'en provided an ideal model of how life could be: different traditions co-existing in a non-threatening, celebratory way. It is fitting that Hallowe'en, a festival that I see as bringing together a great many oppositions, brings together political oppositions as well.

Hallowe'en in Northern Ireland allows people to find common ground with each other even where meaning might otherwise be contested. The history of Ireland and the events that led to the creation of Northern Ireland are unique to that society, as are its problems. But they are at the very least analogous to other societal problems internationally, such as the Arab-Israeli disputes, the problems in South Africa, and race relations in the United States, to name only a few. The study of the customs, traditions, and contemporary social dynamics of one major calendrical festival in this one place may help us understand and even deal with similar situations plaguing humanity throughout the world.

Notes

1. This article was first published in *Western Folklore*, 1996 55, 213-31, and is reproduced with the kind permission of the publisher.
2. The principal field research for this article was conducted from August 1991 to June 1992, with other trips in 1993, 1994, and 1995. Thus, the overwhelming majority of the fieldwork was conducted before the cease-fires of Autumn, 1994.
3. Soon after this was written in 1996, controlled sales of fireworks for Hallowe'en were legalised (editor's comment).

References

Buchanan, R H, 1963 'Calendar customs part 2' *Ulster Folklife* 9, 61–79.

Buckley, A D and M C Kenney, 1995. *Negotiating identity: rhetoric, metaphor and social drama in Northern Ireland.* Washington D C, Smithsonian Institution Press.

Charsley, S, 1987 'Interpretation and custom: the case of the wedding cake'. *Man* (NS) 22, 93–110.

Cressy, D, 1989 *Bonfires and bells: memory and the Protestant calendar in Elizabethan and Stuart England.* Berkeley and Los Angeles, University of California Press.

Gailey, R A, 1977 'The bonfire in north Irish tradition'. *Folklore* 88, 3–38.

Handelman, D, 1990 *Models and mirrors: toward an anthropology of public events.* Cambridge, Cambridge University Press.

Newall, V J, 1972 'Two English fire festivals in relation to their contemporary social setting'. *Western Folklore* 31, 244–74.

Santino, J, 1983 'Hallowe'en in America: contemporary customs and performances'. *Western Folklore* 42, 1–20.

Santino, J, (ed.) 1994 *Hallowe'en and other festivals of death and life.* Knoxville, University of Tennessee Press.

Painting Landscapes: The Place of Murals in the Symbolic Construction of Urban Space

IN little more than a decade mural painting has developed into one of the most dynamic media for symbolic expression in the north of Ireland. On any journey, real or virtual, through the working-class estates of Belfast one is bombarded by a panoply of visual statements. In recent years these images have become increasingly elaborate and extensive in their design and professional in their execution. Nowadays scaffolding is often erected in front of walls which are to be transformed and painters may spend days working to cover a wall with symbols, icons and images. We have come a long way from 1970 when two men were sentenced to six months' imprisonment for painting a tricolour at Annadale Street, or from 1980 when a 16-year-old youth was shot dead while painting republican slogans on a wall by a policeman who said he thought the paintbrush was a gun. Nowadays such activity is largely acknowledged as an established, if not entirely legitimate, political practice.

Many people have recorded the growing number of mural paintings and analysed their changing symbolic content. But most such discussions focus purely on the murals as images and have only briefly acknowledged another important factor: the materiality of these paintings. For as well as being elaborate visual displays, the murals are also objects. As such they are more artefact than art. As artefacts they are produced to be seen at fixed sites and in specific locales, and an extension of their significance is generated by a semiotic dynamic which involves the images taking meaning from their location and the location in turn having a differing significance because of the paintings. As images they are always open to multiple interpretations, but as artefacts in public space they are also open to multiple forms of use, re-use and abuse. As images they always have had a functionality: as propaganda, as rhetoric, as ideological and symbolic markers etc., but as artefacts their use is potentially more varied. While on one level it is primarily the image that it is being used and transformed, on another level it is the physical artefact, fixed in space, which is the subject of activity; taken still further it is the public space in which the artefact is sited that is changed.

As artefacts all murals are site-specific. Not in an artistic way which suggests they might be designed with a particular location in mind, but rather, their power as political statements and as symbols is enhanced by their location. A sense of place can always be understood in terms of the content of the paintings: the juxtaposition and selection of the varied components and their framing situates each mural on one side of the sectarian divide or the other. But this is still to see them principally as images. To see them as artefacts demands some wider recognition of placing, of the area beyond the immediate frame or the edge of the wall, which all too often is the limit or boundary of photographic reproduction and of verbal analysis. To see them as site-specific requires awareness of the physical and social environment in which the images are produced and with which they interact. Meaning changes as the frame widens. The three-storey-high depiction of the Madonna and Child at the bottom of the Falls Road is transformed when one is aware of the military base, bristling with antennae, at the top of the adjacent Divis Tower, and the 20-foot high steel fence dividing the Falls Road from the Shankill Road on the other side. To regard the murals essentially, or only, as images is therefore to restrict their power. Their very location affects how they are interpreted and what they mean, while the location is used and treated differently because of the presence of the paintings. But as artefacts the power of the murals also extends beyond their immediate position. Many paintings are widely represented and thereby further transformed. Although they may be removed from their original context, they will always be reproduced in another location. The mode and medium of reproduction may in turn suggest a very different chain of meaning and interpretation.

The intention of this paper is not to focus on the symbolic content of murals or the developments in their style and form, as this has been dealt with extensively elsewhere (Jarman 1992, 1996a, 1997; Rolston 1991, 1992, 1995a; Woods 1995). Rather I will discuss the ways in which the murals are used as symbolic objects in themselves. Objects which are used and abused, admired and transformed, replaced and defaced and which, while they ultimately physically disappear, will often survive as reproductions, and thereby transcend their context in time and place. As artefacts they are always situated in an urban landscape which itself adds to, and is altered by, the presence of painted daubs on the walls. But emerging as a symbolic landscape, somewhat paradoxically it is no longer so physically grounded, or so anchored to place, but is itself a highly mobile signifier of violence and danger.

Some elements of the spatial relationship have long been established, if not widely addressed. The large number of murals that are prominently situated on parade routes, or mark assembly points for major gatherings, indicates how they are widely used within the community (Jarman 1993). In contrast it has been more widely noted how murals and other displays are sometimes situated as territorial indicators or as boundary markers – as a warning or challenge to the 'other'. Jeff Sluka addressed a further facet of the relationship between image and place when he described the challenge that has been issued from republicans by painting slogans under a military post on Derry city walls. He has also noted the negative reaction that some people have towards political paintings in their neighbourhoods. But this type of response he curtly dismisses as merely a 'bourgeois' view, and by implication without substance (Sluka 1997). Both of these examples illustrate the significance for their political meaning of the location of mural paintings, a point that is also acknowledged in passing in a recent paper by Bill Rolston (1996). However neither of these authors elaborates or expands on this aspect of the paintings.

This paper begins by considering the historic role of murals in the construction of sectarian space in urban Northern Ireland, before moving on to discuss the ways in which their use has expanded in symbolising resistance and opposition to the state. I then consider some of the recent developments: their use in redefining distinct locales as political sites, as a subject of tourist routes and then their significance as local memorials to those who have died for their cause. Finally I will touch on more critical and negative responses to the increase in painted gables, by looking at mural paintings as objects which provoke both fear and opposition from within the working-class communities.

Segregating space

Mural painting has been a feature of unionist popular culture since the early years of this century when images of King William III and other Orange symbols began to adorn the gable walls of the working-class areas of Belfast. They appeared as part of an assertion of the Protestant people's sense of British identity during an extended period of political crisis. In the later stages of the Home Rule campaign and, following partition in 1921, in the period of consolidation of the Northern Irish state, mural paintings were used to complement and extend the existing forms of Orange displays.

From the early years of the nineteenth century elaborate displays of flags, flowers and bunting were hung from houses and across streets for the July commemorations of the Battle of the Boyne. Each year wooden, metal or floral arches were installed in the centres of many towns and villages and in staunchly Protestant residential areas. These displays were highly formalised and showed little variation in their symbolic content from year to year or from place to place (Jarman 1997). Each area was content to affirm its loyalty to the memory of King William III, and celebrate the victory at the Boyne. Such displays served to mark out those towns, villages and streets which were loyal and Protestant.

These displays on the Twelfth of July marked the beginnings of a visible sectarianisation of place. But they were short-lived. Most lasted for no more than a few days and then the streets and buildings returned to their everyday appearance with no overt demonstration of collective identity. However the introduction of mural paintings in working-class areas of Belfast changed all this, making these hitherto temporary and seasonal affirmations of loyalty much more permanent. Streets could now declare their faith throughout the year. They were no longer simply rows of houses, but terraces of Protestant houses. The permanent displays visually confirmed a status above and beyond mere function. While this may have been a relatively minor step in areas which were already recognised as staunchly Protestant, and much of working-class Belfast was highly segregated, such displays helped to make explicit the fact of residential segregation.

Murals helped to transform 'areas where Protestants lived' into 'Protestant areas'. By implication this should also mean that some areas were accepted as 'Catholic areas'. Mural painting was soon recognised as an established feature of Protestant popular culture, and after partition in 1921, helped to define the political and cultural parameters of the Northern Ireland state. New murals, arches and other displays were ritually unveiled by politicians each July in Protestant areas across the north, but the law and the police were utilised to ensure that the nationalist population did not develop a similar tradition within a British Northern Ireland. Although an area could be acknowledged as inhabited by Catholics, it could not easily or readily be regarded as a 'Catholic area' since all Catholics were regarded as Irish nationalists and therefore a threat to the status of Northern Ireland. Gerrymandering ensured that Unionist politicians controlled some areas with a Catholic majority and no area could be regarded as beyond the actual, or symbolic, remit of the Orange state. Loyalist parades were allowed to pass through Catholic areas but attempts by nationalists to parade or erect visual displays were often highly restricted or banned outright. Even the temporary erection of the Irish tricolour was seen as a challenge and an affront, and more permanent displays were almost unknown (but see Rolston 1991, 72).

Displaying resistance

In the 1960s these inequalities began to be challenged by the Northern Irish Civil Rights Movement. The main thrust of the campaign focused on securing equal access to housing and employment but a challenge was also mounted to the Orange hegemony of the streets. Demonstrators sought to carry their arguments into towns which were regarded as the preserve of

Protestants. They also began to challenge the 'traditional' rights of Protestants to parade wherever they wanted. As ideological and political arguments turned into sectarian violence and outright warfare, Catholic areas in Derry and Belfast were enclosed behind barricades. As the forces of the state were excluded, people began to exert control over their own areas. A key element of this newly claimed control was to redefine the symbolic identity and status of the estates. Allen Feldman has discussed how, in this situation, the areas behind the barricades and away from the interfaces became sanctuary spaces, places in which the nationalist community, and to a lesser extent the loyalist community, could begin to redefine themselves on their own terms. These sanctuary spaces then served as loci of cultural and ideological resistance (Feldman 1991, 36–9). Behind the barricades the power of the state was restricted and the agents of the state were excluded. Initially this included physical exclusion but principally this was symbolic activity.

When the first barricades were erected in the Bogside in Derry, in January 1969, the act of excluding the forces of the state, was proclaimed by the slogan 'You Are Now Entering Free Derry' painted on a gable wall in St Columb's Street. By the time the painting was re-done, professionally, for the visit of the Home Secretary, James Callaghan, in August that year it had become emblematic of communal attitudes and collective resistance (McCann 1980). The mural has remained in place throughout the reconstruction of the Bogside, and although the wall is now isolated on a stretch of dual carriageway, it is far from a passive memorial. The mural is repainted regularly and Free Derry Corner has been established as the focal point for republican commemorations within the city: the annual Bloody Sunday Commemoration march terminates in a rally in front of the wall. In the past few years several other large murals, some related to the early events of the troubles, others linked to the opposition to loyalist parades, have been painted nearby. Although the barricades are long gone and the original buildings are no more, Free Derry Corner remains a defiant public space. In contrast, the loyalist murals in the nearby Fountain area, painted by Bobby Jackson in the 1920s and maintained by his family for many years, were finally demolished a couple of years ago. The divergent fortunes of the two sites seem to encapsulate the dramatic changes in the relationships between the two communities and the city of Derry.

The Free Derry mural was an early example of the transformation of public space by nationalists through the installation of political imagery, but for a time it was an isolated example. It was not until the early 1980s that murals became a prominent form of street display in nationalist areas and the brush joined the armalite and the ballot box as a facet of political strategy. Republican strategy changed after the hunger strikes: the military campaign continued, but at the same time a more open political movement began, culminating in the success of Sinn Féin at the polls. This movement tried to emphasise the distinctive cultural base of nationalism, which was deemed to provide the secure foundations for the political movement. Numerous murals and political slogans appeared across nationalist Belfast, kerbstones and lamp-posts were painted, streets were renamed in Irish, and the tricolour flew freely to assert a permanent and visible, political and cultural dominance over the area. This development was exemplified by the transformation of the republican commemorations to mark the introduction of internment each August. During the 1980s this changed from a day of political speeches and rioting to a week-long celebration of Irish culture. Mural painting was encouraged as part of the new West Belfast Festival. Competitions to judge the best painting were held in the early years, while more recently paintings have been especially commissioned for the Festival. The images were used as a means of conveying political ideas, for displaying historical heroes and role models, and extending the parameters of the movement. As with the emergence of unionist murals earlier in the century, the paintings were a prominent part of a wider transformation of nationalist areas.

The development of a republican mural-painting tradition was matched by a resurgence of loyalist paintings so that at any one time there are well over 100 paintings on the walls of the city. Although these were always very public displays, the messages have been primarily directed at those broad communities of support which sustained the paramilitary groups rather than outside bodies of opinion. In the past, few paintings were visible from neutral areas or from the main thoroughfares that bring people in and out of the city centres. The paintings were used to situate the paramilitary political practices of loyalism and republicanism within the broader political bodies of unionism and nationalism. They were used to refine traditional beliefs in line with the changing circumstances of political and military conflict, to consolidate the support of the faithful and to give substance to an otherwise shadowy presence.

All murals create a new type of space, they redefine mundane public space as politicised place and can thereby help to reclaim it for the community. Place becomes an activated facet of the ideological struggle. Such paintings are therefore also a means of extending the message of resistance. Murals can be used to claim and define new politicised places as readily as refining or restating old arguments on existing sites. In the period since the cease-fires many new murals have been painted on new sites. Some areas, such as parts of the Falls Road, the New Lodge, the Shankill and the Newtownards Roads in Belfast, and at Free Derry Corner in Derry have become repositories of dense concentrations of painted walls, where new images are sited beside, or painted over older ones to create a complex stratigraphy of ideological designs. In other parts of Belfast the cease-fires witnessed the first appearance of murals in areas which, until then, had appeared relatively uninvolved. Some surprise was expressed in the press when a large UVF mural appeared on the Woodstock Road in east Belfast, and a similar reaction greeted another UVF mural at Mount Vernon in the north of the city. This was both because of the threatening sentiments expressed by portrayals of hooded gunmen and because of the visibility of these painting from main thoroughfares. Less attention has been given to a republican mural that appeared in the lower Ormeau area in October 1995, but again its location has some significance. This is an area which had been without political paintings in recent years but which had been the scene of an extensive, and unresolved conflict over parading rights since the spring of 1995. While its location seems designed to confirm the identity of the area within republican political circles, the fact that the mural can be easily seen from the Ormeau Bridge, the recurrent site of confrontation, is surely not mere chance. While historically most murals have been painted to be seen from within the community of support, these recent paintings seem to be used more clearly to look out, beyond the community and into the wider society.

Breaking boundaries

This use of murals, to speak to a wider audience, through their location at interfaces or from neutral spaces, is still a relatively rare occurrence. But at the same time it is important to recognise that while as artefacts the paintings themselves are relatively fixed, as mediated images they can be, and are, easily represented to a wider audience. As such the paintings have often had a complex social life (Kopytoff 1990). Once painted they are only ever partly under the control of the community that produced them and can be taken up and used by whosoever chooses. But the scale and the diversity of use, and reuse, appears to have grown as the importance and significance of their value as a form of propaganda has become more readily acknowledged. Although the painting of a mural may appear to constitute the finished artefact, it actually may be just the beginning of a complex social life, which may well continue long after the original painting itself has been over-painted or destroyed. The paintings themselves are always politically contextualised when they are situated on the streets of Belfast, but their physical presence also allows them to be readily removed, transformed photographically and electronically, and re-presented in a new context. These electronic virtual-murals can then exist in an ahistorical state, where they are often reproduced as no more than empty signifiers of timeless tribal divisions.

Despite their physical solidity there is a sense in which the murals have always been in a state of flux. They have always circulated in other diverse spheres. Their meaning is continuously extended and recontextualised by a variety of technological and electronic re-presentations. Although murals have been widely used as illustrations in party publications, as posters and postcards, and in other forms of political ephemera, their visual power meant that they were also co-opted and used to represent the ideals, intentions and sheer presence of the paramilitary groups in a much broader sphere. After the British government banned the broadcasting of the actual voice of supporters of republican and loyalist paramilitary groups, mural paintings increasingly became an easy way to convey the invisible presence of the gunmen. They could be used to allude to the threat of, or at least the potential for, violence that was concealed by staged press conferences and rational rhetoric. Murals became a staple item of news reports, documentaries, film and television dramas as well as newspaper and magazine articles on the Troubles. A seemingly endless chain of reporters posed in front of one of a number of popular republican murals as they recounted the latest litany of terror or murder (Jarman 1996b). The mural has become such a ubiquitous symbol of Northern Ireland that temporary examples have been painted in Cardiff, in Manchester and in Dublin by film companies who sought to authenticate their location filming of dramas about the Troubles. Although these paintings were disembodied and delocated, they were widely used to conjure up a sense of place. Once the media had established that murals were the pre-eminent symbolic signifier of the northern conflict, the idea of Belfast could now be conjured up by little more than a few frames depicting a painting of a hooded gunman or King William on his white horse. And by the same process it was almost as if a mural had to be included in every film or news report for it to be convincing, thereby establishing a self-perpetuating cycle.

While local, national and international media removed the images from their original, specific context in order to provide the veracity of 'being there', this practice nevertheless simultaneously extended the visibility of the painting and its message. The painters, producers and sponsors of the murals were clearly aware of the possibilities that this offered. In recent years they seem to have had one eye on the use the media make of these paintings, and have used this as an opportunity to extend the audience for their propaganda. Sometimes such a strategy is purely opportunistic. For example, in December 1995 republicans erected a hurriedly-prepared board mural over an existing mural on the Falls Road because it was thought that Bill Clinton might pass nearby and thereby provide a good press image. Furthermore the political representatives of both republican and loyalist movements regularly use specific murals as a backdrop to press announcements, for photo opportunities and sometimes for political rallies where there is likely to be a media interest. Both the Republican Press Centre on the Falls Road and the offices of the Ulster Democratic Party on the Shankill Road have murals on adjoining walls which facilitate this practice. The murals help to provide a sympathetic frame for the politician. In the Sinn Féin case the mural depicts a smiling Bobby Sands, leader of the 1981 hunger strikes, while for the UDP the mural is simply headed by the words 'FOR PEACE'. As backdrops they provide the broader context for the spokesman's newsworthiness. Even if the mural is only a partial image it is evidence of the roots or background of an often otherwise unfamiliar face. The murals act as indicators of place. They show that the political figure is in home territory and, even if place is only defined by which side of the sectarian divide one is on, the mural helps define the nature of that locale. Murals can therefore help to create apposite places for the photo-opportunity with a visiting celebrity. They provide a contrast with the more common political photo-opportunity in more formal or grandiose public setting. As Gerry Adams, in particular, is increasingly seen moving in the realm of international politics it remains important for him to generate balancing images which situate him within his local base. Photographed in front of the Bobby Sands mural helps to reassure that this erstwhile statesman is still a man-of-the-people, and retains his grass roots connections.

The power of the murals have meant that they have become a more self-conscious means by which to propagandise to a much wider public, while still primarily aimed at a local audience. For the global media these remain little more than relatively simple symbols of the Troubles and of paramilitary violence. On the other hand the local media have began to recognise the significance of the paintings, although they are not always sure how seriously to treat them. The local press now frequently reports the appearance of a new mural as a news item in itself. While they are still rarely prepared to analyse the message as offering an insight into paramilitary thinking, it was deemed newsworthy when a murdered loyalist paramilitary, accused of being a police informer, was not named on a UVF memorial mural which was painted on the Shankill Road in July 1995 (*Sunday Life* 30 July 1995). A few months later another UVF mural in east Belfast which depicted hooded gunmen and demanded 'deeds and actions' rather than words became a news story under the headline 'Tension Rising Among Loyalists' (*Sunday Life* 24 September 1995). However although there are occasions when a new image has generated a shock or a surprise it is still rare for the paintings to be analysed in any detail, or for murals to be considered collectively or as part of a body of work. The norm is still to use them as illustrations to a paramilitary story and represent them as little more than superficial images rather than regard them as a significant part of the political process.

Figure 8   *Mural of Loyalist Volunteer Force, Portadown, 1997.* N Jarman.

Tourist trails

For most people the images of murals that are available for consumption
were (and are) mediated by professionals. Most people only see representations of the murals rather than the paintings themselves. And while the
paintings are used in newspapers and on television to imply danger or a
threat of violence, the images themselves are clearly also intriguing and
attractive. The murals therefore have a tourist potential in a way that
localised features of many war zones do. The paintings have had a seduc-
tive effect on many consumers who recognise them as a significant feature
of the local culture of war. Viewing the murals for oneself seems to offer
the opportunity to gain a personal and safe insight into what is otherwise
often a confusing and dangerous situation. Part of that understanding in
turn derives from the ability to see the paintings *in situ*, and therefore in
context. Most tourist guides to Northern Ireland have studiously avoided
any reference to conflict. They prefer to emphasise the natural beauties of
the landscape or the opportunities for fishing and relaxation rather than
draw attention to the violence and conflict (Rolston 1995b). At the same
time there has always been a category of independent tourists who are
attracted to sites of conflict, and there has always been a steady stream of
visitors doing the round of mural sites in nationalist west Belfast. For polit-

ical reasons, however, loyalist areas were less attractive and less welcoming. In spite of a certain wry smile when yet another camera is produced, this tourist activity was encouraged by local groups. Mini-bus tours of mural and other sites have been organised as part of the West Belfast Festival for some years, and local book shops in Belfast and Derry offer postcards of murals and leaflets which indicate the location of, and routes to prominent 'war sites' and political murals for those who visit outside the Festival season.

Some commercial travel guides have also begun to acknowledge the significance of murals as a feature of contemporary life which should be seen by visitors. The 1992 edition of the *Rough Guide to Ireland*, which is part of a series aimed at the independent traveller, gave five of the 13 pages devoted to Belfast and its environs to describing the location of the best mural sites in west Belfast. Half of the section about tourist sites in Derry is similarly orientated to the murals in the Fountain and the Bogside. But while these guides indicate the main sites of interest they still expect people to make their own way into, and around, west Belfast and the Bogside. For many people, whose only experience of these areas is through news broadcasts or feature films, this is still a daunting prospect. However, fear for one's safety is not only a factor which tourists are forced to address, many local people respond to suggestions that one might walk through the Ardoyne or up the Shankill to see a mural with amazement. Let alone that one might walk from the Ardoyne to the Shankill. The high public profile of the murals and their 'dangerous' locations therefore made them an attractive subject for more organised tourism.

During the republican cease-fire of 1994–96, hopes that this would be the beginnings of a lasting peace, led to a resurgence of the stagnant tourist industry. Tourism was welcomed as one of the potential salvations for the heavily subsidised economy. Building started on many new hotels and leisure complexes as tourism surged ahead. One of the early successes was the extension of the various site-seeing tours of the city run by the local bus companies to include the working-class areas of Belfast. These tours proved as popular with Belfast people 'on a voyage of rediscovery of their own city' (*Sunday Life* 9 April 1995) as they did with foreign tourists and the media. The tour offered a social history of the Troubles with a local guide indicating the significance of key areas, however as David Sharrock acknowledged, writing in the *Guardian*, 'everybody agreed the murals which decorate the gable ends were the highlight' (*Guardian* 23 March 1995). In fact without the paintings to punctuate the tour, the Belfast estates would be no more attractive than those of any other urban centre. At the more prominent paintings the tour bus stops to allow the sightseers to disembark to make their own photographic record of their visit. While memories of the sites of bombings and shootings might produce no more than a shudder, images of murals are a visible reminder of the unique complexities of Belfast. And when they are put on display back home, the meaning of the paintings will once again be transformed and extended as they are placed in a new context.

There is a certain sense of opportunism as the tourist operators move into the working-class areas, but these tours also offer an opportunity to see the city in a different light. These routinised repetitions help inscribe new and distinct routes around the city, they help to link up and reconnect many areas that have long been separated. They may only make transient connections, but these tourist routes also offer the possibility of a new way of seeing the city. This is particularly poignant for those residents of Belfast who take the tour. In daily life, routes and journeys to and from the city centre, and between different residential areas, become hardened by routine. Avoiding 'the other side' people remain in the known areas, among their own. The bus tours re-open the possibilities of seeing the city from other perspectives. They make links between areas and across sectarian boundaries in a way that is often not acknowledged or which are made difficult by the blocked entries and the numerous peace-lines. On the bus the sectarian boundaries are dissolved, at least for a short time. As the tours cross between Protestant and Catholic areas they are able to focus on and emphasise the commonality of experience over the past 30 years for those living, for example, in the two west Belfasts. The images on the murals may serve to symbolise the differing aspirations of the two communities, but their presence as artefacts also helps to indicate something of the shared history which may in the future provide the base for shared understandings.

The memory of the dead

For tourists, many of the murals may suggest a romanticised view of the violence of recent years, even a nostalgia for the imagined sense of community which has provided the base for resistance and struggle, and at times encouraged sacrifice for the cause. For the communities themselves the walls have long been regarded as an appropriate place on which to honour and remember the dead and imprisoned. The working-class areas contain many small memorials which record the names of local individuals who have been killed during the Troubles. Although some will include the name of relevant paramilitary organisations many commemorate those not killed by chance or misfortune. A diverse array of small plaques, formal marble memorials, murals and free-standing Celtic crosses is scattered across the city, and permanent reminders to the price of the cause. While all of these memorials have an impact on the sense of place, the murals are probably the most assertive in demanding acknowledgement of their presence. Most formal memorials are self-effacing objects which, while they remain as permanent reminders to death, rarely confront or challenge the passer by. It is usually considered inappropriate for memorials to be colourful; most are constructed from solid, but visually dull stone. For most of the year the memorials merge into the background, forgotten and ignored at the fringe of social consciousness. They only become the focus of collective attention on rare occasions, usually the annual commemoration when they are brightened by floral wreaths for a few days before these colours too fade with the elements.

There have been a number of paramilitary memorial murals painted in recent years, and these have been added to since the cease-fires were declared. Painting a wall is a relatively quick and easy means of honouring a comrade and at the same time serves to reaffirm the presence of the organisation in an area. Many of these paintings were constructed around, and from, images that dominate the sombre rhetoric of formal commemoration: stone memorials, mourning soldiers, crosses, wreaths, plaques and furled flags. But their frequent use of bright colour, as backdrop, on wreaths, emblems and badges also situates them within the wider realm of paramilitary displays and celebration. And while many formal memorials exist in a liminal space, which is carved out and set aside from daily routine, and thereby furthers their invisibility, these murals are placed on main thoroughfares, adjacent to shops and houses, the sites of everyday life. These murals provide a constant reminder to a sacrifices and hardships that the community has put itself through.

Most nationalist areas have paintings which display a simple list of the local men who are imprisoned for paramilitary activity and there are a few republicans murals which are devised specifically as memorials, but recent paintings have tended to focus on the cultural base of nationalism rather than military side of republicanism. In contrast loyalist groups marked their cease-fires by a number of large, elaborate memorials to paramilitary volunteers. Three such paintings appeared in the Shankill area during the summer of 1995, and each was then incorporated into the broader practice of public remembrance by holding commemorative parades around the area. The UVF mural to Trevor King on Disraeli Street, painted adjacent to an earlier memorial to Brian Robinson, was the site of an extensive ceremony at the end of a parade, held to mark the completion of the memorial and the anniversary of his death, in July 1995. Numerous loyalist bands paraded in his honour and laid floral wreaths in front of the painting before an oration was given by Billy Hutchinson, a prominent member of the Progressive Unionist Party. As with the example of Gerry Adams, the emerging loyalist politicians need to retain their street credibility and keep the ear of their supporters. Having established a certain legitimacy as defenders of their community, the gunmen have since become honoured as war dead. Although this initial event was a more elaborate ceremony than normal, the holding of parades around the focal point of a painted memorial is now an established practice. Memorial murals such as these, help to restructure and redefine a hitherto bland and naked wall. They reconstitute it as something approaching a sacred site, analogous to an official war memorial, but always more grounded in daily routine. While many ordinary murals are often allowed to fade and decay, the most significant memorials are kept in good conditions, any graffiti is quickly painted out and there are repainted to keep the colours bright. Murals can and are being used to satisfy the emotional as well as the ideological demands of the political movement.

Voicing opposition

Although they have become an internationally recognised signifier of Belfast, it is not true to say that these paintings are loved by all those who live locally. In fact murals attract opposition from two quarters: from within and from without. The opposition from without has been well documented: murals have often become prominent targets for destruction from paint bombs and graffiti. The defacing of republican paintings has, on occasion, been carried out by members of the security forces (Rolston 1991), and paintings in both communities which express support for paramilitaries have been the target of graffiti from the other side. The damage caused by the security forces has usually been a deliberate, extensive destruction sometimes necessitating the complete repainting of a mural. In contrast, scrawling the letters UVF on the Bobby Sands mural on the Falls Road or the initials INLA on a UFF mural on Sandy Row is necessarily an elusive act. Whether in response to a challenge, a dare, and just an act of bravado, there is a obviously a distinct attraction in such symbolic assaults. But the thrill of entering the enemy territory and leaving your calling card continues to lead to recurrent incursions.

The opposition to murals and other such street decorations from within has been less widely acknowledged. During the early part of the cease-fire period local newspapers carried repeated calls for a similar cessation of paintings. Although Sinn Féin councillor Alex Maskey was quoted as saying that the murals 'echo the feelings of the majority of the people in that area' (*Sunday World* February 1995), for some the murals are too closely identified with the paramilitary culture and paintings are therefore not welcome. It is difficult to gauge how widespread opposition might be since few people have been prepared to put their heads above to wall to declare their objections. The acknowledged close association between the murals and paramilitary groups is both a reason to oppose the paintings and also a reason not to speak out publicly. One woman, quoted in the press, said that although a lot of people did not like the paintings, 'many people are too frightened to complain about offensive graffiti'. Most of the opponents of mural paintings who have been quoted have also remained anonymous. Those few who have been named have been women, perhaps having more licence than men in these matters, since they have more rarely been the targets of physical reprisals should they publically challenge the authority of paramilitaries within their own communities. It is therefore too easy to assume that all the paintings are welcomed, that they represent the 'true' feelings of an area or that any opposition to them may only be concerned with property values. Clearly the paramilitary groups have their base, and considerable support, within the working-class estates, but these areas contain a wide body of opinion who oppose these groups as well. Sometimes such opposition can be more easily focused on a painting than a organisation. Interestingly most of those murals which have received criticism in the local press have been loyalist paintings. In particular the objections have been with the continued representation of paramilitary figures or emblems, rather than the painting of murals per se. These are images which have now largely been abandoned by republican painters.

The most extensive debate over a painting was concerned with a group of loyalist murals on the Newtownards Road in east Belfast. In April 1993, anonymous residents complained of the security risk that they felt was posed by the paintings on houses that were allocated to the elderly. In spite of appeals, by residents, by the local clergy and by politicians, to the police, no attempt was made to remove the paintings (*Belfast Telegraph* 6 April 1993, 12 April 1993, 13 April 1993, *News Letter* 14 April 1993). Furthermore in subsequent years the original paintings have been reworked and repainted and adjacent walls have been included as part of the overall display. In this case the dispute was not just about the content of the images but rather whether the site was appropriate as a locale for mural painting. The elderly residents feared that it might be assumed that they were responsible for the paintings and therefore the target for recrimination. For painters the site is always of importance, if permission is given to paint a wall then all well and good, but if not then prime sites might still be claimed and painted. The site on the Newtownards Road was one such prime site. The buildings offered an extensive frontage on a major thoroughfare, which was also on the route of a number of loyalist parades and not far from the only significant nationalist area in east Belfast (which no doubt added to the concerns of the residents). This was therefore an ideal location to publicise in visual form the ideals and aspirations of the UDA and to confirm their continued presence in the area. Not only were the protests ignored but this series of paintings has continued to attract attention because of the inclusion of Cú Chulainn, hitherto an Irish republican icon, who is here claimed for the loyalist cause. The publicity over this image has made it the most prominently reproduced loyalist painting of recent years. This has in turn helped to feed and stimulate a debate on the nature of Irish culture and the basis of a distinct Ulster identity (*Fortnight* 320, 32; *Sunday Life* 19 June 1994; Graham 1994). The publicity has also made sure that the murals are maintained and where possible extended, and has ensured that the paintings continue to attract a steady stream of visitors.

In another case, residents in Rathcoole actually took it upon themselves to paint out a mural to the Red Hand Commando, only for it to be painted back soon afterwards. This happened three times (*Sunday Life* 27 November 1994). In the end, the mural remained on the wall but over two years later the painting was still unfinished. An uneasy truce seems to have been reached between opposing viewpoints. Similar problems arose over a UVF memorial mural in the Cregagh area during 1996. A spokesperson for the Housing Executive stated that the 'overwhelming majority' of residents in the area wanted the painting removed, but also noted: 'It is a delicate issue. There is considerable artistic merit in some of the murals and it is not a case of removing unwanted graffiti' (*News Letter* 23 April 1996).

While it is true that the overall quality of mural paintings has improved in the past decade, decisions over whether they should remain or be removed are not about artistic merit but are concerned with the power of the paramilitary groups who sponsor them. In each of these examples, the Housing Executive (who own the properties) have ultimately chosen not to remove the paintings, but often the final decision has only been taken after consultation with the police. The Executive have apparently adopted a policy of not removing murals, in order not to put their workers at risk from members or supporters of the paramilitary groups. This issue was confronted however on the Ormeau Road in the summer of 1996 after loyalists had painted the kerbstones, on part of a disputed parade route, red, white and blue. This attracted extensive media attention after it was claimed that members of the RUC had stood and watched the men painting the kerbs, rather than trying to stop them. Residents in the area were concerned that these paintings would serve to raise sectarian tensions. It was seen as a deliberately provocative act, to claim what was a relatively well-integrated area as Protestant territory. In this case the residents were successful in getting the kerb paintings removed, but only after the end of the marching season, when passions had calmed a little.

Over the past decade street paintings and other forms of visual displays have increased in size, scale and number. They have become an established and prominent means of propagandising and elaborating political ideologies. Although some objections are publically voiced towards a few murals and other paintings, this has so far only affected a small part of the total and there is no indication that new paintings will not continue to appear in the coming years.

In conclusion

Considerable attention has been given, and continues to be given, to the symbolic content of murals, but less attention has been paid to their status as symbols in their own right. In this paper I have tried to show how, as objects rather than as images, murals have been, and continue to be used, as part of the political process, in the widest sense. As such murals have perhaps become the primary symbolic artefact of the late Troubles, a signifier and a symbol of place as much as they are bounded constructs of symbols and emblems. This is not in any way to deny their significance as images, but I have indicated that they are always more than mere simple images.

I have argued that murals are intimately related to place, and that some consideration of their location is required for a broader understanding of their wider power and meaning. But this is not to suggest that taking them out of their original context is to somehow limit their authenticity as symbols, because as Roland Barthes (1977) has illustrated, meaning is always contextual, the text always escapes the control of the author, and is always open to new interpretations. Furthermore place in the fullest sense is not a fixed space, the fact that murals can and are used as part of the political and interpretative process means that they are always being relocated, transposed to new locations, both phenomenological and technological, and therefore open to new sets of meanings. To move towards a fuller understanding of the contemporary practice of mural-painting demands some wider recognition of the fact that their power and importance is always in part derived from this capacity to resonate meaning both at a specific localised site and at seemingly endless other sites, at one and the same time. Of course this is not something that is specific or particular to mural painting, it is a factor in the versatility and vitality of both images and objects, and of images as objects, which always makes them so good to think with and so difficult to pin down.

References

Barthes, R, 1977, *Image – music – text*. London, Fontana.
Feldman, A, 1991, *Formations of violence: the narrative of the body and political terror in Northern Ireland*. Chicago, University of Chicago Press.
Graham, BJ, 1994, 'No place of the mind: contested Protestant representation of Ulster'. *Ecumene* 3, 257–81.
Jarman, N, 1992, 'Troubled images: the iconography of loyalism'. *Critique of Anthropology* 12, 133–45.

Jarman, N, 1993, 'Intersecting Belfast'. In B Bender (ed.) *Landscape, politics and perspectives*. Oxford, Berg, 107–38.

Jarman, N, 1996a, 'The ambiguities of peace: republican and loyalist ceasefire murals'. *Causeway* 3, 1.

Jarman, N, 1996b, 'Violent men, violent land: dramatizing the Troubles and the landscape of Ulster'. *Journal of Material Culture* 1, 39–61.

Jarman, N, 1997, *Material conflicts, parades and visual displays in Northern Ireland*. Oxford, Berg.

Kopytoff, I, 1990, 'The cultural biography of things: commoditisation as process'. In A Appadurai (ed.) *The social life of things: commodities in cultural perspective*. Cambridge, Cambridge University Press.

McCann, E, 1980, *War in an Irish town*. London, Pluto Press.

Rolston, B, 1991, *Politics and painting: murals and conflict in Northern Ireland*. Cranbury, N J, Associated University Presses.

Rolston, B, 1992, *Drawing support: murals in the North of Ireland*. Belfast, Beyond the Pale Publications.

Rolston, B, 1995a, *Drawing support 2: murals of war and peace*. Belfast, Beyond the Pale Publications.

Rolston, B, 1995b, 'Selling tourism in a country at war'. *Race and Class* 37, 1.

Rolston, B, 1996, 'Culture, conflict and murals: the Irish case'. In Ziff, T (ed) *Distant relations: Chicano, Irish, Mexican art and critical writing*. New York, Smart Art Press.

Sluka, J, 1997, 'The writings on the wall: peace process images, symbols and murals in Northern Ireland'. *Critique of Anthropology* 16, 4.

Woods, O, 1995, *'Seeing is believing: murals in Derry'*. Derry, Guildhall Press.

Playing Nationalism

CIRO DE ROSA

NTHROPOLOGY has long been concerned with studying the role of symbolic practices in the production and reproduction of ethnic, national and class identities. However, such identities represent multifaceted phenomena which cannot be reduced to their political dimension. This essay is concerned with the significance of parades, processions and demonstrations among nationalists in Northern Ireland.[1] The social boundaries of a community being symbolically constructed, it is necessary to focus on patterns of social interaction which maintain boundaries to fully understand this symbolic construction. Nevertheless, symbols are clearly and powerfully displayed in public rituals, which can be crucial points for interpreting processes of national or ethnic group self-identifications.

I argue that parades in Northern Ireland represent symbolic spaces where negotiation of identities takes place. Furthermore, ritual practices express tensions and conflicts between groups related to competing cultural codes and different symbolic representations. They are an arena within which different actors and interest groups compete and lay claims to group heritage or tradition in their struggle for hegemony.

Finally, rituals and festivals also involve creativity, as subcultures may articulate their own projects, or tend to manipulate and to re-signify hegemonic cultural patterns. In particular, as I shall show here, nationalist symbols provide an important cultural resource for working-class Catholic youths who are members of republican flute and drum bands.

On rituals

It is not easy to define ritual. Here I begin with Kertzer's definition of rituals as 'symbolic, standardised, repetitive social acts' (Kertzer 1988, 9), though I am aware it represents too broad a categorisation of rituals. This is because it emphasises only some aspects of the ritual actions, i.e. standardisation and repetition; we end in conceiving any type of behaviour which includes routine and habit as a ritual. Rather, I will argue that the specificity of ritual is its relationship with symbolism. This is the crucial point of an action whose meaning is not carried inherently. Although some anthropologists (for example Gluckman 1962) differentiate ritual from ceremonial, I consider it useful to employ both terms interchangeably (see Lane 1981).

Anthropologists have interpreted rituals as a reflection of social relationships, following Durkheim's paradigm. That is, rituals have the capacity to produce identities; they have the power in themselves to create social cohesion, or to reproduce the equilibrium in social conflicts. Through Turner's work, this functional link between ritual and social structure has been better elucidated. For Turner (1967) rituals are a useful strategy to maintain social bonds. He argues that ritual is an opportunity to experience the affectionate bonds of '*communitas*', and he sees the fall of '*communitas*' as representing a menace to the existence of society itself.

With Geertz, meaning has become a crucial concern for investigating rituals. Thus, we acknowledge that rituals allow certain groups to interpret the order of things for themselves. Geertz observes that 'in a ritual the world as lived and the world as imagined, fused under the agency of a single set of symbolic forms, turns out to be the same world' (Geertz 1973, 112–13). To sum up, in rituals something is being done and something is being said about groups and individuals (Bloch 1986; Bryan et al 1995).[2]

Now, with social and cultural anthropology engaged in working on social dynamics, rituals are mostly investigated as performances. And performances do not only communicate previous cultural messages, but they can manipulate everyday interactions. So we are urged to question the historical context of the events to understand how rituals give an impression of timelessness. And also how they appear to reinforce the cohesiveness of an ethnic group or a nation, while embracing a plurality of political positions and claims (Bryan and Tonkin 1996). That is because rituals are a particular form of communication, and they use symbols to convey a message. It is in the nature of symbols to be polysemic and to have the capacity to mean different things to different people. Anthony Cohen reminds us that the community has a symbolic dimension and that 'symbols of community are mental constructs [which] provide people with the means to make meaning' (Cohen 1985, 19).

By approaching ritual within a framework of practice and by focusing on the strategies of ritualisation (Bell 1992) we are led to articulate the contradiction between standardisation and uniqueness of ritual actions which seems to constitute their very nature (Bryan and Tonkin 1996). By emphasising practical actions, we recognise that 'ritual is never simply or solely a matter of routine and habit, or the "dead weight of tradition"' (Bell 1992, 92). Rituals are practices of production and description of intersubjective meaning, so they always involve negotiation on control and meaning.

In other words, rituals represent symbolic devices which among other things keep people aware of their sense of belonging to a community. They dramatically define 'us' who are inside the community, and 'them' who are outside it. The participants and bystanders are emotionally involved, and the ethnic boundaries of the group are reinforced by such occasions. But public rituals are also the realm of competing discourses within a group. 'They are an agent of consensus' (Pasquinelli 1989, 86). As such, they can legitimise a whole series of social relations, political authority and positions.

Having said that, we realise that the management of these events is crucial for different interest groups who have different cultural and political capital (Bourdieu 1988) in the political field. A ritual 'may be intended by the group staging it as a display – perhaps implicit, or perhaps overt and triumphant – of the current state of often changing and contested power relations within the group itself' (Harrison 1992, 225).

By ethnographic and historical examination of parades of the nationalist community, I attempt to analyse how rituals produce the symbolisation of community boundaries, and to investigate the competing discourses and the negotiation of meaning which take place during ceremonies.

Parades in the nationalist community

People in Northern Ireland use the term 'nationalist community' to mean that ethnic and political identity which is not unionist/loyalist. Although the community is not homogenous, we can use Anderson's notion of 'imagined community' (Anderson 1983)[3] to refer to a group characterised by a shared sense of history, political allegiance, and cultural forms.

Parading, we know, is a very significant feature of Northern Irish cultural, religious and political life. For instance, in 1994, 2,792 parades crossed the streets of cities and towns in that part of the world, most of them being loyalist parades.

Irish nationalism in Northern Ireland has no unified display of the 'green'. As a matter of fact, a variety of public demonstrations take place. Nationalist imagery is not reserved to the public display as the loyalist one is. Marching or 'walking' seems to be essential to Orangemen, Apprentice Boys, the Royal Black Preceptory, or marching bands which parade around Northern Ireland. On the other hand, Gaelic sports, Irish music and dance, so-called Celtic art, or for more committed republicans, framed copies of the 1916 Proclamation, hand-crafts made by republican prisoners, reproductions of Sheppard's Cú Chulainn, are all part of the celebration of Irishness in many working-class areas of the region (see Loftus 1994). This is due to the Catholic/nationalist sense of themselves as a distinct group which is undergirded by a nationalist ideology, and by the existence of an Irish state in the south of the island. So, unlike loyalism, it does not depend on a religious discourse, or on the notion of exclusiveness, although it is articulated by the social and political reality which nationalists live in the north and their symbolic opposition to the loyalist imagined community.

As regards festivals and commemorations, we must take into account the differences between rural and urban parades, a parade held in a republican stronghold, or one in a town where relationships between both communities are good. These may be very different types of occasions and their diversities need to be questioned.

On St Patrick's Day (17 March), which commemorates Ireland's patron saint, there are parades in numerous venues in Northern Ireland, held by different organisations: the Ancient Order of Hibernians, the Irish National Foresters, or clubs of the GAA; and even some associations in the republican movement have exploited the feast, promoting parades to publicise the current political agenda. The main parade on the island of Ireland is the American-style procession held in Dublin, at which hundreds of thousands often attend. In Belfast's Falls Road, and other nationalist areas, there have been processions for many years.

The Easter Sunday commemorations are a different type of demonstration. The narrative of the 1916 uprising is a basic component of republican ideology. The largest parades are held by Provisional Sinn Féin. Nevertheless, the Irish Republican Socialist Party (IRSP), Republican Sinn Féin, and the Workers' Party all give a special emphasis to this founding sacrifice, whether through parading, or rallying at the cemeteries where fallen volunteers are buried.

In the preceding days in nationalist districts, youth and Sinn Féin supporters will have been mobilised to display bunting, to paint kerbstones and lamp-posts with Irish colours, to painting new murals, or touch up the older ones.

Later on in the summer, August has always been a time for nationalist demonstrations, the most important of the Protestant processions having taken place in early July.

The feast of the Assumption of the Virgin on August 15 has been celebrated since the nineteenth century when the cult of the Virgin received a strong vigour. Indeed, the relevance of the day as a Catholic day of obligation was very clear, and politicians have frequently exploited it. For instance, the 'Liberator' O'Connell organised his massive Tara rally on that day (O'Dwyer 1988, 261). In his account of Belfast sectarian riots in 1872, Boyd underlines its relevance:

A month later the nationalists of Belfast decided that they too, would have a procession. They choose to hold it on Thursday 15 August, the Feast of Assumption of the Blessed Virgin, better known as Lady Day. This was probably an unwise choice. It stamped the nationalists of Ulster as Catholic sectarians, which is the image they carry to the present day, and it is hardly surprising that 15 August came to be known as 'the papish Twelfth'. (Boyd 1969, 89)

In much the same way as the Orange Order's Twelfth of July is preceded with an 'Eleventh Night' bonfire, bonfires used to be lit on the eve of the celebration of the Assumption in nationalist areas.[4] Since 1972, however, bonfires have been burned on the eve of 9 August as an act of resistance and protest to commemorate the introduction of internment without trial. At the top of the pyre, a Union flag, an Ulster flag, or an Orange flag portraying King William III might be burned. Today, most young people in nationalist areas do not even know that bonfires were lit on the 15 August. It is not without significance that some young informants have associated the August 15 with the deployment of the British troops on Northern Irish streets on 14–15 August 1969.

It is hard to say if these occasions are only an imitation of the Protestant bonfires on the 'Eleventh Night', or an influence of international street politics (see Loftus 1994, 36). It is sure, however, that if these dramas of political affirmation are so meaningful, it is because both communities, far from having two separate 'traditions', share a fundamental symbolism.

The process of constructing a consensus has caused the republican movement to promote a culture of resistance in Catholic working class districts. I agree with Sluka who writes that this happened 'by a two-way process involving gradual politicisation of social and cultural events and the opposite, gradual socialisation of political events' (Sluka 1995, 89).[5]

The anniversary of the introduction of internment without trial represents an example of socialisation of a political event. August, as mentioned before, has always been the Catholic month. The religious festival of the Assumption used to be celebrated with bonfires, local processions and different AOH parades held in four or five venues. But since the introduction of internment, the meaning has switched, and the anniversary has been commemorated with rallies which have always been characterised by tensions and clashes with the security forces.

Afterwards, in an attempt to diffuse tension and promote a more positive image of Catholic working-class areas in Belfast and other towns, community festivals were established, and bonfires, once the symbol of resistance, were limited to some open air spaces and transformed into a party with music. People suggested it was just a party, a night out, with children usually involved. I have been given similar explanation in a loyalist area for the traditional 'Eleventh night' bonfires.

However, the burning of flags or effigies shows that bonfires are, at least in part, rituals of destruction. In both the unionist and the nationalist bonfires, symbols of the other side are manipulated, displayed and finally destroyed in what Harrison has described as a 'valuation contest', a type of symbolic conflict in which the values of one group are symbolically affirmed while the symbols of the rival groups are attacked (Harrison 1995).

Since then, the first half of August, which reminds republicans of 1971 (internment and the deployment of the army) has been the time when the festivals take place. In Belfast they are typically opened by a street parade with fancy dress and floats. People participate in the atmosphere, which is also charged with political meaning. The march to commemorate the anniversary of internment is the closing parade on the following Sunday. In Belfast on that Sunday, the demonstrators leave the local nationalist districts carrying banners with political statements for a march and rally that used to be held in west Belfast. Since 1993 the demonstrators have been allowed to march to the centre of Belfast.

Rituals need to be performed in a space which is symbolic in itself (Mach 1994, 61). Moreover, the symbolic control of urban space through flags, colour-coding or parades is relevant. In the past, attempts to march to Belfast city centre were prevented by the security forces. And the ceremony used to be performed within the main nationalist symbolic territory, namely the Falls Road, symbolising the control of its own space and the resistance to what are conceived as the invaders.

However, the march to the city centre means a change in the policy of republican marches, and specifically a change to what is not just resistance any longer, but an acknowledgement of what in nationalist ideology is a 'parity of esteem', or even a 'culture of victory'.

Numerous pipe bands, accordion bands and republican flute bands playing nationalist songs march with the demonstrators. However, they do not seem to play the fundamental role the loyalist bands have had on the Twelfth in the last two decades.[6]

It would be too obvious to think that this mass of people are all supporters of republicanism, as Sluka seems to suggest in his account of republican culture and political resistance (Sluka 1995). We know that symbols are multivocal, and that people participate in the events for different reasons. For instance, in 1995 the Easter commemorations and the anti-internment march had a massive participation of bystanders, more than in the previous years. This was due probably to the paramilitary ceasefires, or to the lack of soldiers in the streets for the first time in many years, or to the capacity of republicans to give a different emphasis to the commemoration. As such, I am not so sure that the numerous girls I saw, in their festive dresses, were asserting a political statement.

Marching with the AOH

Nowadays, in urban areas the first half of the month of August is more devoted to the commemoration of the introduction of internment and to community festivals than to the 'political' celebration of the Assumption.

The members of the Ancient Order of Hibernians (AOH), are sometimes called 'Green Orangemen'. A Belfast priest and historian described them to me as a 'pale shadow' of the Orange Order. Although their main festival on 15 August has lost part of its political and cultural relevance, the AOH nevertheless still holds two processions on that day, one in the north of Ireland, the other in Dublin.[7]

The AOH is an organisation of Catholic Irishmen, created for the protection and promotion of the interests of the Catholic faith and of the Irish nation, 'For Faith and Fatherland' being their motto.

Some people claim its foundation goes back to 1565; others say that it was formed in 1641 when the Leinster chieftain, Rory Og O Mór, attempted to organise a rebellion against the English government. Actually, its present title dates from 1838. Nevertheless, in the quest of an historical legitimacy the AOH claims that it is the descendant of earlier secret societies, such as the Defenders, and the Ribbon Society which emerged in Ireland only in 1820 (Foy 1976, 3).

As a Benefit Society, the AOH is registered as a Friendly Society. Its basic unit is the division. Divisions elect delegates to a district board which will include a county, or a city. District boards and divisions send delegates to the Convention which is the supreme governing body. The Board of Erin is the supreme executive body of the institution when the Convention is not in session. Though primarily an organisation for males, there are also divisions for women and youth attached to the main divisions.

It has been said that the Feast of Assumption on which members of the AOH march corresponds to the Twelfth of July (see Cecil 1993). However, I would claim that apart from the clear similarities in symbolism which the two organisations share, there are striking differences between the two occasions.

First, the AOH, despite being a powerful institution until the first decade of the twentieth century under Joe Devlin's leadership, has not held the same political and economic position as Orangemen have had in Northern Ireland for a long time. Nowadays, they do not play a very significant political role in Northern Irish politics. Second, within the nationalist community the AOH has not been so predominant, as different agencies have played their role as 'curators' (Buckley and Kenney 1995, 9–11) of the so-called nationalist tradition. Third, there is a huge difference between the Twelfth of July, which is a public festival in Northern Ireland, commemorating a foundation myth belonging to the Protestant community, or for those who claim to receive legitimacy from the community, and the Assumption Day parade.

Many towns or AOH divisions apply to have the parade in their area. There is a vote to decide where the parade will take place. The division belonging to the venue runs the parade, and is in control of the parade. They have a band, and their banner[8] leads the parade. Sometimes in the evening the members have a meal, a few drinks, or a function with a ceili and traditional music session.

Bands are an essential part of the Hibernian parades. However, they are mostly accordion bands and pipe bands. Many of the accordion bands are composed of groups of women and girls dressed rather like American majorettes. Neither these nor the pipe bands have a style which could be described as 'triumphalist'. However, some independent flute bands also participate in the parades. The Hibernians, who are a conservative and constitutional nationalist organisation, tend to have total control of the ceremony and to choose the bands to be invited. The republican movement clearly defines itself differently from the AOH, emphasising the Hibernians' sectarian and conservative ethos. Sometimes, however, republicans may keep a stand selling newspapers and knick-knacks, as I saw in Newry on 15 August 1994.

I described certain AOH bands as characterised by a 'majorette' style. Sometimes, however, other kinds of bands take part in the parade. This is not common, because the AOH tends to avoid the involvement of 'troublemakers'. Moreover, the same bands tend not to be associated with the AOH, as they consider themselves part of a different political culture. However, in the 1980s, some flute and drum bands, noted for their republican sympathisers, participated in the parades. For them and their supporters who would walk at their side, the occasion represented an act of rebellion.

For instance, in 1984 at Magherafelt, tension arose when some youths threw stones at the RUC, and the Brendan McConvery band from Bellaghy, named after a dead INLA man, carried an Irish tricolour (*Irish News* 16 August 1984).

In 1985 in Ballerin, members of the same band, again in paramilitary style, marched up and down the field where the speeches were given. They confronted the RUC when the police tried to remove a tricolour they were carrying[9] (*Irish News* 16 August 1985) and continued to play, competing with the official AOH-affiliated band playing the Irish national anthem.

The following year at Toome during another AOH parade on 15 August, police were attacked by stone-throwers and some demonstrators burned a Union flag (*Irish News* 16 August 1986).

In each of these three episodes the AOH hierarchy tried to distance itself from the bands who were not sharing their respectability and policy. On the other hand, the bands and their supporters participating in the parade were talking to both sides of the sectarian divide and the state, asserting their political statement and challenging the conservative values of AOH nationalism. And they were challenging the symbols of the state, i.e. the RUC, perceived as a Protestant force to be symbolically confronted, shouting IRA slogans, or playing republican songs. The celebration represented an occasion which different groups exploited to argue a political statement and to oppose authority at different levels.

The symbolic use of music in public rituals

Musical bands provide an important means whereby young people can become engaged in political activity. The defence of the territorial and symbolic boundaries of their confessional communities are crucial issues, especially for working-class youth who, in contexts characterised by high levels of cultural and political conflict centred on ethnic identification, have an active role in reproducing conflict culture and sustaining ethno-political identities. Far from supporting any type of zoomorphic explanation about territoriality so fashionable in the press when the marching season or any other important commemoration is approaching (see Bryan 1995), I would argue that the politics of territory have become more and more a central concern for a section of the population to whom it provides a sense of belonging to a community, and allows them to symbolise their political arguments. Through the politics of territory, people can act out their ethnic self, their class and status through rituals. For many young people, bands have a crucial role in this enterprise of social drama.

I interviewed several members of four Belfast-based flute bands, attending their practices and following them during parades on different occasions. I also interviewed members of Sinn Féin, and people who were involved in the Band Association who helped me with contacts and gave me their interpretation of the history of the bands.

Republican bands are a comparatively new phenomenon in Northern Ireland. In the past, most bands found among nationalists were of a type nowadays identified with the AOH, such as accordion or pipe bands. In the 1970s, a few republican flute and drum bands grew up. However, the republican press did not give much emphasis to these bands, just describing their colourful presence at parades.

The reason for the diffusion of mainly flute and drums bands,[10] I would argue, is similar to the analogous spread of loyalist bands. Handy, cheap flutes and drums are easier to play than bagpipes or an accordion. Moreover, the wide diffusion of street politics involving young people since the 1981 hunger strikes I believe helped in creating a growth of interest in the flute bands.

At present times, these flute and drum bands are made up of 20 to 30 members. Many are named after dead IRA volunteers, or prominent figures in Sinn Féin. Some use the word 'martyrs' and commemorate a specific area (e.g. Andersonstown martyrs). Or they carry a political statement (e.g. Éire

Nua) or a place (e.g. Sliabh Dubh). Typically, they have a large base drum in the middle which is the focal point of the band. The band's name is painted on the drum together with nationalist and republican symbols. The drummer plays vigorously, sometimes moving out of step with the rest. This is a clear imitation of the loyalist bands' style.[11] The bands are preceded by a colour party carrying flags. Sometimes they are teenage girls.

While loyalist bands are mainly composed of males, most republican bands include girls, who also play flutes and snare drums. It is not easy to give the definitive reason for this difference. However, on one hand, loyalist working-class culture is predominantly male-oriented, and is characterised by 'macho' attitudes. On the other hand, many nationalist women have been involved in street politics since the troubles began.

The flags most frequently carried are the Irish tricolour, and those bearing the arms of the four Irish provinces. But some bands carry the Sunburst (the flag of the Fianna), as well as the Starry Plough. These flags are displayed at the anti-internment march and during some local commemorations, but not at Easter Sunday parades when the Irish tricolour and the National Graves Committee colour party are carried in procession.

As far as the uniforms are concerned, in the early days of the republican bands, that is the 1970s and 1980s, most bands used to wear black v-neck jumpers, black trousers, berets, and sunglasses (many still wear them now). Obviously, they were much more affected by the paramilitary style.[12] According to an informant, people used to have a bad reaction to what was perceived as a menacing style, and tended to consider them as IRA bands. So an attempt was made to change the style by transforming the bands, which now wear richer and more colourful uniforms. Some bands still wear very poor quality clothes, v-neck jumpers and black trousers, or T-shirts in summertime. However, most of the bands have proper uniforms.

Sinn Féin is mostly responsible for creating a republican band, or else somebody will ask them for aid, if they want to run a flute band. To some extent a band is financially supported by Sinn Féin. For instance, the party can help them hire a bus when there is a function to be held outside the city. However, the members need to collect money in different way to supply flutes, or drums, or new uniforms. Quite often they make an appeal while parading in their area, or ask for money in shops, bars, and clubs.

Significantly, some members of a Belfast band pointed out that unlike Orange and loyalist bands, they do not receive any grant. They are not supported by the state. This is obviously neither the case for republican bands, nor loyalist bands. But what is striking is the false perception that some have of the Protestant bands as being state sponsored.

Band members overtly emphasise the necessity of their funding to buy uniforms and new as well as second-hand instruments. However, after more than two decades of war, we are far from the old times when the AOH bands used to borrow bass drums from Orange bands. Belfast shops providing second-hand instruments are located in Protestant areas. So it is difficult to get new stock when needed. Some members told me how sometimes they used to go to a Sandy Row shop, but were worried about the possibility of being questioned about the band they were creating.[13]

Why do people join the bands? A main reason seem to be the fact that the band symbolises but also sustains pragmatically a group identity, whether familial, communal, or political. For example, a band member declared: 'If I were a Protestant I would be in a loyalist band, but we are a republican family, and I am in a republican band'. At times, brothers and sisters persuade each other to join the band, or relatives were involved in bands. 'My father was in a pipe band, then it was dismantled because of internment', said a band member, 'so there is a family background'. Another one added: 'I joined the band because it's a good thing for the community. It keeps children away from the streets. They don't joyride, don't take drugs'. To many band members, probably influenced by their parents' thoughts, this seems to be a very significant reason for playing in a flute band.

Irish heritage often is given as explanation: 'I joined the band mainly because I like to play music; it's also part of my culture, of being Irish. For centuries we were robbed of our language, persecuted for our religion, so for me playing in a band is an expression of who I am. Each band has its own identity, some are named after a volunteer from the district who was killed. There's not much a chance of a job after school, playing is an important part of my life' (Ziff 1989, 58).

So republican band members recognise that bands are very important socially. Through them, they have a role in the republican struggle or support the IRA. When asked about how they differ from AOH bands, they underline that Hibernians are more cultural while they are republican.[14]

But it is more significant that they recognise that bands keep youth engaged in something useful. The bands take children off the streets. They improve their chances. Some people who cannot play an instrument learn after joining a band. It helps them to socialise. For instance, a band member described the band as a happy family where you can have fun.

There is a natural rivalry between the bands. Who are the best? Who have the better presence? Who is most disciplined? These are important issues for these teenagers. Moreover, being in a band allows you to have trips out of the city, participating in parades or in band competitions in Northern Ireland and even in Scotland.

Bands are involved in official commemorations, and in local parades held to commemorate some deceased volunteer. So they play a role in reinforcing the nationalist ideology. Orders are given in Irish during the marches and the rehearsal. This is a symbolic act which consciously helps to produce people's own national identity. Sometimes the bands end their practices, held in leisure centres or republican clubs, by playing the Irish national anthem. Moreover, the older lads who run the band and who mediate between the republican movement or the RUC when a parade needs to be allowed to march in the streets, give details about the reason to participate in a function to commemorate some old or new fellow who entered the pantheon of people who have given their lives for the national cause. I have noticed particularly that the memory of the hunger strikers,[15] as supreme examples of sacrifice,[16] has a deep influence on these young people.

Locality is a relevant element for loyalist bands. In my interview with loyalist band members, they always underlined the significance of the return to the area they belong to which is warmly cheered by residents. This is not often the case for republican bands. Rather, all of them emphasised their first time in the city centre of Belfast in August 1993 anti-internment march. Their excitement and the attitude of bass drummers who played harder and shouted IRA slogans, symbolically marked the city as theirs too. I witnessed the relevance of this while participating in the 1994 and 1995 anti-internment marches.

It is necessary to understand working-class youth sub-cultures as a response to what is the working-class experience of the economic, social and political context (Cohen 1972; Hall and Jefferson 1976). The working-class youth of Northern Ireland, a society which reproduces two endogamous communities, develop their sense of ethnic identity in a context marked by political tension and long-established sectarianism reinforced by a segregated educational system. The ghettoisation of residential life has reduced opportunities both in recreation and in employment. The local economy has been destroyed and patterns of socialisation have been deeply transformed (see Gillespie et al 1992, for a discussion). Furthermore, street confrontations, paramilitary activities and the presence of British Army patrols and RUC high profile policing have all contributed to the worsening of the lives of youth (see Pistoi 1981). For them social interaction, in the form of discos, football matches, or even 'internment' night (that is, the bonfires), or the 'Eleventh' night on loyalist side, provides a relevant cultural space that, however, rarely overcomes the sectarian culture.[17] On each side of the divide young people act as the guardians or curators of tradition (Bell 1990, 9; Buckley and Kenney 1995, 9–11), playing a significant role in the articulation of ethnic categorisation with respect to the opposite group. So they are strongly involved in the celebration of their heritage and in the reproduction of a sectarian ideology.

Hence, nationalist ideology, particularly republicanism, its symbols, and cultural practices which are founded in the rhetoric of an 800-year-old Irish struggle against Britain, provide the marginalised working-class with young symbols of success and social promotion placed beyond the rhythms of working life. In Catholic urban working-class districts a 'Provo' sub-culture exists, which uses the symbolism of rebellion and opposition by violence exists (see Sluka 1995, 93), and has encouraged the institutionalisation of the republican movement in Catholic working-class areas (Sluka 1995, 83).

Conclusions

In this essay, I have drawn attention on the relevance of demonstrations, and parades for the nationalist 'imagined community' in Northern Ireland. Participants have a plurality of perspectives in taking part in rituals. These help the objectification of relationships between individuals and groups because, as symbolic actions, they reproduce the boundaries of an ethnic or national group. Since the symbols are very powerful, competition for, and negotiation of their meaning is fundamental, because by exploiting the meaning, groups can gain symbolic capital within the community.

Through rituals, different sub-groups can articulate their own discourse. Any given section of the nationalist community in Northern Ireland, can exploit ritual as a resource to articulate their sense of ethnic belonging, of their class, gender, and age. The nationalist ideology and the culture of republicanism have provided them with a coherent and organised set of discourses which have been used to claim a political and cultural statement.

Notes

1. I am aware of the politically-charged, non-innocent use of terms like Northern Ireland, Six Counties, Ulster, the North, the North of Ireland, or the Province. However, I have chosen to use the official denomination of the region.
2. Though Bloch provides a useful interpretation of the changes in the ritual actions, inserting a historical dimension to his analysis (see Bloch 1986), he limits social symbolism to its political function, thereby rendering rituals entirely to power.
3. As reality is a symbolic construction, I believe that Anderson's seminal phrase of 'imagined communities' is a useful analytical notion. For Anderson a nation is imagined because though its members will never know most of their fellow-members, 'yet in the minds of each lives the image of their community' (1983, 6). This does not mean that a nation is invented, rather that an ideological process of cultural creation is involved in its manufacturing.
4. For an analysis of the bonfire tradition in Northern Ireland see Gailey 1977 and Loftus 1994, 33–6. Actually, I have no full evidence that bonfires are still lit in Northern Ireland on the eve of the Assumption. Nevertheless, the *Belfast News Letter* (13 August 1973; 15 August 1973, reported preparations for bon-

fires to be lit on 14 August evening. It also reported a confrontation in Belfast's Lenadoon Avenue during such a bonfire (15 August 1973). Some years later, in the *Irish News* (14 August 1978), a reader suggested not to light bonfires as a sign of mourning for the death of the Pope.

5. I do not mean that the republican movement represents a sort of 'godfather' that acts to create a culture of resistance. Consensus is never a one direction process, but is part of complicated social and cultural dynamics. Neither do I deny the right of the people to react to what is their perception – or indeed the historical reality – of discrimination and social injustice.

6. Nevertheless, a republican band member claimed that the bands play a very relevant part in the parade. 'No bands, no parades', he said. I consider this too exaggerated a statement.

7. The AOH used to have four main parades in Northern Ireland before the conflict exacerbated in the late 1960s. As a consequence, they suspended their parades between 1969 and 1974 for security reasons and they held local church parades only.

8. On banners, see Jarman 1994b.

9. The Flags and Emblems Display Act 1954 was repealed with the introduction of the Public Order (NI) Order 1987.

10. One of the first reports about a republican band is in *An Phoblacht* (January 1971) which contains a picture of a new Sinn Féin Accordeon Band formed in Newry. In 1984 *An Phoblacht* gave a special recognition to the band phenomenon at the Wolfe Tone commemoration in Bodenstown: 'The rising calibre of bands attending the commemoration was a talking point amongst the appreciative crowds. The presence of a number of recently formed bands [...] provided an impetus for other areas to follow their example' (*An Phoblacht* 21 June 1984).

11. Some band members argue that the republican bands from Scotland are tougher in their style, and their base drummers walk and play more like loyalist bands. On the other hand, loyalist bands from Scotland also seem rough-and-ready in their uniforms, and harder in their marching style. I believe that this is an issue worth investigating.

12. On the paramilitarisation of style of the bands, namely the loyalist ones, see Bell 1990: 173. I have noticed that some members of AOH bands or Independent bands who participate in the AOH parades wear sunglasses. This may be just an useful and fashionable instrument to be protected by sun rays. However, I would argue that there is an influence of the paramilitary style, or they will a tougher look.

13. In fact, the shop is so small that it is difficult to avoid interacting with other customers.

14. Actually, they categorise three types of bands: AOH, independent and republican bands.

15. I was surprised that in an exhibition I visited in 1994 about *Symbols* in Northern Ireland organised by the Cultural Tradition Group there was no reference to the hunger strikes of 1981. Probably that had to do with the politics of the exhibition. However, if one has walked the streets of nationalist working-class areas,

if one has talked to people of republican political persuasion, or has visited their houses, the significance the 1981 hunger strikes cannot be ignored. Mine is not an apology for republicanism, or for political violence. This is to discuss and analyse what is of real importance to some people. The study of 1981 republican hunger strikes is extremely relevant to explore the intertwinement of historical, political and cultural processes (see Aretxaga 1993).

16. In analysing republican ideology, an obvious reference to sacrifice and martyrdom is often proposed. Though ideology of sacrifice is the backbone of lots of nationalist ideologies, it is not enough to say that the mythology of sacrifice determine IRA support within the Catholic community. Myths do not carry in themselves the capacity to make people act. As Aretxaga argues: 'myths as meaningful frames of interpretation require a social context in order to become more than interesting stories' (Aretxaga 1993, 239). Sacrifice is part of Irish republican ideology, however it is only in specific historical times that it has become significant for a political action.

17. Of course I am not suggesting that everybody has sectarian attitudes, or is involved in activities related to the celebration of ethnic pride. There are lots of young people, probably the majority in Northern Ireland, who have leisure activities of a different nature.

References

Ancient Order of Hibernians Div. 284, Official booklet, August 1994.

Anderson, B, 1983 *Imagined communities: reflections on the origins and spread of nationalism.* London, Verso.

Aretxaga, B, 1993 'Striking with hunger: cultural meanings of political violence in Northern Ireland'. In K B Warren *The violence within: cultural and political opposition in divided nations.* Boulder, Westview Press, 219–53.

Barth, F, (ed.), 1969 *Ethnic groups and boundaries.* London, Allen and Unwin.

Bell, C, 1992 *Ritual theory, ritual practice.* Oxford, Oxford University Press.

Bell, D, 1990 *Acts of union.* London, Macmillan.

Bloch, M, 1986 *From blessing to violence.* Cambridge, Cambridge University Press.

Boissevain, J, (ed.), 1982 *Revitalising European rituals.* London, Routledge.

Bourdieu, P, 1988 *La parola e il potere.* Napoli, Guida. (*Ce que parler veut dire*). Paris, L'economie des échanges linguistiques, 1982.

Boyd, A, 1969 *Holy war in Belfast.* Tralee, Anvil Books.

Brown, T, 1985 *Ireland. A social and cultural history 1922–1985.* London, Fontana.

Burton, F, 1978 *The politics of legitimacy.* London, Routledge and Kegan Paul.

Buckley, A D and M C Kenney, 1995 *Negotiating identity: rhetoric, metaphor and social drama in Northern Ireland.* Washington D C, Smithsonian Institution Press.

Bryan, D, 1995 'Orangutango'. *Fortnight*, 341, 14–15.

Bryan, D, T Fraser and S Dunn, 1995 *Political rituals: loyalist parades in Portadown.* Coleraine, Centre for the Study of Conflict, University of Ulster.

Bryan, D and Tonkin, J E A, 1996 'Political ritual: temporality and tradition'. In (ed.) A Boholm *Political Ritual*. Gothenburg, Institute for Advanced Studies in Social Anthropology.

Cecil, R, 1993 'The marching season in Northern Ireland: an expression of politico-religious identity'. In S MacDonald (ed.) *Inside European identities*. Oxford, Berg, 146–66.

Cohen, A P, 1985 *The symbolic construction of community*. London, Tavistock.

Cohen, A P, 1972 'Sub-cultural conflict and working class community'. *Working papers in cultural studies*. Birmingham, Centre for Contemporary Cultural Studies.

Durkheim, É, 1912 *Les formes élémentaires de la vie religieuse*. Paris, Alcan.

Eriksen, T H, 1993 *Ethnicity and nationalism*. London, Pluto Press.

Foy, M T, 1976 'The Ancient Order of Hibernians'. Unpublished MA thesis, Queen's University of Belfast.

Gailey, R A, 1977 'The bonfire in Northern Irish tradition'. *Folklore* 88, 3–38.

Geertz, C, 1973 *The interpretations of cultures*. New York, Basic Books.

Gillespie, N, T Lovett and W Garner 1992, *Youth work and working class youth culture: rules and resistance in west Belfast*. Buckingham, Open University Press.

Gluckman, M (ed.), 1962 *Essays on the ritual of social relations*. Manchester, Manchester University Press.

Harrison, S, 1992 'Ritual as intellectual property'. *Man* (NS) vol. 27, 225–44.

Harrison, S, 1995 'Four types of symbolic conflict'. *Man* (NS), 255–72.

Hobsbawm, E J and T Ranger (eds), 1983 *The invention of tradition*. Cambridge, Cambridge University Press.

Jarman, N, 1994a 'Intersecting Belfast'. In B Bender (ed.) *Landscape: politics and perspectives*. Oxford, Berg, 107–38.

Jarman, N, 1994b 'Displaying faith'. *New Ulster*, 23, 10–12.

Jefferson, T and S Hall (eds), 1976 *Resistance through rituals*. London, Hutchinson.

Kertzer, D, 1988 *Ritual, politics and power*. Yale University Press.

Kertzer, D, 1992 'Rituel et symbolisme politiques des sociétés occidentales'. *L'Homme*, 32, 79–90.

Lane, C, 1981 *The rites of rulers*. Cambridge, Cambridge University Press.

Loftus, B, 1994 *Mirrors: Orange and Green*. Pictures Press, Dundrum.

Mach, Z, 1993 *Symbols, conflicts, and identity*. Albany, State University of New York Press.

O'Connor, F, 1994 *In search of a state: Catholics in Northern Ireland*. Belfast, Blackstaff Press.

O'Dwyer, P, 1988 *Mary: a history of devotion in Ireland*. Dublin, Four Courts Press.

Pasquinelli, C, 1989 'Il ritorno del rito'. *Problemi del Socialismo*, 3, 78–89.

Pistoli, P, 1981 *Una comunità sotto controllo*. Milano, F. Angeli.

Sluka, J A, 1989 *Hearts and Mind, Water and Fish*. Greenwich, Jai Press.

Sluka, J A, 1995 'Domination, resistance and political culture in Northern Ireland's Catholic-nationalist ghettos,' *Critique of Anthropology*, 15, 71–102.

Turner, V W, 1967 *The forest of symbols*. Ithaca, Cornell University Press.

Ziff, T (ed.), 1989 *Still war: photographs from the north of Ireland*. London, Bellew Publishing.

Acknowledgements

My fieldwork in Northern Ireland was part of my research project for the fulfil-ment of the *Dottorato di Ricerca in Scienze Antropologiche e Analisi dei Mutamenti Culturali, at the Istituto Universitario Orientale, Napoli.* My thanks are due to the Department of Social Sciences at IUO, Naples which supported me financially during my stay in Northern Ireland.

There are many to whom I am indebted in Ireland, Tony Buckley of the Ulster Folk and Transport Museum, Hastings Donnan and Roseanne Cecil of the Queen's University of Belfast for their helpful comments. Also I would like to thank Karen McCartney, Angela Daly, Dominic Bryan, Neil Jarman, Noel Maguigan and David Officer who have all provided invaluable help.

Furthermore, special acknowledgements are due to some people who helped me in my research: Frank Kieran, National Secretary of the AOH, and Joe Austin, Sinn Féin councillor for North Belfast. Special thanks are due to Danny, Colm and Jim.

Motor-cycle Dress and Undress

LINDA MAY BALLARD

IT is a familiar enough idea that since Marlon Brando's appearance in the 1950s film *The Wild One*, the black leather jacket has, like the motor cycle itself, been synonymous with rebellion. The jacket may for some even have made the statement without recourse to the more expensive and potentially more dangerous bike. The image of rebellion emerging in the 1950s was no doubt reinforced by the fact that during this decade the Hell's Angels began to appear in the USA, in the wake of the Second World War.

This paper, drawn from field-work carried out among motor-cyclists and former motor-cyclists in Ulster, explores aspects of the personal presentation of local bikers, and the way in which dress and adornment may express, or contribute to a symbolic expression of, self and social values. It will also show that the motor-cycling fraternity is very diverse, and that within its ranks, one man's rebellion may simply be another woman's leather or even denim jacket. There are many potential gradations between these two points.

Given the diversity of the motor-cycling fraternity, it may be useful to outline some of its component parts. Many motor-cyclists are individual-ists belonging to no group or club, but for others, a sense of group identity is crucial.

There are several styles of motor-cycle club. Some, usually referred to as MCC organisations, hold meetings, organise runs and other social events, may involve themselves in charitable work and often provide prac-tical help to members, for example by advising on matters of insurance. Most clubs of this sort produce small fabric badges known as 'patches' which members usually wear attached to the sleeve of a motor-cycle jacket. These clubs may be groups of motor-cycle enthusiasts from a given area (the North Down Motor Cycle Club, for example); they may consist of owners of a particular type of bike (for instance the Goldwing Owners' Club); or, like the Christian Motorcyclists' Club, members may share a specific commitment or interest apart from motor-cycling.

Others are commonly referred to as MC organisations, otherwise known as Outlaws. These are structured clubs, the prototype for which are the American Hell's Angels. Some clubs regard themselves as existing on the margin between these kinds of organisation. For example, the all-female motor-cycle club, the Black Widows, describe themselves as being neither MC nor MCC (both sets of initials stand for 'Motor Cycle Club').

A fundamental point common to all of these groups is that members ride motor-cycles, not motor scooters. The scooter was the mode of transport favoured by the so-called Mods who, by their tidy, sophisticated dress in the 1960s and in the Mod revival in the 1980s, differentiated themselves from the leather clad, motor-cycle riding Rockers. Research and fieldwork to date has not revealed any Outlaw scooter clubs in Northern Ireland, but scooter organisations parallel to MCC groups have existed locally at least since the 1950s.

While among motor-cyclists, and more generally as an item of dress, the black leather jacket may undoubtedly be both seen and used as an expression of rebellion, its primary importance is much more prosaic and mundane. It offers protection both from the elements and from abrasions and even more serious injury. The advantages of leather clothing as a means of keeping out bad weather were fully appreciated by early car drivers and their passengers, and were equally well understood by the first generation of bikers, some of whom were well aware that the leather jacket could contribute to the wearer's raffish style. It has been suggested that the jacket

Figure 9   *Competitors in the Isle of Man Grand Prix, 1912.* J F R Martin.

was borrowed from the pilots of the First World War (Farren 1985, 22) but in fact leather was being worn by bikers in the era before the war (see Fig. 9). In later years, notably during the 1950s, leather clothing was beyond the pocket of many local bikers, and rubber garments were the practical if not always comfortable substitute (see Fig. 10).

As motor-cycle racing became an increasingly popular and established sport, many meetings began to regulate the dress of competitors (Ballard 1995). By the 1930s, it was quite common for race rules to stipulate that entrants had to wear leather clothing, and this seems to have encouraged the use of the same material among motor-cyclists, who often model styles on those used by heroes of the race track. Incidentally, decades before the helmet law was passed, competitors in many races had to prove that they had adequate protection for their heads, and the styles and decoration of helmets worn on the race track have also influenced the everyday wear of helmets.

In recent years, racers have increasingly chosen brightly-coloured leather suits, and these too have been copied for every-day motor-cycle wear. Nowadays, riders and pillion passengers often have costly, matching one-piece suits of brightly-coloured leather which may co-ordinate with

Figure 10 *Rubber-clad self-styled mad motor-cyclists, Belfast, 1950s.* W Middleton.

the motor-cycle itself, or in some cases may closely replicate the outfit of a famous racer, but for many there is no substitute for the colour black.

Ironically, the fact that leather garments provide motor-cyclists with a degree of protection meant that they were deliberately rejected by early American Hell's Angels. 'Professional motor-cyclists who have learned the hard way wear helmets, gloves and full-length leather suits ... But not the Hell's Angels. Anything safe, they want no part of' (Thompson 1967, 89).

These archetypal rebels, models of 'rancid, criminal sleaziness' (Thompson 1967, 18), therefore eschew the very symbol with which they are popularly thought to be most closely associated. Early Hell's Angels were virtually confined to California, where, while they may have been indifferent to personal safety, the climate was equitable. Outlaws in less hospitable regions are more likely to appreciate the robustness of leather clothing.

As a colour, or to be technically more accurate, as an absence of colour, black can carry many symbolic meanings. When applied to clothing, it may contribute to the expression of authority, for example in clerical or academic dress; it may suggest chic and sophistication, as in the 'little black dress'; the punk movement of the 1970s used a certain style of black outfit to help express an aggressively rebellious stance and the rejection of more apparently normative social values; black may also convey a sense of mystery. In European cultures, it is the colour most readily associated with mourning and therefore by extension with death. It can be argued that all these symbolic qualities contribute to the choice of black for the dress of motor-cyclists.

Leathers, not necessarily black, are often perceived as a type of marginalised dress. One young man who regularly uses his motor-cycle as a means of transport came a short walking distance during his lunch break from work to be interviewed as part of the field-work on which this paper is based, wearing a sober business suit. He had travelled to work on his motor cycle that morning and would return home on it that night. When asked if his dress was of a type suited to motor-cycling he explained that he kept his suit hanging up in work, changing into his leathers every morning and evening (UFTM R95.6; see also Ballard 1997). Another motor-cyclist, encountered on one occasion fresh from work, not in his biking costume but in a two-piece suit, had his usually conspicuous and extremely long pony tail tucked down the back of the suit jacket.

The colour black has the capacity to suggest the sinister and threatening; these attributes may be extended to other items of biker clothing, in addition to the jacket. The helmet is usually understood to be the most important piece of protective wear available to the motor-cyclist. Many bikers consider it very foolhardy to ride without wearing a helmet, but some bikers question this wisdom and believe that legislation introduced in Britain during the 1970s and compelling them to wear helmets, is an infringement of their civil liberties. In addition to this debate about helmets within the motor-cycling fraternity at large, there is a problem of perception in relation to helmets which can create a threatening appearance when in wear. Many business premises insist that bikers remove their helmets before entering.

This is of course a matter of practical concern. Motor-cycle helmets, especially the full-faced and visored variety, offer great potential for disguise. While the motor-cyclist who wears a helmet of this or any other style will on the balance of probability be a careful, law-abiding citizen whose main concern is to give maximum protection to his cranium, this may not be the image he or she externally conveys. This is a point which is not lost on some members of the motor-cycling fraternity at large. Customised motor-cycle helmets, particularly those decorated in a style stipulated by the owner, often draw on threatening imagery inspired by certain styles of film, literature and other sources of fantasy art. One custom painter working from Carrickfergus remarked on the fact that to don a full-faced and visored helmet decorated with imagery suggesting, for example, transformation from man to mechanoid, was in effect to become the creature of fantasy. Wearing the helmet, one complies with the law, ensures one is protected from the elements and from injury in the event of an accident, but one may also more or less consciously be donning a mask which helps in assuming the somewhat threatening persona of the motor-cyclist. The example of the helmet provides a clear example of many of the issues which may be confused in the general perception of motor-cycle dress.

Some motor-cyclists may choose to tap into certain of these elements and be well aware of the impact of their appearance, while others may innocently create an image simply by dressing practically. Yet others may borrow and extend certain implications of the dress typical of the motor-cycle scene, for example those who perceive leather (or for that matter the cheaper substitute, rubber) as a fetish. The motor-cyclist who dresses in leather for no other reason than practicality may therefore find himself in a situation parallel to that of the girl who wears a short skirt (for example) because it suits her, only to discover that this is conduct which may be assessed as sufficient to justify the actions of a rapist.

Other items of dress in addition to the helmet may be customised. Jackets are often treated in this way, and customising may extend to the machine itself. Tanks and mud-guards lend themselves to decoration.

So does the body of the motor-cyclist. Internationally, tattooing is an increasingly popular art form and it has an enthusiastic local following, as evidenced for example by the show now held annually in Belfast's Ulster Hall. Tattooing is not the preserve of motor-cyclists, nor do all motor-cyclists sport tattoos, but there is a strong and growing association between the two. Many large-scale annual motor-cycle meetings and events both locally and elsewhere now number an on-site tattooist among the attractions.

Bikers' tattoos are often but not exclusively on a theme related to motor-cycling both in direct and in more abstracted ways. For example, they may illustrate straightforward motifs associated with specific brands or models of motor-cycle. By using a variant on the 'ride hard, die free' theme, they may refer to the inherent risk in motor-cycling. Tattoos may also express this idea more symbolically, without reference to a legend, by using motifs associated with mortality. The Death's Head, which is closely associated with Hell's Angels, is widely used in this way. Some members of certain styles of motor-cycle club, especially Outlaw clubs whose members generally have a strong sense of brotherhood and of shared identity, will express their club membership by having various components of the club regalia tattooed on their bodies.

Outlaw clubs also use dress and other aspects of personal presentation, for example hairstyles, to express club membership. The style of dress and the symbolic nature of the motifs selected by these clubs is modelled on those characteristic of Hell's Angels, and is itself of interest. Aspects of this behaviour can be traced to the earliest stages of development of the Hell's Angels in America during the 1960s.

An Angel known as 'the Mute' was stopped for speeding by a policeman near the beach in Santa Cruz ... The Mute was proudly displaying his colours on a ragged Levi jacket. The Mute stripped off his Levi jacket, exposing another Angel decal on his leather jacket. 'Take that off too,' the irate patrolman ordered ... And under that was a wool shirt, also emblazoned with the club colours. 'Off with it ...' With a smirk the Mute removed his undershirt and ... brought into full view the Hell's Angels grinning Death's Head which had been tattooed on his body (Thompson 1967, 72–3).

'Colours' have also been associated with Outlaw clubs since they first appeared in the 1950s. The club which figures in *The Wild One* is such an organisation, and Colours in a rudimentary form are sported on the backs of their jackets. Once again, it appears to have been the Hell's Angels who established the accepted form to be taken by Outlaw Colours.

In August 1966 the Angels officially changed their patch to read 'Hell's Angels' on top of the skull, 'California' underneath. New chapters in the East and Midwest were expected to be operative by 1967. They would be allowed to wear the traditional patch, but with the name of their own State (Thompson 1967, 85).

Colours thus defined have become the prototype for those worn by Outlaw clubs. Each club will have its own motif, which while distinctive will draw on the symbolic resonances suggested by the Death's Head. The motif will be surrounded by 'rockers', components carrying the name of the club and the area of operation, as established by the style formalised three decades ago by the Hell's Angels.

In addition to identifying the Outlaw as a member of a clearly-defined group, the back patch or Colours he wears expresses his degree of initiation into the club. (Irish Outlaw clubs are exclusively male). The number of components of the back patch which have been achieved reflects the degree to which the wearer is a club initiate. After a period of time in which a potential member associates with a club, he achieves one rocker which is displayed on the back of his jacket. After a time a second rocker is acquired. An incomplete patch of this sort illustrates that the club member is a 'prospect'. Full members wear full patches, complete with the relevant motif denoting his affiliation (see Ballard 1997).

These patches are generally to be found not on a leather ground but attached to a sleeveless denim cutaway gilet or bodice worn over a leather motor-cycle jacket. Once again, this is a style originally established by Hell's Angels, in part because the denim gilet is more appropriate to their philosophy of courting danger, in part, it has been suggested, because it is readily removed. This helps to explain the logos so consistently displayed by the Mute, and gives an insight into the reasons why Outlaws sport club tattoos.

Club colours are exclusively the right of club members, and must be given up if membership ceases for any reason. Members who leave amicably have their club tattoos endorsed with their dates of membership. Those leaving as the result of a dispute generally have a certain length of time in which to have any tattoos reflecting club membership covered or removed.

Outlaws represent the extreme of biker culture. In Ireland, there is a limited number of such clubs, and each one tends to operate in a given territory, resisting any attempts to set up a rival group in the same region. This means that the wearing of Colours is jealously guarded. Members of other types of clubs may wear badges expressing their membership, but these are usually discrete patches worn on the arm or perhaps on the front of the jacket. There are a few exceptions, but their Colours are carefully designed to be easily distinguished from the composite style favoured by the Outlaw clubs. It is not the leather jacket, black or otherwise which truly expresses rejection of normative social values, but these patches or Colours. These form a stylised and deliberate symbol expressive of club membership, and, at a deeper level symbolise the shared values which also define the group's identity.

It should not be imagined that this identity is unremittingly anti-social. Outlaws include the charming, the witty and the articulate among their numbers. Partying is a popular social activity. At their annual custom bike show in 1995, the Waterford Freewheelers were raising funds to help the children of Chernobyl.

Outlaws give further expression to the sense of shared values by wearing a patch carrying the legend '1%' (or '1%er'). This is an overt statement that the rider considers himself to be part of the one per cent of motor cyclists who like to cause trouble. 'All Angels wear this patch as do most other Outlaws, and it means that they are proud to be part of the alleged one per cent of bike riders whom the American Motor-cycle Association refuses to claim'. (Thompson 1967, 18)

Some Outlaws also wear a patch carrying the number '13', and of these some explain that this stands for the letter 'M', and is therefore an indirect reference to use of the drug marijuana. This patch has been worn by Hell's Angels since the 1960s and since then has carried this connotation.[1] However, field-work among Outlaws suggests that for some who wear this patch, the allusion to marijuana has been lost, and that for them the patch has become another essential component of Outlaw regalia. Of course, the number 13 carries quite different connotations, being widely regarded as a symbol of ill luck. It is a number often consciously avoided by motorcyclists. For instance, few motor-cycle races will compel a rider to enter at 13 (Ballard 1995, 55). To sport a badge featuring this device is therefore in a way to court disaster, and in this way is in keeping with other aspects of Outlaw philosophy.

While the associations between 13 and marijuana seem to have become obscured, more direct reference is sometimes made to the drug. The marijuana leaf may be worn as a tattoo, and occasionally motor-cyclists (not necessarily members of Outlaw clubs) wear metal or other badges depicting the plant. It is reasonable to assume that such badges may also be worn by non-motor-cyclists, but to hint indirectly or more openly at drug use is to express ideas about freedom to choose irrespective of the law or of the possibility of personal risk, and is again appropriate to the Outlaw identity.

In addition to tattooing, body piercing is another means of self-presentation popular with some contemporary bikers. Again it may contribute to an apparently threatening or unwelcoming image which may be (and may be deliberately cultivated as) the perceived persona of an individual who is actually both approachable and affable.

Body piercing is, of course, also a popular aspect of contemporary culture more generally and is neither confined to nor universally espoused by motor-cyclists. While some bikers adorn their piercings with conventional ring decorations, some select from a range of jewellery on recognisable themes including for example representations of skeletal hands and tattoo guns, once again reinforcing the message by drawing on a relevant symbolic range.

There is a clear and integrated range of symbols represented through various methods of dress and adornment upon which a motor-cyclist may choose to draw in order to express his or her persona. Patches and badges are very popular and may embrace an enormous and diverse range of ideas and motifs associated with motor-cycling. The composite back patches worn by members of Outlaw clubs are a fairly extreme example, but many organisations, including the Christian Motorcycle Association, identify themselves by means of discrete fabric badges usually worn on a jacket sleeve. Specific events, club runs for example, are often commemorated by a special fabric patch so that these too may have a wider symbolic valency than simply that of expressing club membership.

Together with studs, chains and paint, metal badges made an important contribution to the style of decoration characteristic of the typical Rocker jacket of the mid 1960s to early 1970s. These jackets are of great interest, for, being studded and decorated in this way, the protective nature of the original leather jacket is completely subverted. Pierced, it is no longer waterproof; the metal adornments make it extremely heavy and if these should come into contact with the ground while travelling at speed they are more likely to cause the jacket to produce sparks than to protect from abrasion. They fulfil the role of dress uniform or costume, and are in no sense practical, protective garments. Some local motor-cyclists of the same era avoided the use of studs etc. on the very grounds that these undermined the functionality of the leather garment, but one man commented that he liked the idea that he conveyed the mystique of the 'black rider' by his unadorned black leathers (UFTM C 95.4).

Rocker jackets often feature Nazi insignia, original or reproduced, as part of the applied surface decoration they carry. Similar devices were also favoured by the early Hell's Angels, and they remain popular with many Outlaw bikers. The message they convey is apparently unambiguous but it is possible that, for at least some Rockers, these insignia were worn subversively, more as a rejection of authority and acceptability than as a expression of the values actually represented by the insignia. Rocker jackets had no influence on the 'rocker' components of Outlaw patches. These are named because of their shape, and are intended to suggest the outline of a wheel. However, some bikers still echo in their dress aspects the style espoused by Rockers, applying to their clothes, particularly jackets, decoration which pays tribute to the chains favoured by some members of an earlier generation of bikers. Miniaturised tools, spanners for example, may be worn almost like brooches, and suggest the practical skills which may be required to meet some of the technical challenges with which a motor-cyclist may be confronted by his machine. Badges may also be worn, examples generally referring to a liking for certain illicit substances.

The fact that patches, badges and the like sometimes express a group identity may seem to be at odds with the image of the motor-cyclist as a free-spirited individual. There are in fact many individuals who, while they may draw on available and familiar repertoire of imagery in order to express their interest or way of life, do not belong to an organised, identified club or organisation.

Lynn and Ian Gourley of Bangor Co. Down are clear examples of individuals (or to be exact a married couple) who see the motor-cycle as much more than a means of transport. The motor-cycle forms part of their means of expressing the fact that they espouse a life-style which in some ways departs from that which might be considered the norm. Dress is consciously used by them as a means of both stating and reinforcing their general attitudes. This can clearly be seen for example in a dramatic denim jacket designed and meticulously hand-embroidered on a theme appropriate to motor-cycling by Lynn herself for her own use, and even more radically in their wedding photograph, which shows bride and groom uncompromising in black leather and blue denim in the elegant setting of Bangor Castle.

Ideas of freedom inform much of the symbolism chosen for the customising of motor-cycles and accessories. In addition to drawing on threatening and menacing themes, customising often features motifs with a different emphasis. Native American Indians and Vikings are among the cultural groups which carry resonances for bikers, suggesting as they do a combination of the free, the uncompromising and the marginalised. Fashion and therefore a more open conformity is also an issue.

Celtic interlace design, in this context often referred to as 'tribal' in style, is increasingly popular both for tattoos and for custom decoration. At least one young local motor-cyclist sports a personalised, custom painted helmet and tattoo to match, both on the theme of the currently extremely popular 'Diesel' logo (which itself is sometimes interpreted as being derived from the death's head favoured by the Hell's Angels). Once again, expression of individuality is fused with a statement of communal identity.

For some motor-cyclists, machismo is an overt factor influencing and expressed by their self-presentation. For example, mild eroticism often features as a theme for motor-cycle customising, and undercurrents of machismo may be perceived in many aspects of motor-cycling. Some motor-cycles are advertised as being among other things, 'sexy' in the particular rather than the more generalised sense of the word.

In addition to expressing various aspects of attitude and philosophy, customising is an art form, and as such symbolises the quality of the relationship between the biker and the bike, the pride a rider takes in ownership of a machine. Good engineering is also appreciated, so that a machine, whether customised or factory-made, may be highly regarded as a piece of kinetic art.

This attitude is common to riders of both motor-cycles and motor scooters. Italian-designed scooters are particularly highly regarded. With their enclosed engines, scooters were the form of transport favoured in the 1960s by the Mods whose style of presentation differed radically from that of the contemporary Rockers. These groups were less well represented in Ireland than in England, and their activities were certainly less highlighted by the press, but it can safely be said that they had their adherents in this country, and that the animosity between them sometimes expressed itself in violence. Members of either group could readily be identified by their distinctive dress style as well as by choice of machine.

Mods re-emerged quite strongly in Ulster during the 1980s, when their differences were not with Rockers, who did not make a contemporary comeback, but with Skinheads to whom they were historically and stylistically closely related. Dress and machine again helped to express the carefully-studied and cultivated image, smart but in no way soft, which is clearly illustrated by the brooding photographic self-portraits of the Belfast-based mod, Joe McGilloway, who during the early 1980s was a Art student in the city (Fig. 11). McGilloway's carefully-studied self-image extended to mannerisms of speech, to dance style and to other aspects of presentation, dress being the most immediately conspicuous.

Dress provides motor-cyclists with a potent means of self-expression. This is a matter which they clearly understand and frequently exploit. As has been demonstrated, it is a grave misunderstanding to imagine that all this symbolic expression is invested in a single garment, the black leather jacket. While this garment was brought by the Rockers to a symbolic apotheosis which totally subverted its practical function, by other groups it has been rejected outright. There are many contradictions inherent in the symbolism of the black leather jacket, and in popular perceptions and understandings of that symbolism.

The garment itself is at once a rather conservative and sensible form of dress, and an evocative and sinister emblem. Even the subversive quality of the Rocker jacket may be reinterpreted. One couple found themselves gripped by a 'collecting mania' in the 1980s. This mania was for motorcycle badges and the like which they wear, Rocker-style, on leather jackets. As they point out, 'the studs traditionally used to adorn Rockers' jackets are not what they used to be'. For them, while embracing Rocker culture may provide an alternative to current values, the message appears to be retrospective, rather than a matter of subversion of contemporary values. They comment: 'We're proud to be real Rockers like they were in the old days. It's in our blood. What we'd love to do more than anything would be to go back to the Fifties wearing all this stuff' (May 1966).

The Rocker jacket has thus acquired another set of connotations. With the black leather jacket, as with beauty, much of the message may be in the

Figure 11   *Joe McGilloway 1980s Mod in Belfast.* J. McGilloway.

eyes of the beholder. It is illuminating to draw a parallel between this example of coded dressing and that worn by those in mourning, particularly widows, in the nineteenth century. Mourning dress was governed by sets of rules which were generally agreed and understood. Superficially, black was intended to express profound sorrow, but mourning could be used as a means of expressing many aspects of social relationships and outlooks (Taylor 1983, 133). As the nineteenth century progressed, it became an increasingly fashionable mode of dress, one which was more and more removed from its original ostensible purpose. The difference is that while mourning was espoused by society in general, so that social credibility could be derived from displaying a knowledge of the associated rules, the codes of motor-cycle dress are more arcane, and credibility is derived by illustrating that the wearer as access to secrets of means of subversion.

At the heart of the matter is the nature of the motor-cycle itself. The bike is a demanding and unforgiving means of transport, one which may expose its rider to dangers much graver than those posed by the elements. The motor-cycle may become mechanically temperamental, often without warning. No rider, no matter how carefully dressed, is going to come off better in an encounter with a four-wheeled vehicle. The motor-cyclist therefore puts her- or himself into a position of tremendous vulnerability which thoroughly informs the style of self-presentation.

Black leather itself has more to do with self-presentation than with rebellion, but some motor-cyclists choose for various reasons (which may include a sense of rebellion or of rejection of normative values) to emphasise certain aspects of their appearance. This action is invested with symbolic meanings. Much of the associated imagery suggests a kind of *danse macabre*. This is reminiscent of the custom of hanging religious memorabilia and images of Death from the rear-view mirror, one which is observed, for example, in many European and North African counties. The fluffy dice and plastic skeletons favoured locally by some car drivers are also symbols of a sense of the element of chance involved in (and the potentially lethal nature of) the activity of travelling by road. The symbolism of decorative customising of both the person and the machine may express a range of ideas, including the exhilaration of the experience of motor-cycling and an awareness that to engage in the activity is to court disaster if not to dance with death. The Death's Head and the skeletal biker, among the most popular images chosen for tattoos, are less an expression of a death wish than a statement that the odds have been weighed. On one level, therefore, the images may be talismanic. On another, used for example as a component of club regalia, they function as the expression of group identity.

In recent years, even the advertising industry has repeatedly exploited the popularly conceived image of the motor-cyclist to various ends. The depth of popular misconception may be gauged from the fact that the term 'hell's angel' is often used to refer to a biker, without any understanding of the fact that Hell's Angels is a distinctive and highly organised motor-cycle club.

Misinterpretations of many aspects of motor-cycle dress are similarly grounded, and due to the diversity of the motor-cycling fraternity, valid broad generalities about the symbolic nature of motor-cycle dress are difficult to draw. While there are those who interpret the black leather jacket as a threatening and ominous emblem, it seems that the appeal of the Harley Davidson is virtually limitless. The Harley Davidson, closely associated with Hell's Angels, and popular with a wide range of motor-cyclists, is a highly evocative symbol. An enormous range of merchandise bearing this name is available. Recently, Harley Davidson toiletries have appeared on the market, and the name carries connotations of a reverse sophistication which appeals to many non-bikers.

Bikers and non-bikers alike often find off-the-peg t-shirts decorated with themes closely associated to motor-cycling and specifically with customising to their taste. These garments are quite widely available, and like the black leather jacket, provide the opportunity to express though dress, an espousal of or sympathy with a certain set of values without necessarily having to ride a motor-cycle. More exclusive are club t-shirts available only to members of specific motor-cycle organisations. Many clubs, including Outlaws, have garments prepared to express club membership or to commemorate a particular event. Club t- or sweat-shirts are usually intended for wear only by members of the named group. Any garment carrying a direct reference to an Outlaw club will be available only to members.

While it is true that many motor-cyclists operate as individuals, not belonging to any identified group or club, it is also true that a strong sense of unity binds many bikers together. When on the road, most motor-cyclists will acknowledge one another by means of a wave or by flashing a headlight. Few will pass a motor-cyclist who has obviously broken down without stopping to offer practical help or at least moral support. In some, this sense of camaraderie is much stronger, extending to the urge to belong to a club or organised group. In a few, the sense of camaraderie is registered so strongly that the motor-cycle becomes a symbolic focus for an entire way of life. This is reinforced by specific ways of dressing and manners of self-presentation which themselves help to re-emphasise the nature and boundaries of the group. A specific repertoire of resonant motifs may be drawn on to strengthen this expression. This repertoire is not in all aspects the exclusive preserve of a single sector of the motor-cycle fraternity, and its range may be extended as individuals choose to draw upon it.

In summary, while motor-cycle dress may readily lend itself to symbolic expression, it may also readily be misread, so that for example perfectly respectable individuals may have to change from leather clothing to lounge suit every day on arriving at and leaving work. The valency of this symbolism is not lost on motor-cyclists, some of whom exploit its potential to the full. Motor-cycle dress provides a potent means of expressing a wide rage of ideas, some closely interrelated, others widely diverse. At heart, even the most conservative and practical of motor-cyclists, while justifying the choice of black leather on grounds of prudence alone, may secretly cherish the mystique of his projected image as the 'black rider'.

Notes

1. See the Hell's Angels motorcycling clubs quoted by Thompson (1967, 17–18). This also describes the colours and other aspects of dress favoured by Hell's Angels in the 1960s.

References

Ballard, L M, 1995 'Jack Martin, racing motor-cyclist'. *Ulster Folklife* 41, 52–61.
Ballard, L M, 1997 'These youngsters change all these traditions'. *Folklore* 108.
Farren, M, 1985 *The black leather jacket*. New York, Abbeville.
May, G, 1966 'Pin ups'. *The classic motor-cycle*, Jan 1966.
Taylor, L, 1983 *Mourning dress*. London, Allen and Unwin.
Thompson, H S, 1967 *Hell's Angels*. Harmondsworth, Penguin.
UFTM, Sound Archive of the Ulster Folk and Transport Museum.

Titanic: Out of the Depths and Into the Culture

MICHAEL McCAUGHAN

In June 1994 our family went on holiday to the Isle of Man. We crossed the Irish Sea in the Isle of Man Steam Packet Company's new 37-knot 'wave-piercing catamaran' *SeaCat*, which by chance was making her maiden voyage from Belfast. Owing more to aircraft design and construction than to conventional naval architecture, this high speed, hi-tech innovative craft, 'fitted with a special ride control system', whizzed us over calm waters, 'foot down all the way', just as advertised. However, the return passage ten days later was a seagoing experience of a different order. Running late because of stormy conditions, we were given instructions for 'our comfort and safety' in an airline-style presentation, before putting to sea at much reduced speed. As soon as we cleared Douglas harbour, *SeaCat's* motion became violent as the lightweight aluminium vessel pitched and crashed into steep and rolling white-topped waves. The large passenger cabin creaked and groaned alarmingly and sick bags began to appear. Suddenly a young woman cried out, in a Belfast accent, 'It's the *Titanic!*' A momentary silence was followed by a ripple of nervous laughter, as if the invocation of *Titanic* – the ultimate symbol of disaster – had acted as a lightning conductor for our fears and anxieties. Of course, there was no real danger of us sinking, but the association of historic disaster with that which we were experiencing had fused past, present and future in our collective imagination. For a moment, symbol and reality had conjoined and we were vulnerable and human in our labouring, technological cocoon.

The wreck of the *Titanic* is an epic tale of the twentieth century. On the evening of 14 April 1912, *Titanic* – the essence of modernity and technological achievement – was steaming across the Atlantic on her maiden voyage from the Old World to the New. On board, her passengers and crew were oblivious to the iceberg's presence and the imminence of destruction and death. Enshrining the values, self-confidence and social fabric of the era, *Titanic* was a microcosm of western civilisation in 'a gilded age' before the First World War. The *Zeitgeist* was reflected and proclaimed, with unknowing irony, in the White Star Line's grandiloquent advertising of *Titanic* and her sister ship *Olympic*:

The White Star liners *Olympic* and *Titanic*, eloquent testimonies to the progress of mankind, as shown in the conquest of mind over matter – will rank high in the achievements of the twentieth century ... the Staterooms in their situation, spaciousness and appointments, will be perfect havens of retreat where many pleasant hours are spent, and where the time given to slumber and rest will be free from noise or other disturbance. The friendly intercourse, mutual helpfulness and bonhomie of third class passengers is proverbial ... The new field of endeavour is looked forward to with hope and confidence. In these vessels the interval between the old life and the new is spent under the happiest possible conditions. (*White Star Line* May 1911)

The sinking of *Titanic* had a traumatic effect in both Europe and the United States. The great ship, a signifier of the civilised world, now lay fractured on the ocean floor after plunging down through two miles of freezing water. Millionaires and emigrant poor on board had gone down with her. It was a mighty blow to the self-confidence of the age. An American writer, Bruce Jackson, has interpreted the impact of the disaster from a modern perspective:

The rising star of modern technology had a sudden loss of magnitude, as that sleek and enormous ship that could not be sunk tore its hide and collapsed. It was the major disaster of the era, and it struck the imagination of the rich, who lost friends and relatives on the ship ... and the poor, for whom the ship represented the great shining and glistening world forever denied them and anyone they would ever know. (Jackson 1972)

Throughout the twentieth century, *Titanic*, and all that her loss implies, has maintained a powerful hold on the imagination of people, not only in Europe and North America, but virtually throughout the world. Yet with the passage of time attitudes have changed and for us today, *Titanic* has a significance beyond tragedy and death. So we are not surprised to learn, for example, that in Costa Rica buses are given dramatic titles like *Sport, Goofy, Victor Hugo* and *El Gran Titanic* (Travel Weekend, *Guardian*, 5 March 1990). However, in the north of Ireland the tragedy retains a special significance for, of course, Belfast was the birthplace of *Titanic* and there remains a thwarted pride in her memory. Perhaps this is most poignantly reflected in a photograph of 97-year-old Sam McLaughlin, a riveter on *Titanic*, holding a plastic model of the ship (Hammond 1986, 104). But the imagery entails a mystery, for we do not know if the model belongs to Mr McLaughlin or if it was perhaps placed in his hands by the photographer. We begin to wonder if the photograph is disclosing a poignant reminder or a pathetic imitation.

In a retrospective way the tragedy of the Belfast-built ship can be seen as mirroring that of the city itself. But today there is a spirit of optimism in Belfast and new possibilities for the future are being envisioned. With unerring commercial sensibility these include re-appropriations of a

Titanic past. For example, on 20 June 1994 the *Belfast Telegraph* reported that:

> A Northern Ireland construction firm is hoping to launch a *Titanic* twin – by building an exact replica for a mystery Japanese buyer ... the life-size model of the 270m vessel, minus engines, would be permanently moored in Tokyo Bay for use as a luxury conference centre ... we are talking big, big money.

In September 1992, *Belfast Special Dry Gin* – 'The Spirit of our City' – was launched as a new premium-quality drink, 'made to the original Belfast recipe using a careful balance of pure spirit, essence of juniper and orange'. Marketed in a distinctive nautical-style bottle, the gin is claimed to be 'as much part of Belfast's heritage as the ocean-going liners built by generations of the city's craftsmen'. A back-of-bottle listing of famous Belfast-built ships, 'which conjure up romantic images of that "Golden Age of Travel"' of course includes *Titanic*. To reinforce this nautical heritage, each bottle carries a romantic image of a liner that appears to be *Titanic*, but possibly due to sensibilities of taste, it is in fact her look-alike sister-ship *Britannic*.

As builders of the original *Titanic*, Harland and Wolff are looking to the new millennium with a proposed technology-based *Titanic Park*. In lavish promotional literature, the company stakes out this dynamic new territory, confidently predicating its futuristic proposals on the resonating name of its most famous and symbolic ship.

> *Titanic Park* will form Northern Ireland's central focus for the high-tech, innovative corporations of today and the future. It will be Belfast's most striking business landmark, a hub of technological excellence and a nationally important flagship development situated on Queen's Island ...
>
> *Titanic Park's* construction will utilise innovative design and superb finishes throughout. External elevations will be clad in aluminium panels and energy-efficient blue-tinted glass, while the entire interior will be finished to full office standard including suspended acoustic tile ceilings, integral lighting, full air-conditioning and state-of-the-art security systems (*Titanic Park* nd; see also *Irish News* 5 April 1995).

Within these *Titanic* appropriations and commercial frames, irony and parody are unconsciously present. The proposed transfiguration of *Titanic* from substance to pastiche is a retro-visionary proclamation that millennial post-modernity is alive and well in the city of Belfast.

While potent images of the stricken liner have endured for eight decades, the multiplicity of metaphors resulting from the catastrophe have been equally powerful. Cultural processes of absorption, transformation and diffusion began immediately after the sinking and as resonances of *Titanic's* disaster, they perhaps have significance for humanity greater than the event itself. *Titanic* and the mythic proportions of her loss have become the subject, generator and carrier of all kinds of signs, messages and meanings, from the sublime to the tacky. They embrace the cultural spectrum, from high culture to low culture, from popular culture to consumer culture. The *Titanic* litany includes books, verse, vaudeville, religion, songs, music, opera, dance, drama, art, poetry, film, cartoons, jokes, fantasy, graffiti, advertising, satire, politics, pornography, propaganda, romantic fiction, science fiction, museum exhibitions and cultural discourse (Biels 1996, Foster 1997, Larabsee 1990, McCaughan 1994, 1997). So firmly is *Titanic* embedded in our consciousness that it can be invoked and responded to simply by inference rather than specific reference, as in the recent newspaper headlines 'Risk of the banking iceberg' (*Independent on Sunday* 13 June 1993) and 'Britain sinking fast' (*Observer* 31 July 1994). Although the human tragedy of the *Titanic* disaster retains its potency and evoked, for example, in the press reporting of both the *Herald of Free Enterprise* and *Estonia* ferry disasters, *Titanic* has also been exploited as a carrier of messages and meanings which may or may not be in the best possible taste. Besides the ship itself, the recurring disaster motifs are lifebelts, dance-bands, deckchairs and icebergs, especially the tip of the iceberg. Although these motifs, both visual and textual, have been so overworked as to become clichés, they still retain a metaphorical power, despite their predictability. Here is an above-average example, combining topicality with a surreal flourish of disaster imagery.

> Down in the City something stirs. The people who make money from money are suddenly making a lot more money again ... the sackings, the tears on the steps of broking houses, all of this now floats astern like an iceberg successfully navigated in the night. The band switches, mid-tune, from 'Abide With Me' to 'Happy Days Are Here Again'. (Leader, *Independent on Sunday*, 29 September 1993.)

The huge scale and diversity of Titanicism has made *Titanic* a glittering star of popular culture. In April 1987, for example, an English provincial newspaper (*Chipping Valley Youth News* 3 March 1987) reported the premiere of a new Titanic pop-musical by the Howard of Effingham School. The performance incorporated many special effects, including dry ice. Special guests attended. Mr Philip Trumble, Head of School Music, said, 'I have invited Nickey Slater 'the ice-skating star' to the show. He may be interested in performing *Titanic* on ice'. For *Titanic* consumption at home, why not curl up with a good book? If it's romance and a bit of a weep you want, try Danielle Steel's *No Greater Love* (1992), or if you're into the Hammer House of Horror go for the ghastly thriller *Something's Alive On The Titanic*. For more intimate moments alone or with a friend, there's a *Titanic* 'bathberg', a *Titanic* beer stein, *Titanic* phone cards and a *Titanic* teapot. However, for real wall-to-wall Titanicana you might have visited the National Maritime Museum's 1994–95 blockbuster exhibition *The Wreck of the Titanic* (see McCaughan 1996). Surrounded by 'a sea of controversy', it featured over 150 artefacts, including personal effects, recovered from the ocean floor around the wreck. The Museum said: 'The range and nature of artefacts on display will bring to life – like nothing else can – *Titanic's* brief but legendary history and the way things were at the twilight of the British Empire'. One person unlikely to have visited the show is the British politician Norman Lamont MP. As Chancellor of the Exchequer he was interviewed by the *Guardian* newspaper on 27 May 1993 and concluded with the remark, 'I am sure I seem responsible for the sinking of the *Titanic*'. Alas within hours, and quite coincidentally, a humiliated Mr Lamont was relieved of his office and a new Chancellor appointed. Next day the *Guardian* asked, 'But is this merely a switching of the deck chairs on the *Titanic?*'

Titanic, or rather Titanicism, is an international cultural phenomenon. It shows no sign of abating and indeed it is clear that the scale and potency of Titanicism has increased rather than diminished since the remains were located on the seabed in 1985. Despite the magnitude of other twentieth century horrors, *Titanic* has achieved the status of ultimate disaster symbol, or root metaphor, in our cultural consciousness.

Titanic, both real and imagined, has become a key icon of twentieth-century popular culture and one of the great metaphors of our time. However, in reviewing the cultural currency of *Titanic*, past and present, it is necessary to be mindful that the phenomenon derives from the horrific death of hundreds of people in the freezing cold black waters of the North Atlantic. Ultimately this is the perspective that applies to any consideration of *Titanic* as a cultural superstar. But this sensibility hardly stacks against the current exploitation of the physical wreck of *Titanic* as a consumable product. Today, the grave site of hundreds of people has become a tourist destination for cruising sightseers and a mega-souvenir hunting ground for predatory promoters.

Primarily, it is the passage of time that places *Titanic* in a different social taboo category to contemporary tragedies, such as the TWA Flight 800 disaster. To organise voyeuristic displays of aircraft fragments and personal effects recovered from Flight 800 would be unthinkable. This tragedy is part of our present and the dead are still mourned. In contrast, the tragedy of *Titanic* belongs to the past, but it's not the distant past, where archaeologists feel safe. For many, the *Titanic* disaster is not quite history, it's still too close to the present. In a way, the iconic *Titanic* is in limbo or a time warp between the present and the past. The debates and controversy generated by the recovery and commercial activities of RMS *Titanic* Inc. are a reflection of this shifting status. For some, the *Titanic* disaster is still memory fresh, and many people regard the wreck and debris field as grave sites which should not be violated. However, 84 years on, the reality is that attitudes to the *Titanic* dead have changed and that entrepreneurs have set a long sell-by date on the exploitable remains of the wreck.

News of the catastrophic loss of *Titanic* had a shattering effect on both sides of the Atlantic. As survivors began to tell their stories and facts became known, every conceivable aspect of the disaster was documented and debated. Scapegoats were found and heroism acclaimed. The chivalric commands, 'Be British' and 'Women and children first', struck sentimental and patriotic chords. Captain Smith was widely believed to have rescued a child before he perished with his ship. The wireless operators had stayed at their posts to the end, as had the engineers and the ship's band. It was rumoured that the band had played 'Nearer My God To Thee' as *Titanic* went down. Although this is now considered to be unlikely, it was believed to be true and the sheet music became an international best seller (Lord 1956; Eaton and Haas 1986).

Public expressions of grief knew no bounds. Entrepreneurs, catching the mood of emotion, flooded an eager market with mementos of the disaster. This was the modern *Titanic* industry in embryo, a profitable symbiotic relationship between production and consumption, keyed initially to a prevailing sense of human loss.

Commemorative postcards were especially popular, as they combined a high level of memorialisation with the commercial advantage of low cost. Most commonly the cards depicted the ship with an appropriate inscription. Often, however, it was *Titanic's* sister ship *Olympic* which was represented rather than *Titanic* herself, as the public were not aware of the slight differences between them and of course relatively few photographs of *Titanic* were available. More imaginatively the English postcard firm, Bamforth & Company, published a six-card set illustrating verses from 'Nearer My God To Thee'. To describe these as bizarre is, of course, a judgement of our day, but their iconography does provide a valuable insight into popular religious attitudes to the disaster. By incorporating the sinking ship with a figure of Christ, shining crosses, beckoning angels, wreaths of flowers, drapes and pillars, together with mourning vestal virgins, the cards memorialise the dead and provide theatrical reassurance of a heavenly home for one and all! The publication of specially-composed *Titanic* sheet music and songs was another commercial activity and market opportunity generated by the disaster. In the United States the first commercially published song was copyrighted on 25 April 1912 and within 12 months more than 100 *Titanic* disaster songs had been composed, copyrighted and published in America. Over 50 of these songs were published by the Washington D C firm of H Kirkus Dugdale, who organised a promotion whereby members of the public submitted lyrics and company hacks set them to music (Goodman 1985).

Figure 12   *Titanic memorial postcard 1912.*

Characteristically, sheet music songs were banal, sentimental and sanitised. For example, in the first US copyright song, *Just As The Ship Went Down*, the lyricist evoked the tragedy with:

> The sky grows black, the icebergs crack,
> And Death hangs o'er the water,
> But 'Women first!' the orders rang,
> For mother and for daughter.

With a limited range of possibilities, music titles were fairly predictable. Nevertheless, *Titanic's Angel Band* did suggest something of a surreal ascension when compared to *My Sweetheart Went Down With The Ship; The Titanic's Heroes Grave;* and *Rest in Peace Titanic*. Of course, consumer demand for such material was essentially transient and within a year or so the output of new titles by American sheet music publishers had fallen dramatically.

In Britain, in contrast to the United States, it appears that relatively few *Titanic* songs and musical sketches were published. Surviving examples include Haydon Augarde's *The Wreck of the Titanic*, a descriptive musical sketch for the piano. It incorporated Chopin's *Funeral March*, but otherwise it was a remarkably jolly piece. Dedicated to the gallant and ill-fated crew of *Titanic, Be British* was a descriptive song and recitation, for which illustrative coloured lantern slides could be bought or hired from the publisher. The recitation began after the second verse and included these immortal lines:

> All went well, and the laugh and jest
> And the dance went gaily on,
> Till they met the ice, and a rasp and a jar,
> Told there was something wrong.

Be British was also available on an early gramophone record produced in remembrance of the *Titanic*. Ernest Gray recorded it in 1912 on the Winner label, together with the song *Stand To Your Post*. The latter was both a commemoration and an exhortation for contributions to the relief fund for the widows and orphans of *Titanic's* crew. Listening to Ernest Gray's voice crackling over the years from 1912, the shortcomings of the commercially-inspired lyrics are transcended by an authentic and poignant engagement with history.

The generally ephemeral *Titanic* sheet music and songs were products of music consumerism and so were relatively quickly displaced by other novelties. They contrast with the *Titanic* narrative ballads of folk tradition, where origins are more diverse and where informal development and continuity occur. Relating strongly to, and informed by, the emigrant and immigrant experience, *Titanic* traditional songs have been transmitted in vernacular oral culture, not only in English, but also in Yiddish, Hebrew, Czech, Swedish, Danish, German and Dutch. Curiously there are no known *Titanic* songs in the Irish language. For many years an American folklorist, the late D K Wilgus, studied the *Titanic* traditional ballad complex, not just in the United States, with all its rich diversity of tradition, but also in Ireland and other parts of Europe. He considered that the *Titanic* disaster 'contributed to what seems to be the largest number of songs concerning any disaster, perhaps any event in American history'. Of the traditional ballads in English, Wilgus suggested 13 song types of North American origin and nine individual songs of Irish origin. No songs appear to have originated in England. Considering significant differences between Irish and American songs, Wilgus felt that most Irish songs tended to praise the captain and the crew of *Titanic*, while the American songs tended to lambaste them (Wilgus 1977). Certainly the songs and related material in Black American tradition are characterised by assertions of superiority over the white authority structure on board *Titanic* (Jackson 1972).

For many in 1912, the loss of *Titanic* was rich in symbolic significance. Her sinking called into question the established order of things. It deeply troubled those who implicitly believed in a good and merciful God. For others, the disaster was widely regarded as a fateful warning, or confirmed their belief in divine retribution for human conceit and arrogance. It seemed to demonstrate the folly of man's presumption and vanity that nature could be a conquest of science. In a speech in 1909, Winston Churchill had proclaimed the advent of a new *Titanic* world.

> We have arrived at a new time – and with this new time, strange methods, huge forces and combinations – a *Titanic* world – have spread all around us (Rees 1993).

Now in 1912 the Bishop of Winchester preached its nadir:

> When has such a mighty lesson against our confidence and trust in power, machinery and money been shot through the nation? The *Titanic*, name and thing, will stand for a monument and warning to human presumption (Brinnin 1972, 378).

Feelings of loss, bewilderment and the pointing of lessons were expressed in a cathartic outpouring of popular verse. There was an irresistible urge to string the lyre, invoke the Muse and, in the seventeenth-century phrase, indulge in pious ejaculation. Although often written from the heart, most of it comprised a desert of doggerel. However, this is not to diminish its social, cultural and historical significances, which are often considerable. In Belfast, a shipyard versifier composed *The Big Boat 401* and this evocative eight-verse poem provides a valuable insight into post-disaster shipyard attitudes. A number of shipyard men were lost with *Titanic,* including Thomas Andrews, the Chief Designer and Managing Director of Harland and Wolff.

> In a shipyard we're all workmates,
> No matter what our state,
> For a falling plank has no respect,
> When sealing a man's fate.
> That ship was flesh and bone of us;
> We loved her, and with pride
> We admire the men and women
> Who like heroes on her died.

> We know although we've lost them,
> And their work on earth is done,
> The world has learned a lesson
> From the big boat 401.
> The greatest wisdom of mankind
> Is foolishness with God;
> If he denounces anything,
> Then man must ne'er applaud.

Retributional religiosity characterised post-disaster *Titanic* folklore in the Belfast shipyards and beyond. Its key theme was come-uppance for wrong-doing in the form of vanity or bigotry. Many shipyard workers believed that an apprentice painter working on *Titanic* daubed the challenge, 'Let God sink this vessel if He can!,' in large letters on the hull, before painting it over (Johnson 1996). Following sectarian assaults on Catholic shipyard workers in the highly charged political atmosphere of 1912, the belief spread among many Catholics that the sunken *Titanic* had enshrined anti-Catholic messages, such as the alleged ship number '3909 ON,' which of course was a mirror image of the sectarian slogan 'No Pope' (Hayes 1994, 194–6; Plunkett 1978 311–13). That the ship was a demonological carrier, classified Ulster-positive, was of course of no relevance to the oblivious humanity on board *Titanic* when she steamed into the night in 1912.

With fearful symmetry, *Titanic* had sailed on her maiden voyage the day before the third Irish Home Rule Bill was introduced in the House of Commons on 11 April 1912. Unionist Ulster was in political turmoil. Inevitably, the creation and destruction of *Titanic* became a popular text which reflected the political, religious and sectarian tensions fissuring Ireland in the Home Rule crisis of that time. The remembered *Titanic* was adopted by some as a symbol of Ulster unionist identity, while others rejected this and regarded it as the symbol of a workplace from which they themselves had been rejected. Despite the passing years, this semiology of the past is still plangent with meaning today.

> The Orangemen carried lush ornate banners portraying scenes of Ulster's darkest days – the sinking of the *Titanic* in 1912, the Battle of the Somme in 1916. 'Prepare to meet thy God', 'The wages of sin is death', were the messages (Suzanne Breen reporting the Belfast Twelfth of July in the *Irish Times*, 13 July 1996).[1]

The cultural response to the sinking of *Titanic* was a remarkable phenomenon. Overwhelmingly it was popular and vernacular, but artists and writers also expressed the catastrophic event in terms of their individual imagination and vision of humanity. For the novelist and poet, Thomas Hardy, the destruction of *Titanic* was a dramatic confirmation of his view that man existed at the whim of nature. The collision of ship and iceberg precisely reflected Hardy's sense of an 'ironic will' governing a universe where man was the victim of destiny rather than its master. Hardy's poem *The Convergence of the Twain* was a powerful working of this theme.

> And as the smart ship grew
> In stature, grace, and hue,
> In shadowy silent distance grew the Iceberg too.
>
> Alien they seemed to be:
> No mortal eye could see
> The intimate welding of their later history.

The monumental dimension of the disaster and its meanings for humanity were also refracted through the imagination of the expressionist painter

Max Beckman, in his painting *The Sinking of the Titanic*. In 1912 Beckman was photographed in his Berlin studio seated beside the giant canvas. The photograph was intended to project a self-image of the artist who, in the view of the critic Hans Belting, 'interprets the world and thereby asserts his dominion over it'. Belting has suggested that Beckman's depiction of the ocean-liner catastrophe in the icy waters was intended to portray a human fable in contemporary guise, the tragic life and death struggle and the stubborn self-assertion of man (Belting 1989, 17–18).

The destruction of *Titanic* by a spur of ice shattered popular faith in the supremacy of technology, progress and privilege. The age of self-confident belief in the inexorable progress of society through the appliance of science was over. In retrospect, the utter failure of this microcosmic machine and all that it represented, symbolised the end of the nineteenth century. The twentieth century had begun. The day of Salman Rushdie's *'Titanic Verses'* and other *Titanic* jokes was at hand!

Jokes constitute a familiar genre of Titanicism. They range from the *Iceberg/Goldberg – I don't care what your name is –* variety to the formulaic question and answer type such as, 'Q. What is the difference between *Titanic* and Saddam Hussein? A. The *Titanic* had a band when it went down.' Of course, *Titanic* jokes form part of a wider constituency of disaster jokes, many of which are a play on technological dependence and subsequent failure. The corpus of disaster jokes includes a large number of American *Challenger* jokes, together with eastern European and Russian jokes on the Chernobyl experience (Oring 1987, Kürti 1988). In general, the more recent the disaster the more such jokes are regarded as being in bad taste. For example, jokes about the 1994 *Estonia* ferry disaster would be considered less socially acceptable than jokes about the sinking of *Titanic* in 1912. However, all such jokes tend to depend on paradoxical juxtapositions for their effect and are rooted in the disparity between real disasters and the view of them from safe and distant perspectives. The incongruities of modern media reporting, in which the horrific and the banal are routinely juxtaposed, also contribute strongly to the genre (Davies 1990). Essentially disaster jokes, including *Titanic* jokes, subvert authority and establishment, which of course is a key characteristic of popular culture and its contradictions.

Titanic as a religious metaphor is associated particularly with Protestant fundamentalism. Today in Northern Ireland ephemeral religious tracts are widely circulated and often incorporate a message based on the loss of *Titanic*. The disaster is perceived as an ideal propaganda device, both for warning the unconverted about the perils of disregarding God's word and as a means of propagating the means of personal salvation, or being 'born again' before it is too late. In May 1988, for example, the 'Every Home Crusade', based in Belfast, distributed a tract entitled *The Tragedy of the*

Titanic. After a lengthy descriptive narrative, the tract concludes:

> The tragedy of the sinking of the *Titanic* brings before you Jesus' question 'What shall it profit a man, if he shall gain the whole world and lose his own soul?' Suddenly these 1502 persons were called away from this world. Away from loved ones and friends. Away to spend Eternity in Happiness or Woe. Where will you spend Eternity? If you trust in the Lord Jesus Christ as your personal Saviour, you will spend Eternity with Him in Heaven. If you reject him, you will perish.

Many Northern Ireland tracts are locally prepared and printed, but others have more distant origins and employ a more sophisticated means of communication. The Californian-based Chick Publications, for example, have produced a *Titanic* religious tract in the form of a cartoon booklet. It stars a 1912 go-getter called Chester who takes passage in Titanic to make his fortune, but fails to ensure that his name is in the Book of Life, with predictable results. Infused with appropriate emotion, the cartoon pictures are drawn with clarity of line and remarkable attention to historical detail. The use of *Titanic* for evangelical purposes seems to be a widespread tradition of long standing. In the early 1920s, for example, Scottish travelling evangelists, Seth and Betty Sykes, prepared a *Titanic* lecture, with slides, for presentation in gospel and mission halls. At appropriate points in the story, gospel choruses would be sung, the words provided on the lantern slide. The Sykes composed their own material and many of their songs were recorded by others and broadcast by American evangelical radio stations. In their presentation the *Titanic's* iceberg was a central motif, used to demonstrate the ease with which the Sykes's considered lives could be shipwrecked on the icebergs of atheism, Sabbath-breaking and the taking of strong drink. Although Seth Sykes died in 1950, his wife Betty was still delivering the *Titanic* lecture slide show in Glasgow as recently as 1980.

By way of contrast, here is a highly selective and compressed presentation of contemporary secular manifestations of Titanicism, beginning with Harry Chapin's remarkable album *Dance Band On The Titanic* (1977). The album cover is pastiche *Titanic* and the record notes include a Chapin poem which complements the title song and suggests its covert seriousness.

> A familiar name is being etched
> on the bow of Space Ship Earth.
> There are icebergs up ahead
> but life goes on as usual.
> Down in the cramped quarters of steerage
> up to the sumptuous salons of first class
> the ever multiple variations
> of oft repeated themes
> make a dancing counterpoint
> to the long low melancholy dirge
> of the fog horn. H.C.

In *Zany Afternoons,* Bruce McCall presents a White Star parody guide to RMS *Tyrannic* – the biggest thing in all the world:

> An area equivalent to Hindustan is devoted to food and its preparation aboard *Tyrannic.* Steerage is reminded that eating toffee in bed is forbidden. The boat deck is reserved for first class – the right crowd and no crowding. Gentlemen are requested to refrain from riding ponies through steerage after 8.00 p.m. (see McCall 1985, 21–31).

The sinking *Titanic* is a favourite motif for political cartoonists. For example, the front cover of the February 1987 issue of *Fortnight* magazine carried an Irish general election cartoon with party leaders Charles J Haughey and Garrett Fitzgerald fighting for deckchairs on board the sinking *Titanic.* More recently, on 4 July 1995, the *Daily Mail's* front page headline 'Time to Ditch the Captain', was augmented by a cartoon of the 'Toryanic' sinking with all hands.

Titanic has generated a tidal wave of books – mostly fact, but also fiction – from 1912 to the present day. Survivor Lawrence Beesley was the first to publish his personal account of the disaster and in 1989 he reappeared in Julian Barnes's best selling novel, *A History of the World In 10½ Chapters.* Walter Lord's *A Night To Remember* is perhaps the seminal factual work on the sinking and in 1958 the book was the basis for a highly successful film of the same name. In recent years, and especially since 1985, *Titanic* publishing has been very vigorous and profitable. Shortlisted for the 1996 Booker Prize, but alas not the winner, Beryl Bainbridge's new novel *Every Man For Himself* is a splendidly deep addition to *Titanic* literature.

In 1985 the *Titanic* Brewery Company brewed its first beer in Captain Smith's home town of Stoke-on-Trent. The first pint was pulled to the sounds of the *Titanic Brewery Stompers.* Other 'feeling good about *Titanic*' marketing devices and merchandising include:

1. *Titanic* t-shirt – 'pre-shrunk and washable. Remember the RMS *Titanic* by proudly wearing it'.
2. Rare coal from the *Titanic* in limited availability for $25.
3. *Titanic* fridge magnet.
4. *Titanic* Surprise ice-cold drink.
5. *Titanic* – 'the world's largest investment coin – still available but only a few can own one. The world's largest ship deserves the world's largest coin'.

Fulfilling all expectations, the eighty-fifth anniversary of the sinking of *Titanic* in 1997 was a vintage year of Titanicism. Of course, its advent had been proclaimed in 1996. On 25 November, *Time* magazine ran a feature headlined 'Disaster: that's entertainment', which listed current and upcoming manifestations of *Titanic* frenzy. The feature identified a CBS television mini-series, a Discovery Channel documentary, new books – including a cultural history of the *Titanic* disaster – together with a major feature film and a Broadway musical. During the same month of November 1996, the enormous selling power of *Titanic* and its place in the American psyche was further demonstrated in a *Titanic* shipwreck-illustrated advertisement carried in the *New Yorker* magazine for the Sonicare electric toothbrush: 'If sonic technology can find the *Titanic* two miles below the ocean, why not use it to reach plaque bacteria just below the gumline? . . . Sonicare. Amazing, isn't it?'

By June 1997, it was possible to have checked out a $6 million *Titanic* exhibition in Memphis, become a secret agent in a *Titanic* CD-ROM, attended the Ulster Society's '*Titanic* At Home' international convention in Belfast, visited thousands of *Titanic* sites on the Internet, experimented with a *Titanic* cookbook, and flown to New York for the $10 million, Tony award-winning musical, '*Titanic*'; dubbed by one newspaper as the 'Sing as You Sink Show' (*Daily Mail*, 21 October 1996), the production led the fleet of spring musicals on Broadway, not least because of its elaborate tilting set and dramatic upbeat songs (Franklin 1997). Prior to the show's opening, *Titanic* jokes swept theatre-land. They included the prediction: '*Titanic* opened on Broadway last night . . . There were no survivors.'

The 1997–98 blockbuster film, '*Titanic*' – 'the biggest movie of all time' – is also the most expensive film ever made at an estimated cost of over $200 million. During production, the director, James Cameron (creator of *Alien, Terminator* and *True Lies*), said unrepentantly 'We're doing spectacle. Spectacle costs money'. A studio insider has described the film as '*Love Story* meets *The Poseidon Adventure*'. It is believed more man-hours have been spent constructing the full-sized mock-up of *Titanic* than went into the original. However, to save some money, only one side of the great ship was reconstructed in the Mexican beach town of Rosarito. On set, the realism that Cameron demands resulted in numerous injuries to the professional stunt team and cast of extras in steerage. Reflecting on the meaning of *Titanic* in *Time* magazine during production, Cameron said, 'It's a metaphor for the inevitability of death. We're all on the *Titanic*'. 'Maybe so' responded *Time*, 'but at the moment executives at Fox and Paramount are probably feeling it more than the rest of us'(see *Time* 25 November 1996; the *Sunday Telegraph* 13 April 1997; the *Observer* 18 May 1997; the *Sunday Times* 27 April 1997; the *Mail on Sunday* 16 March 1997).

By mid-January 1998, just before '*Titanic*'s' European release, the film already had begun to look like a commercial and critical winner. Following its release in the United States at the end of 1997, the film grossed $157 million in only three weeks. With massive publicity, rave reviews and Golden Globe awards, '*Titanic*' now (in January 1998) seems likely to sweep the 1998 Oscars. Film critic Ciaran Carty reckons there hasn't been anything like it since *Gone With the Wind* (*Sunday Tribune* 18 January 1998). In Belfast, excitement and positive possibilities engendered by the imminent premiere of '*Titanic*' was reported under the headline 'Belfast told to stop feeling guilty and hold Titanic Day' (*Sunday Times* 18 January 1998). Writing the foreword to Twentieth Century Fox's lavish spin-off book of the film, James Cameron concludes: 'I know that my team and I have given our hearts to it, and tried to pass on the baton of telling *Titanic's* story with respect, with dedication, with humility and with love. Welcome to the ship of dreams. You'll find the life-belts on top of the wardrobe, just in case' (Marsh 1998). Cameron's '*Titanic*' is a rich cinematographic entertainment whose simulated reality powerfully projects the vulnerability of life and its dreams in a capricious and uncertain world. This is a major millennial movie, a *Gone with the Waves* of the 1990s.

By way of a satirical antidote to the contemporary American preoccupation with the *Titanic* disaster, Bruce McCall, provided a 'verbal lifeboat through the conversational icebergs of the social season's number one topic'. His 'titillating *Titanic* tidbits' included the following quiz questions:

The name of the *Titanic's* onboard band was:
(a) The Ti-Tones
(b) Salty Waters and the Nep-Tones
(c) The Tone-Tanics

And their closing number was
(d) Nearer my God to Thee
(e) Autumn
(f) All-request programme. (*The New Yorker* 14 April 1997)

Whilst McCall's lampoon is aimed at contemporary revelling in the *Titanic* disaster, it also encompasses the prevailing preoccupation with catastrophes and disasters in general. Of course calamity fascination has endured for centuries, but the present boom is not just remarkable, it is also big business, especially for the entertainment and media news industries. From movies like *Volcano* – 'the coast is toast' – to the Disasterama website and news stories about crashes, floods, plagues and genocide, we are voyeuristically and comfortably fixated on other people's tragedies, past and present, real and imaginary, and of course *Titanic* is the most immaculate and regularly occurring disaster of them all. Satiated on the historical facts of the sinking, quality magazines and newspapers are now offering commentaries on the wider meanings of the disaster for us today. For example, the June 1997 issue of *Life* featured the sinking ship on its front cover with the headline, '*Titanic* fever – why we can't look away from disasters'. The 12-page main article included disaster insights by sociologist Denis Mileti:

> People who are drawn to their TV after disasters are not goremongers. Their empathy is kicking in. What we're observing is the fundamental social mechanism that has enabled our species to survive. When the chips are down, we come together.

Writing in the *Independent*, on 14 June 1997, Reggie Nadelson was somewhat less optimistic. Under the headline 'The disaster to die for', Nadelson argues that the enduring legend of *Titanic* – from the seabed to the Hollywood Hills – provides vicarious sensations for an age and culture bereft of news, especially in the United States:

> Nervy times, though the end of the century is in sight. There's a millennial unease, a low grade paranoia brought on by the constant hum of stuff that lulls us, the white noise of infotainment and factoids, non-news and tab TV . . . But what consumes us, what holds us all in thrall is the safe adventure with a one-way ticket, the crisis in a theme park, the celluloid *Titanic* that, having gone down once in 1912, can go down over and over again.

In considering Titanicism as an aspect of popular culture, three key and interconnected characteristics can be identified. These are profit, pleasure and memorialisation. The first of these, profit, is premised on the mass consumption and commercial exploitation which are endemic to Titanicism. This commodification is nothing new. In a sense it was begun by the White Star Line, whose essential purpose in building and operating *Titanic* was to turn a profit. As the lost ship deconstructed on the seabed, it continued to make money for an increasing number of entrepreneurs. With the discovery of the wreck in 1985, its 'real presence' created new market opportunities for *Titanic* products, publications and attractions. In short, *Titanic* is a very profitable commercial property. With its critical mass, *Titanic* is the business!

It has been argued that popular culture is concerned with meanings, pleasures and identities (Fiske 1989). Pleasure is, of course, a mainstream feature of Titanicism. Part of the continuing consumer appeal of *Titanic* is that simultaneously it makes you feel good and glad you weren't there. The deriving of pleasure and satisfaction from the tragedy of *Titanic* seems to suggest that Freud's pleasure and reality principles can operate in reverse order. But what the hell! *Titanic* is big, it's sexy and it's a star. It's up there with Madonna, Pamela Anderson and possibly Joan Collins!

Naturally the keepers of *Titanic's* sacred history tend not to see things this way, for the obsession here is the memorialisation of *Titanic* and all who sailed in her. Just as museums are holy temples for *Titanic* relics, so *Titanic* enthusiasts are custodians of historical truths and gnostic possessors of arcane knowledge. The *Titanic* Historical Society is the largest and most senior enthusiast organisation in the *Titanic* pantheon. Based in the United States, but with a world wide membership, the mission of the THS is that the ship's 'memory and history be preserved for future generations'. To this end the Society publishes a regular journal, holds conventions and, most recently, organised *Titanic* Heritage Tours. As the pilgrimage advertising says, 'Hurry, Act Now, Get on Board!! We have only a few spaces still available.'

Beyond popular culture, *Titanic* continues to engage the imagination of artists and writers in whose work the tragedy takes on meanings beyond the event itself. Poets, and Irish poets in particular, have explored *Titanic* themes. Perhaps the most compelling contemporary poem is *The Sinking of the Titanic* by Hans Magnus Enzensberger (1978). Translated from German into English by the poet, it is an extended metaphorical discourse on human loss and the foundering of western society (Enzensberger 1981).

I can see my fellow beings going down very gradually, and I call out to them and explain: I can see you going down very gradually. There is no reply. On distant charter cruises there are orchestras playing feebly but gallantly. I deplore all this very much, I do not like the way they all die, soaked to the skin, in the drizzle, it is a pity I am severely tempted to wail. 'The Doomsday year,' I wail, 'is not yet clear/so let's have/so let's have/another beer'. (From the 33rd canto)

Figure 13   *Titanic: detail from publicity leaflet of Lagan Lifeboat Visitor's Centre 1994.*

Why is *Titanic* so powerfully rooted in our cultural consciousness and why does her sinking continue to preoccupy and fascinate us? What is the cultural significance of *Titanic* today and how can we decode its symbolic meaning? Part of the answer might be that the epic story of *Titanic* is a parable, or universal lesson, in the mystery of the human condition. The tragedy can be perceived as a dramatic revelation of human fallibility, but also nobility, in the enduring relationship of humanity, machine and implacable nature. The cataclysmic failure of *Titanic* was, and remains, a paradigm for the inevitable failure of flaunted technology. *Titanic*, the sunken signifier, resonates with us today because it is emblematic of a change of era, both past and present. *Titanic* symbolises and pre-figures our fears and anxieties about the precariousness of existence, the frightening possibilities of science, the failures of technology and the indulgence of vanity as we prepare to enter the new world order of the twenty-first century. We know that the *Titanic* advances of science, technology and late twentieth century capitalism, while bestowing material well-being, have yet no answers to the really big problems of the world. They are out of synchronisation with popular trust and confidence. As the twentieth century draws to a close, there is a feeling that in a way, we've caught up with *Titanic* and are recreating the future. *Titanic* is our *fin de siècle*.

Notes

1. See Brearton 1997 for further discussion of *Titanic*, the Somme and Ulster Protestantism.

Bibliography

Belting, H, 1989 *Max Beckman: tradition as a problem in modern art*. New York, Timken.
Biel, S, 1996 *Down with the old canoe: a cultural history of the Titanic disaster.* New York, Norton.
Brinnin, J M, 1972 *The sway of the grand saloon*. London, Macmillan.
Brearton, F, 1997 'Dancing unto death: perceptions of the Somme, the Titanic and Ulster Protestantism'. *The Irish Review* 20, 89–103.
Davies, C, 1990 'Nasty legends, "sick" humour and ethnic jokes about stupidity'. In (eds) G Bennett and P Smith *A nest of vipers: perspectives on contemporary legend* 5, 1990, Sheffield, Sheffield Academic Press, 49–67.
Eaton, J P and C A Haas, 1986 *Titanic, triumph and tragedy*. Wellingborough, Patrick Stephens.
Enzensberger, H M, 1981 *The sinking of the Titanic*. London, Carcanet.
Fiske, J, 1989 *Understanding popular culture*. Boston, Unwin Hyman.
Foster, J W, 1997 *The Titanic complex*. Vancouver, Belcouver.
Franklin, N, 1997 'The gem of the ocean'. *The New Yorker* 12 May, 102–3.
Goodman, S, 1985 'Titanic disaster music copyrights'. Manuscript in the Archive of Folk Culture, American Folklife Center, The Library of Congress, Washington, D C.

Hammond, D, 1986 *Steelchest, nail in the boot and the barking dog.* Belfast, Flying Fox Films.

Hayes, M, 1994 *Sweet Killough, let go your anchor.* Belfast, Blackstaff.

Jackson, B, 1972 'The *Titanic* toast'. In (ed.) H Levin *Veins of Humour.* Harvard, Harvard University Press.

Johnston, S, 1996 Information in a letter to author dated 12 March 1996.

Kürti, L, 1988 'The politics of joking: popular responses to Chernobyl'. *Journal of American Folklore* 101, 324–34.

Larabsee, A E, 1990 'The American hero and his mechanical bride: gender myths of the Titanic disaster'. *American Studies* 31, 5–23.

Lord, W, 1956 'A night to remember'. London, Longman's Green.

Marsh, E, 1998 *James Cameron's 'Titanic'* London, Boxtree.

McCall, B, 1983 *Zany afternoons.* London, Pan.

McCaughan, M, 1994 'Titanicus de profundis'. In (ed.) C Orr *The small Titanic: the work of Chris Orr 1990–1994.* Buckingham, Pinko, 1994.

McCaughan, M, 1996 'National Maritime Museum, reading the runes: *Titanic* culture and the wreck of the *Titanic* exhibit': *Material History Review/Revue d'Histoire de la Culture Matérielle* 43, 68–72.

Oring, E, 1987 'Jokes and the discourse on disaster'. *Journal of American Folklore* 100, 276–86.

Plunkett, J, 1978 *Strumpet city.* London, Arrow.

Rees, N, 1993, *Dictionary of phrase and fable.* London, Parragon Books.

Steele, D, 1992 *No greater love.* London, Corgi.

Titanic Park, nd *Titanic Park.* Belfast, Harland and Wolff Properties Ltd.

Wilgus, D K, 1977 'Prolegomena to a study of *Titanic* ballads'. Unpublished paper delivered to the American Folklore Society, 3 November 1977.

The Phoenix and the Lark: Revolutionary Mythology and Iconographic Creativity in Belfast's Republican Districts

MARY CATHERINE KENNEY

O
N the walls of republican-dominated Catholic districts of west Belfast are to be seen symbolic images of two kind of bird. One is a comparatively old image, that of the phoenix of Irish nationalism rising out of the ashes of the defeat suffered by the martyr-heroes of the 1916 Easter Rising. The other is more recent, that of the lark, symbol of the IRA rebel-poet Bobby Sands, flying eternally to freedom over the barbed wire of the Maze prison where Sands died as one of the republican hunger strikers in 1979.

The motifs of republican murals such as these are often copied from illustrations, either photographs or drawings, appearing in or on the covers of republican publications, such as the *Republican News* or the occasional glossy magazine *Iris*. The original 'Lark' mural design appeared as the cover illustration of Bobby Sands' prison poems, following the deaths of the ten republican hunger strikers.

This paper is concerned with the creativity found in the symbolism used by nationalists and republicans in Belfast; with the way this symbolism draws upon both old and new images and forms; and indeed with the cross-fertilisation between Protestant and Catholic symbols. I shall argue that there is much evidence of cultural exchange between Catholics and Protestants in Northern Ireland. There is also much evidence of innovation. Northern Irish culture (especially political culture) has emerged as a mixed form without the two groups losing their separate and frequently antago-nistic identities.

In this creative process, however, the Catholics now appear to have the upper hand. A concrete example of this is provided by the presence (in the mid-1980s) of two painted statements, one on Flax Street in Ardoyne and the other not far away in the Woodvale side of the Crumlin Road in Belfast.[1] One slogan (occupying approximately eight metres of wall space) in Ardoyne proclaimed 'This is Free Ardoyne'. The other, on the Crumlin Road in Woodvale, was more primitively executed but similarly announced 'This is Free Woodvale'. Both were copies of the famous 'You are now entering Free Derry' mural that had announced that the Catholic Bogside in Derry was a 'no go' area for the police and army.

Further evidence will follow of the creative use of symbolism in the context of conflict. By a creative choice of the more successful metaphors, slogans and symbolic motifs, nationalists have come to dominate the political discourse in Northern Ireland. Collectively, they have become masters of post-modern modes of communication even when they use religious or other apparently 'traditional' symbols.

They do not seem generally to have done this purposefully. The effect is partly based on the liveliness of folk arts among the population in combination with the global nature of mass media. Since imperialism has largely faded as a major ideology in the Western world, the Catholics with their folk-nationalism, are better equipped to participate in main-stream international political discourse characteristic of the post-colonial twentieth century.

Using Barth's 'generative approach' to cultural variation in Highland New Guinea (1987), we do not have to assume that, just because neighbouring groups fight each other, that they do not borrow cultural elements from each other and transform them. This process of symbolic sharing is a function of cultural and physical proximity. As Northern Ireland shows, generative processes of folk ideology, and the symbolic canons of political movements, are distinct even in highly rational and modernised places such as certain regions of Western Europe.

An active political argument is carried out in Belfast by means of a range of cultural genres including murals, graffiti, public demonstrations and riots. The opposed ideologies compete through the use of the same culture forms revealing the existence of a shared political culture characteristic of Northern Irish Catholics and Protestants. Diane MacDonnell (1986) suggests that an element of conflict is a normal aspect of 'discourse'. She writes, 'No ideology takes shape outside a struggle with some opposing ideology'. MacDonnell bases her theory of discourse on Louis Althusser's idea that 'formed as means of domination and resistance, ideologies are never simply free to set their own terms but are marked by what they are opposing' (1986, 33–47).

The Northern Irish argument is not always a direct exchange of messages between Catholics and Protestants. This is, of course, because of the historical roles of other parties involved in the situation in Northern Ireland. The third major party in the conflict in Northern Ireland is 'the British' (meaning the Crown, the British army, the police in Northern Ireland) but American and other international opinion is also frequently addressed within the Northern Irish discourse of conflict. In terms of formal ideologies (of, for example, Sinn Féin and the loyalist paramilitary groups respectively) the Catholics oppose the British and the Protestants oppose the Catholics. Thus the argument, and the violence, is somewhat unbalanced in terms of the choice of targets. But on the level of popular cultural forms (exactly who is being spoken to in any specific culturally coded message) there is also a great deal of direct debate going on locally between Catholics and Protestants. The 'This is Free Ardoyne/This is Free Woodvale' example demonstrates this complexity. Are the neighbouring parties (Ardoyne republicans and Woodvale loyalists) talking to each other or separately to the British army?[2]

This article documents the development and use of a considerable breadth of nationalist symbols from the mid-1980s to 1990. It looks at murals, processions and bonfires, but it moves on to consider the appropriation of images from foreign as well as more traditional Irish sources. The ethnographic data provides evidence for new approaches to the study of symbolism and metaphor in day to day life in Western cultures and especially for other societies characterised by serious ethno-political and sectarian conflict.

Murals

I want first of all to consider the tendency towards symbolic creativity and innovation in broad terms looking at a range of issues from mural painting to processions and bonfires.

Political mural-painting is an old Belfast custom. Walls in Protestant districts are often adorned with images of a triumphant King William of Orange on the banks of the River Boyne in 1690. These 'traditional' Protestant murals are executed alongside many newer-style loyalist paramilitary murals depicting the UDA (Ulster Defence Association) and UVF (Ulster Volunteer Force) and their insignia.

It may well be that the practice of painting murals in nationalist areas was itself something that arose from Protestant practices. Sluka states that before the 1980s 'there was no mural tradition in Catholic districts' (1989, 6), suggesting that youthful supporters of Sinn Féin spontaneously started painting murals in response to the hunger strike crisis at the end of the 1970s. He even implies Catholic murals are unrelated to Protestant murals.

Sluka is, however, probably overstating his case when he claims that Catholic mural painting is totally unrelated to the tradition of loyalist mural painting that was flourishing in the Protestant working class neighbourhoods existing in immediate proximity of the Belfast republican strongholds.

For example, he divides the nationalist mural themes into four phases: (i) before 1981, a preliminary phase; (ii) 1981–82, murals emphasising the hunger strike; (iii) 1983–84, armed struggle murals; and (iii) from 1985 onward, party-political murals (Sluka 1989, 9).

This schema is basically correct except that it excludes some other, less frequent, themes of Catholic murals, such as those observed by the present writer from 1984 to 1991 in Catholic districts in Belfast. One of these was a full gable-end mural of the Blessed Virgin (adapted from the Mary image on the miraculous medal) with the twin spires of Ardoyne's Holy Cross Monastery church rising in the background. This picture may reflect deliberate competition with the republicans for local cultural dominance by Church-oriented Catholics in Ardoyne.

Nor does Sluka include 'flute band' murals in his typology, possibly because they are a mainly Protestant theme. This writer, however, observed and photographed a mural honouring a republican flute band in Belfast's Short Strand area in 1990. In contrast to the usually aggressive or sometimes (para)militaristic names of these bands on both sides, this latter mural proudly proclaimed the 'Short Strand Martyrs' with a life-sized representation of a Catholic bandsman. Its relatively primitive artistic quality seemed to indicate that it was painted by youthful members of the band. Except for its use of a tricolour rather than a union flag, and a green (and not red) bandsman's sweater the mural was indistinguishable from comparable representations of loyalist flute bands.

In addition, however, although many loyalist teenage flute bands are named 'Conquerors' (South Belfast Young Conquerors, for example). I

Figure 14   *'Short Strand Martyrs' east Belfast, 1990.* M C Kenney.

maintain that only Catholics in Northern Ireland could conceive of identifying themselves symbolically as 'Martyrs', at least on the level of flute bands. The martyr – 'Another martyr for old Ireland' goes the song – appears to be a key symbol (Ortner 1973) for Irish Catholics but not for Protestants. An example of this difference is to be found when, in attempts to copy a successful republican tactic, loyalist prisoners went on hunger strike several times during the 1980s to win concessions from prison authorities. Whereas republican prisoners famously starved themselves to death, self-starvation never resulted in the case of Protestant paramilitary prisoners. This is possibly because individual martyrdom by voluntary starvation is not part of their collective historical and cultural scenario (see Turner 1979), and thus unavailable as a tactic in contrast to Irish Catholics.

Except for those painted during the hunger strike period, many republican murals do obviously belong to the international 'new left' and liberation movement tradition of political murals. Many republican movement murals in Belfast and Derry resemble, for example, SWAPO (Southern African Peoples' Organization) murals which the present author has seen in Namibia.[3] It is a genre that can be traced to the 'new left' student revolt of 1969 and to Marxist movements in the non-western world.

As Sluka also notes, the incorporation of purely religious symbols into the murals occurred during the hunger strike campaign. The republican prisoners who were 'on the blanket' or participating in the so-called 'dirty protest' against wearing prison uniforms, and the loss of political prisoner status in general, had long hair and beards and were naked except for a blanket wrapped around their emaciated forms. Photographs of these men resemble Jesus at different stages of the crucifixion ordeal, as portrayed in the Stations of the Cross displayed in every Catholic Church in Northern Ireland. This incorporation of religious images – in one major mural of the hunger strike period, located on the Falls Road, the Blessed Virgin appears to bless a rosary-praying prisoner – suggests a significant degree of potential cultural independence from official Sinn Féin ideology on the part of Catholic mural painters.

In the case of mural painting, then, a tradition which may have its origin among Protestants, has been used quite creatively by nationalist mural painters who have drawn on images from the non-western world, from religion, and indeed from their Protestant opponents themselves, to create messages appropriate to their own situation.

Processions, bands and bonfires

The cross-fertilisation between loyalist and nationalist traditions is clearly apparent in the context of the marching tradition, and the closely related tradition of lighting bonfires. This cross-fertilisation seems to have quite a long history. For example, Baker notes the existence of a Irish nationalist triumphal 'arch' during an earlier period of Belfast history. She states, 'When Sandy Row raised its Orange Arch for the Twelfth in 1835, a Green Arch fluttered derisively from the Pound (Baker 1973, 95).[4] And nowadays the cross-fertilisation is still very apparent with loyalists increasingly copying republican styles. In response to the images of the IRA appearing in the mass media, republican publications and in the proliferating murals of their neighbouring Catholic districts, loyalists began to appear personally, and to portray themselves in murals in a ritual battle-dress similar to that worn by members of the Provisional IRA and the INLA.

And indeed, the tendency to imitate is often remarked on by individuals on the ground. As Michael King, the drum major of the Everton Accordion Band from Dundonald, a Protestant suburb of Belfast, sees it:

> Nothing that the one crowd has, the other doesn't have because its a copying thing. When the Falls Road had their Feis, and they were all doing their Irish dancing, the Shankill had their loyalist competition and loyalist concerts. Of course they couldn't use the word 'feis'. It just means festival in Irish. But the Shankill Boys just copied and had an Orange concert and had all the bands out. And if they could get Scottish dancers they got them, just not to be in the Irish tradition ... There will be a Hibernians' parade somewhere about the Falls on the 15 August. The bonfires are on the 14 August night. You see, there's nothing that the one side does that the other doesn't really.

Outside of Northern Ireland, the so-called marching season, which John Blacking called 'one of the most important folk festivals of Europe' (personal communication 1982), is generally associated with the Ulster Protestants since the largest marches occur as part of the Orange Order sponsored Twelfth of July celebration of King William's historic victory over King James at the Battle of the Boyne in 1690.

However, nationalists in Northern Ireland participate in their own marching season. The Catholic marching season is less symbolically and socially elaborated, and on a smaller scale, but is similarly based on their annual cycle of rival national and religious holidays. The celebration of these holidays are marked by parades sponsored by organisations like the Ancient Order of Hibernians and Sinn Féin. Many of the customs (formal and official as well as localised and informal) that are associated with these Catholic parades are remarkably similar to those of Northern Irish Protestants.

The bonfire customs, popular among Belfast children and teenagers of both religious groups, are a good example. The mid-summer bonfire custom is widespread in rural areas of Northern Ireland and corresponds to St John's Eve or the summer solstice in the Northern hemisphere (Gailey 1977). On the eve of the 12 July in Protestant districts and on the eve of 15 August (the Feast of the Assumption, called locally 'Lady Day') in many Catholic districts, giant bonfires are ignited. Buckley and Anderson explain this curious association of bonfires and parades by citing the historical patterning of organisations like the Orange Order and the Ancient Order of Hibernians on the Masons. 'As with the guilds, Freemasons annually celebrated their patron saint's day (the Feast of St John the Baptist) with a procession at which were displayed flags regalia and emblems' (Buckley and Anderson 1988, 1). St John's Day (22 June) has as its eve the date of the midsummer bonfires burned in Ireland and other parts of Europe from quite early times. In this way, according to Buckley (personal communication 1991), bonfire celebrations probably became linked with parades in popular custom.

As the date of the communal holiday approaches, children and youths collect firewood and all other flammable debris and carefully construct a cone-shaped pile (often quite large) to serve as their street's bonfire. During the 1980s, it was the prevalent custom for teenage males to venture into enemy territory (an adjacent neighbourhood primarily inhabited by members of the hostile religion) and steal flags and other symbols (usually Irish tricolours in the case of Protestant raiders and Union Jacks and Ulster flags in the case of Catholics) to display as the crowning touch on the top of the bonfire piles and thus to burn on the night of the bonfire parties in an expression of political and communal solidarity with one's own and to insult and symbolically injure the other group.

Republican symbolic innovation is also evident in the successful adaptation of the Northern Irish Catholic 'marching season' or calendar of communal rituals to the political programme of Sinn Féin. Informants (young adults) in Ardoyne said that, when they were children, the bonfires were burned in the Catholic districts on the eve of 15 August – the eve of the Feast of the Assumption – when the Hibernians marched.[5]

A new date and a new meaning have been associated with bonfire customs in Belfast's Catholic districts by the Provisional IRA and Sinn Fèin's community politics. Since the beginning of the 1980s the republicans have officially defined what was historically a communal celebration as a political commemoration.[6]

It is of interest that the children who collect wood for the bonfires do not always manage correctly to understand the official ideology associated with the new version of the holiday.

In August 1985, I asked one boy, who was busy arranging boards and pieces of derelict furniture on one of the smaller bonfires located in a side street of Ardoyne:

M C Kenney: Why are you and your friends building this bonfire?
Boy: It's some kind of anniversary.
M C Kenney: Of what?
Boy: Of when lots of people got killed. There is one big bonfire that burns through to the 15 August when the bands march.

Another bonfire was topped with a primitive effigy. It was constructed out of a Union Jack muscle shirt stretched on crossed sticks and stuffed with a wad of rags. A plastic Halloween mask was tacked on as the head. I asked a little boy, aged six or seven, about it and, smiling proudly, he replied, 'We've got a big provie on top of our bonfire'. Why do you think he's a provie (an IRA man)?, I asked. 'Because of the flag'.

The ideological confusions of both younger and older youth in republican districts suggest that Sluka's explanations of the motivations for Catholic mural painting are slanted too much in the direction of the official ideology of Sinn Féin. The Provisional IRA and Sinn Féin represent, even in the Catholic enclaves of Belfast, distinct factions within the nationalist community. The republicans by no means enjoy the unconditional approval of all Catholics in Belfast's Catholic working class districts. As a newcomer to Ardoyne (a Provisional IRA stronghold in North Belfast) put it, 'You don't have to like the IRA but you do have to be anti-Brit', (i.e., to be socially accepted as a outsider in the district). In this case, the newcomer was herself a Northern Irish Catholic from rural County Down.

Symbolic innovation: warriors on the Falls Road

Northern Ireland can impress an outside observer as a very strange place. That may be one reason why many sociologists and anthropologists strive relentlessly to represent the political situation there as highly rational. Social scientists often screen the anachronistic and carnivalesque aspects of events out of their accounts possibly because such perceptions are incompatible with dominant theories of conflict or even out of fear that readers may question the author's objectivity. But these seemingly contradictory aspects invoke, in Stephen Tyler's words, 'the fragmentary nature of the post-modern world' (1986, 132). However, this can be interpreted, in the context of Belfast's paramilitary dominated districts, as a substantial capacity for cultural creativity among Northern Irish nationalists, (especially among republicans) combined with the ability to catch the attention and attract the sympathy of the world.

An example of the 'decentered' (Jameson 1981) nature of the post-modern situation in Northern Ireland occurred in the Falls Road area of Belfast in 1985 when native Americans were to be seen on the Falls Road. This event also provides an example of the way that ideas with symbolic import can be quickly taken up across the sectarian divide.

Sinn Féin was host to the delegation from AIM (American Indian Movement) that was touring Western Europe to publicise their cause against the government of the United States. One of the events, connected with the visit of the group of Native Americans from the Pine Ridge Reservation in South Dakota, was a public meeting in an empty factory used as a community centre for the lower Falls Road district. The old flour mill is located across the Falls Road from the high-rise tower of the Divis Flats housing estate – the scene of many confrontations between the British army and the Provisional IRA.

The delegation consisted of about 12 young Lakota men and women from the Pine Ridge Reservation in South Dakota. It included some well-known AIM (American Indian Movement) leaders. Floyd Westerman, the Sioux folk singer and film actor (he later had a major role in Kevin Costner's Hollywood movie *Dances with Wolves*), started the event with a concert that included the satirical song 'Here Come the Anthros'.

Then, Clyde Bellacourt, looking very romantic and exotic in his shoulder length hair, beads and feathers, cowboy boots and blue jeans, addressed the 100 or so people present in the little hall in the old Conway flour mill. He greeted the crowd by warmly thanking the people of the Falls for their hospitality, since the AIM delegation were staying with families in the district. He said that the members of his group felt very close to the Catholic people of Belfast because they had the experience of staying with them in their homes and enjoying their hospitality. He said that his group was impressed because they 'had never seen white people living in such miserable conditions'. Bellacourt repeatedly referred to the members of the AIM delegation as 'warriors' and expressed 'solidarity with Sinn Féin and the warriors of the IRA who are here tonight'. Comparisons were made between republican prisoners in Maze Prison and the imprisoned AIM leader, Leonard Peltier, who took part in the armed confrontation with the FBI at Wounded Knee, South Dakota, in the 1970s. The AIM spokesman expressed sympathy for his hosts saying: 'The Irish are a native people' who possess 'a high culture', who were conquered by alien invaders.

The Sinn Féin spokesman, in turn, announced that Sinn Féin and the nationalist people of the Falls Road district supported AIM's struggle against the United States government and he commented that they had all learned a great deal about the conditions and struggles of Native Americans though the experience of the having the members of the AIM delegation staying in their homes.

At intervals during the programme, four Native American men drummed in the Plains Indian style (four men, one drum), simultaneously singing in the Lakota language. The same group appeared the following day to drum and sing in front of Belfast City Hall, which, at the time, was never used as the location of republican demonstrations.[7] When asked by a BBC television journalist about the purpose of their visit, the AIM representative responded that the group was in Belfast 'to support the IRA'.

This event suggests the diversity of influence affecting the official ideology and symbolism of Sinn Féin and the Provisional IRA. The republican movement officially affiliated itself with the Palestinian Liberation Organization (PLO) and the African National Congress (ANC), and the iconography of republican murals of the 1980s reflected these diplomatic links. On at least one occasion in the mid-1980s, PLO members, wearing head scarves in the style made famous by Yassir Arafat, participated in the Sinn Féin Easter Commemoration march on the Falls Road.

This arrival of American Indians in Catholic West Belfast had something of an impact on loyalist thought. AIM's visit was extensively and, in this writer's opinion, rather enviously) reported in the UDA's (Ulster Defence Association) monthly magazine *Ulster*. At one point, reporter Jim Dunbar claimed in his article:

> It must be said that we Ulstermen can find a lot of common ground with the Red Indians. In particular, we share a similar history in that their land was captured by American explorers.
> Ulster faces the same situation at the hands of the IRA. We too face near extinction at their hands. (*Ulster*, March 1985, 3)

A photograph, accompanying the second article on the AIM visit to the UDA's republican rivals on the Falls Road, showed a native American man dressed in full Plains Indian costume, including a eagle-feather war-bonnet adorned with ermine tails, probably participating in the Twelfth of July celebrations of the Orange lodges in Toronto Canada.

This attempt by loyalists to hijack the public relations success of nationalists was in fact only one aspect of a significant shift in loyalist thinking. There has been in fact a considerable attempt to redefine unionists so that (as in the traditional rhetoric of nationalists) they are perceived not as the invaders but as the aboriginal natives of Ulster.

On a more scholarly level, the writings of Ian Adamson, Belfast physician and amateur prehistorian, have introduced the concept of 'the Cruthin' into Northern Irish political discourse. In his book, *The Identity of Ulster* (1982), Adamson claims that the Ulster Protestants are the direct descendants of an ancient folk called the Cruthin. These ancestors of the present day Ulstermen were the pre-Gaelic inhabitants of the northern part of Ireland who were conquered and dispersed by the invading ancestors of the modern Irish. Hence, the Ulster Protestants are a 'native' people and thus entitled (under the rules of European folk-nationalism and of nationalism in the post-colonial word) to political control of their home territory.

In Adamson's scheme the partition of Ireland reflects an historical and cultural boundary between north and south, one which has been argued in more mainstream scholarship (see Heslinga 1962), and indeed, seen within the combined frameworks of Irish nationalist mythology and academic prehistory, many of his speculations are not unreasonable. By the mid 1980s, Adamson's idea, that Ulster Protestants are natives rather than settlers, had been accepted by significant numbers of unionists, among them members of loyalist paramilitary leadership circles in Northern Ireland (Buckley 1989).

'In concert live': a mass-media rebel performs

For some areas of the world, the distribution of cultural and political information through 'pop' music is now a major form of cultural production, and the use of the symbolic messages of nationalism through popular music is well established.

The lark-flying-over-the-wire symbol has, indeed, escaped from the local, and even the Irish, context and is to be seen as the design of a record cover. The Irish folk singer Christy Moore (formerly with the band *Moving Hearts* but now performing and recording on his own) recorded an LP, in 1986, with the lark and tricolour motif, entitled 'The Spirit of Freedom'. This recording is produced and distributed by a major company (Warner) and includes songs by and about Bobby Sands. It is marketed in Western Europe and North America, where interest in Irish traditional-style music continues to grow.

The recording also includes a song about Francis Hughes, also one of the ten hunger strikers who died. The song is interesting because it is written and performed in the ballad style, as a lament that eulogises a slain Irish revolutionary. The song is a variation on a traditional one. In an older rebel ballad, sung to the same tune, the verses describe the deaths of a band of IRA men, in a gun fight, during the Anglo-Irish War.

In the text of the song a young woman, somewhere in the lonely and wild Sperrin Mountains of County Tyrone, can be heard lamenting the death of Hughes. As she mourns, she tells how he eluded the British enemy by hiding out in the 'hills and glens' of his native country and how he thus frustrated the will and power of England. The mourner relates how he was captured only when badly wounded and how he was taken away to the urban landscape of Belfast to be tried and imprisoned. Upon his arrival in prison he immediately joins the protest, dons the famous blanket instead of the despised prison uniform and goes on hunger strike. She tells how he finally suffered a martyr's death in an H Block cell. As she laments, in the setting of the lonely mountain pass, she repeats that the 'likes' of young Francis Hughes will never be seen again in Ireland.

The melody and text of Moore's ballad are reminiscent of another famous Irish rebel song called 'The Wild Rapparee'. Moore's ballad represents a process of political legitimisation through folklorisation. These events and actors are in no way uncontroversial in the context of Catholic–Protestant relations, however.

The region referred to in Moore's lyrics is the Sperrin Mountains, a highland area in central Ulster, inhabited mainly by Catholics with a strong local republican tradition. A Protestant farmer, living near the foot of the Glenshane Pass (in the Protestant lowlands north west of Lough Neagh) expressed to me a quite different view of Francis Hughes and his exploits.

While telling of a particularly bad IRA bomb attack in the town some years before, he told me that Hughes was one of the 'outsiders' (Catholics from outside the locality) whom local Protestants suspected of carrying out the attack. In this case a bomb had been wired to the ignition of the car of a Protestant RUC man. The bomb exploded in the driveway of the man's home, killing him and his young daughter and seriously injuring his young son, according to the farmer. He complained bitterly that 'They knew that the children might be with him in the car that morning, for he often took them to school himself'.

The political folklore found in the song is not only produced for a foreign market. Christy Moore often sings his songs about hunger strikers and paramilitary members in context, like during his concert held at the Beechmont Leisure Centre on the Falls Road, Belfast, 25 July 1985. There he performed his rebel songs to cheers of 'Up the RA' (IRA) from a republican audience and he joked about the droning of British army surveillance helicopters overhead drowning out the sound of his music.

This process of the legitimisation of political violence, through its representation in folkloric idioms, has post-modern aspects. These involve the creation of a modern style of Irish rebel and the representation of rebels to themselves through the images presented by Christy Moore, a mass-media rebel. This is a process of the mirroring of images in time and space. Moore creates an international representation, out of local events and characters, and reflects it back to its local sources in stylised form.

The notion of folklorisation reflects Jameson's discussion of nostalgia as an aspect of post-modern cultural production (1983, 116–17) as well as Hobsbawm and Ranger's idea of the invention of tradition (1983). Paradoxically, these folklorised images of themselves have meaning for the people of the Falls Road (a rebel community) because such images are part of a global system of communication. People living in Belfast's working-class districts live in a media-saturated environment. Television and the consumption of pop music are a major aspect of daily experience in communities characterised by high levels of unemployment. Yet, unlike most of us, they also participate in a local 'oral tradition' (singing, telling stories, joking and other conversational arts). In practice, the two symbolic and expressive (global and local) forms are not distinct. They crossfertilise each other to produce new expressive forms, styles and cultural artefacts.

This process also has roots in the nature of 'the oral tradition' itself and in the history of Irish political culture. If tradition and mass media are now linked up in an increasingly undifferentiated system of communication and cultural production (as they now are in the third world), the oral tradition in Ireland has been linked to written forms in the past. Maura Murphy clarifies the role of the broadside ballad (a printed medium) in popular traditions of rebellion and resistance in nineteenth-century Ireland.

Broadside ballads were sheets of printed lyrics, meant to be sung to familiar airs, that were performed and sold by itinerant street singers. In nineteenth-century Ireland such texts often had a politically seditious (anti-British or anti-Protestant) intent and meaning (Murphy 1979, 79). This historical evidence indicates that the concept of a pure folk culture (orally transmitted and non-literate) is inaccurate in the case of ballads and other folk idioms in the British Isles. The dynamics of popular culture and of folk culture have been intertwined in this part of the world for a long time. Participants in living oral traditions have learned to apply the criteria of 'pure' or 'traditional' to their own materials, from academic sources and that is where the authority of the concept comes from. Pop versus folk is not a 'native' distinction.

Murphy discusses the role of songs and singing as political action. She says that 'the broadside was ... the medium of political stimulus for the peasantry and for the urban lower classes' but while 'public house singing ... belonged to the secret revolutionary tradition, street ballad singing belonged to the masses whose political attitudes were open, naive and – in the south of Ireland – aggressively Catholic'. She notes, however, that 'The Protestant and Presbyterian north had its own stream of (Orange) ballad singers'. It is apparent that the sharing of elements of (political) culture between Catholics and Protestants in Northern Ireland has been going on for a long time.

Seen in historical perspective Christy Moore's concert on the Falls Road becomes political, not in a way that can be analysed mainly in terms of rational or instrumental theories of modern political processes, but rather in terms of political culture. The singing of what Murphy calls 'the revolutionary song', along with other symbolic and communal acts, continues to play a central role in the organisation of resistance and rebellion.

Murphy's observations also suggest that similarities in symbolic and organisational strategies between Catholics and Protestants are not trivial. These similarities are based in common Irish patterns that reflect a mix of political and social conditions in the north that are as characteristic of pre-modern rural Irish, and pre-World War Two urban, society as they are of late twentieth-century Western Europe. Popular political action in Northern Ireland has its local pattern and modern revolutionary tactics mix, naturally enough to participants, with older political strategies.

The new strategies have by no means rendered the old obsolete. New methods of organising resistance and rebellion have been integrated into older patterns of conflict and social relations in ways related to the integration of mass media based symbolic processes with the practice of local folk culture. Thus patterns of local particularism persist to influence globally determined outcomes (Clifford 1988, 17).

Now, as during the nineteenth century, Catholic (Irish nationalist) symbols escape from the local context of their origins and become incorporated into world history as representations of Ireland and the Irish. This frustrates Ulster Protestants, who are highly ambivalent about being Irish, and who are highly conscious of having missed the main current of late twentieth-century history in terms of communal identity and its representation.

Conclusion

With the story of the hunger strike, and in the person of Bobby Sands and his symbol the lark – but also much more generally – Northern Catholics have succeeded in creating a set of internationally recognised symbols which escape the local, regional and national 'discourse' to join the electronic repertory of international political symbols.

Ulster Protestants have been rather less able to accomplish this feat of effective communication with the outside world during the past 30 years and, partly for this reason, lack significant outside recognition and support for their cause. Irish symbols escaped to the outside world both at the beginning of the twentieth century (the phoenix of 1916) and at the end (Bobby Sands' lark) and have been associated with other anti-colonial movements during the last 50 years.

The example of successful cultural creativity by republicans in Northern Ireland is partly based on the 'fit' of a localised political ideology with large-scale developments in the outside world but also with nature of a folk and oral culture which is still widely practised by Catholics and Protestants in Northern Ireland. In the post-modern world, folk traditions and mass-media phenomena are often mixed up. One does not necessarily destroy the other and the ability of individuals and local groups to instrumentalise elements of local culture is not usually lost.

In a post-modern paradox, we see how conflict actually contributes to the continuing practice of folk traditions of artistic and oral performance. 'Folk culture' is political in Northern Ireland and singing, mural-painting and story-telling are practised enthusiastically by both sides. At the same time they all participate in global culture. But this is why the republicans can benefit from, but cannot really harness the symbolic process to further the sectional interests of their movement. For, as we have seen, other members of the society can seek to use these expressive elements of their culture to mobilise for somewhat different (or even opposing) purposes.

From car bombs to political ballads to parades, all these forms are expressions of the shared political culture of Northern Ireland and thus available to all parties in the conflict. The actual patterns of iconography in republican districts should alert us to the fact that the Northern Catholics are not solely represented by one political faction. There are other voices to be heard if one listens to the discourse going on between all parties in Northern Ireland. Anyone who is interested can go and read 'the writing on the wall' in the working-class districts of Belfast.

Notes

1. Woodvale is the major Loyalist residential enclave bordering on Ardoyne. When Ardoyne was 'invaded' by Protestant mobs in 1969, heralding the beginning of the current phase of the Troubles, the invasion came from Woodvale (Scarman Report 1972).
2. Exactly who is talking to whom in my example is debatable. The location of the Woodvale slogan (facing the Crumlin Road and thus highly visible to Ardoyne residents) would suggest that the Protestants were primarily talking to Catholics but they were also challenging the British army and the Royal Ulster Constabulary at the same time. During the period that the display was observed (mid-1980s), the time of Orange parade re-routings and the Anglo-Irish agreement, loyalists were rioting against the police and protesting against the policies and actions of the British government. As part of this violent protest, Woodvale residents erected street barricades in their district and fire-bombed homes of police officers living in the district.

   The location of the Ardoyne mural (several hundred metres from the boundary with the loyalist neighborhood, across from the Shamrock Club on Flax Street) would suggest that the message was directed at the British army. But the question remains, how then did residents of Woodvale know that it existed, and thus respond to or imitate it, considering that the 'Free Ardoyne' slogan was displayed deep in republican territory?
3. These murals feature the clenched fist motif and incorporate weapons notably the 'armalite' and 'AK 47' automatic rifles as symbols of the IRA.
4. The Pound was the original Catholic settlement on the Falls Road. The maze of red brick terraced houses and narrow streets was largely demolished in the 1960s to make way for the partly high rise Divis Flats housing complex. The loyalist Sandy Row bordered on to the Pound.
5. The Ancient Order of Hibernians represent a rival and more moderate branch of Irish nationalism. Where republicans march, as in Belfast, the Hibernians do not march.
6. The Catholic bonfires in urban areas of Northern Ireland (and other republican strongholds) now burn on the eve of 9 August – 'Internment Eve'. 8 August is the evening proceeding the anniversary of internment when, in 1971, male residents of the nationalist districts of Belfast were arrested in mass raids by the British army and interned, without trial, on suspicion of IRA involvement. This 'Anniversary of Internment' is commemorated each year with a large Sinn Féin parade and political rally on the Falls Road.

7. At the time, the city centres of Belfast and other large towns in Northern Ireland were Protestant communal territory, meaning that only Protestant organisations, such as the Orange Order, could parade or otherwise hold political demonstrations there.

References

Adamson, I, 1982 *The identity of Ulster.* Belfast, Pretani Press.
Baker, S E, 1973 'Orange and Green: Belfast, 1832–1912'. In (eds) H J Dyos and M Wolff *The Victorian city.* London, Routledge and Kegan Paul, 789–811.
Barthes, R, 1988 *Mythologies.* New York, Noon Day Press.
Bardon, J, 1992 *A history of Ulster.* Dundonald, Blackstaff.
Bell, D, 1985 'The loyal sons of Ulster march anew: the new marching bands of Ulster'. *New Society* 73, 79–81.
Barth, F, 1987 *Cosmologies in the making: a generative approach to cultural variation in Inner New Guinea.* Cambridge, Cambridge University Press.
Buckley, A D, 1989 '"We're trying to find our identity": uses of history among Ulster Protestants'. In (eds) J E A Tonkin, M McDonald and M Chapman *History and ethnicity.* Routledge, London, 183–91.
Buckley, A D and T K Anderson, 1988 *Brotherhoods in Ireland.* Cultra, Ulster Folk and Transport Museum.
Buckley, A D and M C Kenney, 1995 *Negotiating identity: rhetoric, metaphor and social drama in Northern Ireland.* Washington D C, Smithsonian Institution Press.
Clifford, J, 1988 *The predicament of culture.* Cambridge, Mass, Harvard University Press.
Darby, J, 1986 *Intimidation and the control of conflict in Northern Ireland.* Dublin, Gill and Macmillan.
Fabian, J, 1983 *Time and the other: how anthropology makes its object.* New York, Columbia University Press.
Gailey, R A, 1977 'The bonfire in northern Irish tradition'. *Folklore* 88, 3–38.
Gibbon, P, 1975 *The origins of Ulster Unionism.* Manchester, Manchester University Press.
Hall, S and T Jefferson, (eds), 1975 *Resistance through rituals.* London, Centre for Contemporary Cultural Studies, University of Birmingham.
Heslinga, M, 1962 *The Irish border as a cultural divide.* Assen, Van Gorcum.
Hobsbawm, E and T Ranger, 1983 *The invention of tradition.* Cambridge, Cambridge University Press.
Jameson, F, 1981 *The political unconscious.* Ithaca, New York, Cornell University Press.
McDonnell, D, 1986 *Theories of discourse.* Oxford, Basil Blackwell.
Murphy, M, 1979 'The ballad singer and the role of the seditious ballad in nineteenth century Ireland'. *Ulster Folklife* 25, 79–101.
Ortner, S, 1973 'On key symbols'. *American Anthropologist* 75, 49–63.
Robinson, P S, 1986 'Hanging ropes and buried secrets'. *Ulster Folklife* 32, 3–15.
Scarman, Hon. Mr Justice et al, 1972 *Violence and civil disturbance in Northern Ireland in 1969.* Report of the Tribunal of Inquiry, Vol. 1. Belfast, Her Majesty's Stationary Office.

Stewart, K, 1988 'Nostalgia – a polemic'. *Cultural Anthropology* 3, 227–41.

Sluka, J A, 1989 *The politics of painting: political murals in Northern Ireland.* Unpublished MS.

Turner, V W, 1974 *Dramas, fields and metaphors.* Ithaca, Cornell University Press.

Turner, V W and Turner, E, 1978 *Image and pilgrimage in Christian culture.* Oxford, Basil Blackwell.

Young, M and Wilmott, P, 1957 *Family and kinship in east London.* London, Routledge and Kegan Paul.

The Symbolism of Womanhood

ROGER SAWYER

IT has often been thought that the condition of women under both Irish political dispensations is such that an apt symbol for them would be one which showed them in fetters or chains. Those, for example, who have campaigned on either side of the border for 'a woman's right to choose' or, in the Republic, for the right to divorce one's spouse, have seen women as, at best, 'slaves of the hearth'. One writer, indeed, has implausibly described the women of the Shankill Road area of Belfast as 'slaves of slaves' (Fields 1977). While it is true that, in legislation, women's rights have only belatedly found their way into law in Northern Ireland, and the process has been much slower in the Republic, the reality of Irish attitudes to women has often been very different from these stereotypes. Other views of Irish femininity have been reflected, accurately or imaginatively, in gender symbolism for some 2000 years.

The purpose of this essay is to show how more widely held, and possibly more accurate, perceptions of Irishwomen have developed. This involves consideration of how images of women in ancient Irish mythology have been used to give definition to Irish social and political thought in the nineteenth and twentieth centuries. After some exploration of the way in which women are portrayed in certain Irish texts, the interpretations and alterations made by later writers are considered. Attention is then given to the influence, partly in the context of a feminist-nationalist dilemma, of symbols, and their past, present and potential effects.

Oral traditions

In common with other cultures, the origins of Ulster's social attitudes are to be found in oral traditions; what distinguishes Ulster and the rest of Ireland from verbal manifestations elsewhere is both the richness and the multiplicity of the material which has survived. The richness speaks for itself; the multiplicity has had many causes, including the intervention of Victorian and Edwardian revivalists who took an already vast collection of myths and legends and breathed their own personalities and prejudices into them, thus virtually doubling (as well as confusing) this part of Ireland's heritage.

A large proportion of the rural inhabitants of modern Ireland, and many who only recently migrated to towns and cities, are only separated by a generation from an essentially peasant oral tradition. Illiteracy, which persisted among much of the population until the present century, undoubtedly gave story-tellers freedom to embellish, and in doing so they would only be following the example set by the scribes of the seventh to the twelfth century (and some as late as the fourteenth), who did not hesitate to impose their own interpretations of events. This means that, to the extent that they have not assimilated the values of late twentieth century industrialised society, people of all the provinces of Ireland have been influenced by a broad spectrum of colourful narrative in which women are often portrayed as having the upper hand. It may be argued that Northern Ireland, having been the principal industrial region of the island since industry began, has been cut off in part from the main thrust of this tradition. But Northern Ireland is more than an industrial community, and by one means or another old Gaelic stories, and the stereotypes which they produce, have found their way into the province's symbolism.

The earliest stories are unremarkable in one respect: in many societies the birth of an entire race is credited to some larger-than-life mythical woman, simply because the ability to give birth is limited to her sex. On the other hand the nature of the primordial women, despite certain outrageous characteristics, separates them from equivalent first beings of other civilisations. According to the earliest legend contained in the lost manuscript, *The Book of Druim Snechta*, Banba was there while Noah was building his ark, and the Flood did not reach the top of her chosen peak (Rees and Rees 1961, 115). But another tradition credits Cessair, supposedly a granddaughter of Noah, with peopling the place (Macalister 1938–56, II, 176ff). She was not as lucky as Banba; despite her alleged antecedents, her group of 50 women and three men were all turned away by Noah, who regarded them as a motley collection of thieves. Cessair only lived 40 days in Ireland, before the Flood came. The mathematical balance of her party, given that there were only three consorts, led to a brief division into three smaller groups. Then, when one of the men died, either because of an excess of women or because the shaft of an oar had penetrated one of his buttocks, two groups each of 25 women were left with two men. Only Cessair's consort, Fintán, survived the Flood.

Although Banba and Cessair are manifestly fictitious characters, their very survival in the memory of the Irish races must tell us something about those who believed in them.

As in the Biblical stories, '40' cannot have meant anything more precise than 'quite a long time', and years were periods of more impressive duration. Cessair found the time and the opportunity to introduce sheep into Ireland, and the one male who survived the deluge did so because he fled from the women and hid in an underwater cave for a year. For the most part, the names of these mythical characters are now either forgotten or confused by the folk memory. What is not so easily forgotten, though, is that so many of the early stories are female-dominated. Of the earliest colonisers of Ireland and Scotland (some five groups) most were reputed to be female, if not exactly feminine, in character. Putting to one side the Fir Bolg and the followers of Nemed, apart from Cessair's people there were the Tuatha Dé Danann, 'the Peoples of the Goddess Danann' and the Fomoire, among whom in the time of Partholon women outnumbered men by three to one. Danann was called 'mother of the gods', and her peoples, led by a king, had to cope with their rivals, the Fomorians. The Fomorian fleet consisted of four ships' crews, each of 50 men and 150 women. The matriarch of this formidable force was Lot, who had swollen lips in her breast, four eyes in her back and strength equal to that of her entire tribe.

The significance of all this extravagant mythology may seem to have been lost today. The overall message could be no more than that, in savage times, women were much to the fore. But other essential features of tribal attitudes to womanhood did become embedded in the consciousness of the kingdoms which became provinces. From the early period few names have come down to virtually all members of the present generation: the best known would be that of Maeve (Medb), Queen of Connaught. She still enjoys a dual symbolism on the island as a whole, having one type of symbolic power in Northern Ireland (traditionally, and more accurately, within the wider confines of Ulster or Ulaid) and a completely different one in the Republic. She is the embodiment of the external aggressor, or she stands for (female) militancy in the pursuit of a great cause.

The basic idea of the story of Queen Maeve could hardly be simpler: because her 'King Consort' Ailill possessed a fine bull, she wanted to acquire for herself a famous one that was kept on the Carlingford peninsula. At first she tried to buy it, but her messengers were ill treated. So she resorted to force, her adversary being Cú Chulainn, a warrior whose fame was no less than her own. This simple story has been told so many times that it can be used to prove almost anything. But as it was first written down (probably by Senchan Torpeist, Ireland's senior poet in the seventh century), the *Táin Bó Cuailnge* was little more than a series of bloody fights. It demonstrated that during the time of Christ, the early inhabitants of Ireland, like the early inhabitants of most places, were savages. Oral tradition, however, did not leave it like that; nor did the revivalists. The story was imbued with a 'Golden Fleece' quality; and a parallel has even been drawn with the quest for Helen of Troy (Gwynn 1923, 7). Later the Irish Amazon (though one of several) could be seen to be in the vanguard of insistence on female rights; alternatively she could represent Irish aggression pitted against an embattled Ulster.

The medieval manuscripts which are the first written records of Ireland's oral tradition, have been divided into four cycles, labelled the Mythological, the Fenian, the Historical and the Ulster. Maeve's exploits, including bloodthirsty accounts of her battles with Cú Chulainn, are recorded in the Ulster Cycle, where they have been adapted accidentally or deliberately, to fit different approaches to Irish/Ulster society.

Because of their distinct geographical and cultural origins, the larger-than-life characters who are principal players in the *Táin* have acquired dual symbolism in today's divided society. The unionist and the nationalist can hardly be expected to react in the same way to the names of ancient antagonists who appear to personify modern divisions. Rebel women have, as mothers, identified with Maeve by, for instance, naming children after her (though, doubtless, many Maeves were innocently baptised in the name of the pagan queen). Cú Chulainn can only have been spared equivalent unionist replication because his name is too cumbersome for the parents of today. But there might be another problem; Cú Chulainn has long been claimed as hero by nationalist and unionist alike; not only does he appear in modern Belfast on the walls of nationalists and of loyalists, but his statue stands in the hallowed sanctum of Dublin's GPO, commemorating the 1916 martyrs. Maeve's behaviour did not endear her to all traditions, but she is a much more potent symbol than, say, Deirdre. The reason for this must lie in the easier simplification of Maeve's performance which, in fact or fiction, was anything but simple.

Deirdre's story, recorded in various contrasting versions of *Lays of the Red Branch* (e.g. Ferguson 1897), may have spawned even more namings than Maeve's; but for most Deirdre is a name, perhaps a romantic name, lacking specific symbolic connotation, even though she is known as 'Deirdre of the Sorrows'.

Generalisations and their consequences

A remarkable feature of the supposed attributes of womanhood, which have been recognised from the earliest times, is that it is not as though women were or are a rare species. To endow half of the inhabitants of Ireland with special powers can seem to be a little odd, to say the least. One way of explaining it is to attribute it to generalisation of the characteristics of a limited number of outstanding individuals. Dominant women were regarded as the source of sovereignty. From the Historical Cycle, another Maeve, Queen of Leinster 'would not allow a king in Tara without his having herself as wife' (Ó Maille 1928, 129). Consequently she was wife to nine Irish kings. And Maeve of Connaught made at least three kings by offering them 'my own friendly thighs' (Kinsella 1970, 169). Women, not all of them at the summit of the tribal hierarchy, frequently arbitrated when succession was in doubt, and this continued well into times when the veracity of story-tellers was less in doubt. Qualities special to womanhood were not, however, solely the prerogative of women who were well-placed to exert influence. Another characteristic of womanhood, not limited by caste, was possession of magical powers. In the Celtic realm of the supernatural, according to *The Adventure of Conle*, 'there is no race there but women and maidens alone' (Rhys 1901, II, 661).

As the mythological period gives way to the beginnings of recorded history, additional specific powers of womanhood become clearer, and can be seen even during times when a *cumal* or female slave was a constituent of the tribe. Ireland's slave trade existed long after Christianity had reached Ireland and was not finally extinguished until the Church imposed its will shortly before the introduction of Norman law. Indeed, when St Brigid was alive, a *cumal* was worth three cows, and the institution of slavery persisted long after the Irish slave trade had disappeared. The coming of Christianity might have heralded the downfall of the old pagan stereotypes, but Patrick has been credited with using existing cultural traditions to serve Christian ends. If he really was as clever as this, his diplomacy does something to account for Brigid's translation into something of an icon for a broad spectrum of religious and secular admirers.

St Brigid is a suitable example of the duality of Irish symbols. She was either a member of 'Ulster's hereditary ruling class' or was born of 'a Leinster chieftain's liaison with a slavewoman' (Donovan 1994, 209–10). Commentators have been known to become quite heated if the approved choice is not made unequivocally. Whatever the truth of her antecedents, she has much to offer to feminists of both main political traditions. After a monastery had been established beside the convent that she founded near Kildare, the relationship between the two institutions shed some light on the place of women in fifth- and sixth-century Ireland. The bishop at Kildare was the nominee and the functionary of Brigid, the abbess, and of her successors. This official relationship derived from a combination of ecclesiastical precedence; Brigid, possessing both the spiritual and the temporal rights of a chief who had become a Christian, would recognise the bishop's authority within his area of responsibility; nevertheless, as the early Church followed the existing organisation of society, he was subject to her.

For women in general, despite the withering away of chattel slavery, Christianity inadvertently helped to bring about the division of labour which pushed and pulled them into a narrow domestic scene (Gwynn 1923, 31–2). Ideas long associated with womanhood, especially supernatural powers and the essential part which they might play in the endowment of sovereignty, never disappeared entirely. But religious influences in the form of monastic settlements shifted life from a tribal basis to a system of more stable communities, each with its own tract of land. Tied to a particular place, the roles of the majority changed. But the old order lingered on until the seventh century, when general acceptance of a woman's role as warrior virtually ceased, about a century after 'Adamnán's Law' was passed.

Adamnán, author of the famous life of St Columba, (Stokes, 1886, 99–100) was believed to have been persuaded by his mother to use his influence in high places to ensure that women were exempt from military service, and to make it a crime to kill them in war. According to legend, when travelling with her son she witnessed a fight in which a woman's breast was impaled on a hooked pike wielded by another woman; she then refused to move until he swore he would prevent such horrors from happening again. Only recently has an Ulsterwoman's right to be a combatant returned.

Gradually, at the lowest level of society, a woman's role was narrowing down to the hearth, and to what passed for the nursery. But in specialised fields, mainly at or near the top of the social scale, women did escape from the restrictions of domesticity. After the arrival of the Normans and until the Reformation, the lives of Ulsterwomen, and in most respects the lives of the women of other provinces, fell mainly into four categories: some lived the celibate religious life; the wives of freeholders accepted responsibilities at the higher level of the domestic scene, including making sure that wool and flax were spun, woven and dyed; poor peasants and serfs scraped a living from the soil; noble women carried on as before. When things went well, as they did, comparatively speaking, throughout the European Dark Ages, there were aesthetic bonuses, in terms of beautiful creations of embroidery, jewellery, and other products typical of an ancient Gaelic cultural tradition.

The Reformation served to consolidate this structure of society, in the sense that the gulf between what could now be discerned to be classes, despite the continued existence of the old tribal divisions of the island, began to widen (Sawyer 1993, 13). The aristocracy had sufficient education both to evaluate the doctrine of the new religious dispensation, and to appreciate the material advantages to be gained by accepting it. The lower orders were suddenly faced by the prohibition of the saying of mass, and nothing was made available to them in their own language that might have made them sympathetic to change. Those priests in sympathy with the reforms knew no Irish. The converted aristocratic women became more aristocratic; as a general rule, socially inferior women either settled for the domestic scene, which was sometimes little better than slavery, or aspired to be nuns. Admission to convents, though, was carefully restricted. Considerable preference was given to those who had some assets which, in another age, would have categorised them as 'middle class'. Others were admitted to carry out menial tasks, thereby to some extent freeing nuns for spiritual duties.

St Brigid's symbolic value never went away but, while pagan Irish women might draw inspiration from the last of their Amazons, pirate chieftainess Grace or Grania (Gráinne) O'Malley, for those who remained faithful to the old religion the Virgin Mary was the supreme focal point. An extreme expression of devotion to Mary, which made her a symbol without peer to those of the Roman Catholic Irish who veered towards Mariolatry came from Saint Oengus the Culdee: 'Mistress of the Heavens, Mother of the Heavenly and Earthly Church, Recreation of Life, Mistress of the Tribes, Mother of the Orphans, Breast of the Infants, Queen of Life, Ladder of Heaven' (*The Catholic Encyclopedia* 1912, XV, 463).

What effect did old Irish symbols of womanhood have on the attitudes to women in Northern Ireland in the twentieth century? To answer this question it is best to start with that part of the cultural revival which spanned the last years of Queen Victoria's reign and much of the reign of Edward VII.

This was a period of creative misinterpretation, or reinterpretation, of myths within which unionists and nationalists alike fashioned a whole host of characters to fit their own preconceptions. Few of those whose works were widely published understood Irish, and the climate of the time made the most prolific revivalists shrink from accurate portrayal of some of the habits of their heroes and heroines. As Lady Gregory said to the people of Kiltartan, 'I left out a good deal I thought you would not care about for one reason or another' (Gregory 1902, Dedication of Irish edition). And Lady Ferguson quoted her husband, Sir Samuel, as saying:

> Much of the material of the best classic literature is as crude and revolting as anything in Irish or Welsh story. Raw material, however, to be converted to the uses of cultivated genius, is not all that we might reasonably hope for from such sources (Ferguson 1897, xix).

Ferguson went on further to justify extreme forms of poetic licence. As he was quite open about such things, it is easy to forgive him, and to see his work for what he meant it to be. The emphasis by Douglas Hyde on 'pure Aryan language' (Ferguson 1897, xi) does, though, with benefit of hindsight, give pause for thought.

The revival was especially strong in the Glens of Antrim, but though cultural activity attracted the support of such southern unionists as Sir Horace Plunkett, the loudest voices were female and nationalist – perhaps the shrillest being that of Alice Stopford Green. Mrs Green, widow of the historian John Richard Green, was one of the most formidable nationalists. Unlike her husband, she found it difficult to express herself even-handedly on historical matters; single-minded devotion to the nationalist cause led her to pour forth a torrent of information which took no real account of alternative points of view. From Dublin, the Ferguson method of presenting what was not purported to be history had no political motivation behind it. In his *Deirdre*, for instance, he took the outline of one version of a myth and translated it into verse. Ferguson's Deirdre tells Noísiu, with whom she has eloped, that life in hiding has no disadvantages as his presence is all that she needs. His reply conveys a message that directly contradicts all the assumptions about womanhood that have long been associated with the crude realities of the Gaelic tradition:

> Not so with me. Love makes the woman's life
> Within-doors and without; but, out of doors,
> Action and glory make the life of man (Ferguson 1897, 370)

While the Gaelic Deirdre was fairly explicit when she wished to seduce a male – 'I'd pick a game young bull like you', (Kinsella 1970, 12) she said, preferring Noísiu to the king of Ulster – Ferguson's heroine became an idealised figure who belonged in a romantic age of chivalry; the visual imagery became distinctly Pre-Raphaelite. When he writes about Maeve, he regrets 'turgid extravagances and exaggerations', (Ferguson 1897, 142) and no references are made to urination or copulation. The trouble is that, shorn of excesses, the figure of Maeve has little to offer to posterity – a point that more politically-minded revivalists seemed quick to appreciate. Which goes to show that symbols may be just as likely to be engineered as to evolve.

Effects of education

Naturally the schools provide a principal means of perpetuating or ignoring potent symbols and stereotypes. As far as the oldest subject matter goes, relevance to today's curriculum is not a clear-cut issue. It does not, in a conventional sense, come within the remit of history departments, if for no other reason than that much magic intrudes. For scholars, the material has a considerable bearing on archaeological studies, as the myths and legends often celebrate events at places which can be identified. In the Republic, where educators have, for cultural or political motives, laid great stress on the teaching of the Irish language, there has been no problem in preserving a good deal of what Lady Gregory wanted to be known. But its place in the schools of Northern Ireland is a little more complicated.

Ever since Northern Ireland accepted responsibility for its own internal affairs, the almost exclusively Protestant grammar and secondary intermediate schools have, for the most part, placed virtually no emphasis on this aspect of Ulster's heritage; though there has been a late recognition of the fact that the nature of Ulster's part of this tradition is not necessarily subservient to an all-embracing island culture. This, in itself, means that a political as well as a cultural judgement is being made.

The schools which came under the management of the Council for Catholic Maintained Schools, if only because the majority of their parents belong to the nationalist tradition, can cope to some extent with this pagan material, at any rate in the sanitised versions which the late Victorian revivalists provided for them. Not for nothing is it more reliable to detect the religion of citizens of Northern Ireland on the basis of their Christian names rather than their surnames, if both have not already been transliterated into a modern brand of Gaelic. As the bulk of the Roman Catholic pupils of Northern Ireland have customarily attended single-sex schools, there will be much instinctive selection of what is appropriate for girls, and what is appropriate for boys – something which is not always recognised as a problem for integrated state schools and co-educational independent schools. All denominations should be happy to find promotion of this part of their heritage as the responsibility of the English department. As Lady Wilde put it, much of it is expressed 'in the Irish-English which preserves so much of the expressive idiom of the antique tongue' (Wilde 1888, xi).

Religious symbolism – though often differing dramatically according to denomination – does not represent such wide gulfs when seen in terms of moral attitudes to women. The Reverend Ian Paisley has said that Roman Catholic families embrace 'the ethos of the nunnery – seen and not heard', (Sawyer, tape recorded interview, 1988) whereas the Protestant ethos was one of liberty for the female. This did not prevent Protestants and Catholics alike from responding identically, though not for identical reasons, when the Northern Irish Brook Advisory Centre was opened in Belfast in 1992; moreover, representatives of each major denomination picketed the twice-weekly sessions. Both religious traditions deplore abortion, and neither is too happy about contraception – which is believed to encourage loose living, and actually to lead to an increase in the number of foetuses aborted. Indeed, uniform attitudes to sex before marriage have led one commentator to remark that 'The Irish museum of puritanism straddled the border' (Fitzpatrick 1991, 265). But, of course, the main visible symbol of ideal womanhood for the Roman Catholic is not an anonymous nun or even St Brigid; inevitably it is the Virgin Mary, whose singular attribute is a unique form of motherhood. Happily, gone are the days when a defensive Catholic headmaster cried out: 'They say we worship women!' (Sawyer 1993, 14)

Protestant symbolism is very different in form, even though in the final analysis the idealised version of womanhood differs little from that of Roman Catholics. Despite centuries of religious disputation, many areas of which have not been resolved, attitudes to women, and to 'women's issues', if actions speak louder than words, are similar. Each denomination has a core of those whose private lives are 'closer to Victorian puritanism than to Gaelic licentiousness' (Fitzpatrick 1991, 264); each, too, has its share of militant feminists striving to make the province discard what they claim to be outdated concepts of a woman's role in society.

If Roman Catholicism was symbolised by the Virgin Mary, it was likely that a corresponding female symbol would embody Protestant beliefs about the place of women in the scheme of things. Apart from general acceptance over the ages that a female personification of Ireland itself was the mother of its inhabitants – the Cathleen ni Uallacháin of so many nationalist, and purely cultural, writings – educated Protestants had been inclined to look to members of their own aristocracy for role models. At the summit of this hierarchy stood the Queen-Empress, too lofty a figure to be a role model but, having had nine children, and especially as Defender of the Faith, she was well-qualified to be the supreme mother-figure of her peoples. Simple parallels between two hierarchies, one entirely spiritual, one predominantly secular, might have been sustained had the course of events run smoothly. However, mainly in the early years of the twentieth century, new versions of old symbols came into existence because of the development of three powerful causes: suffragism, resistance to Home Rule, and response to the outbreak of the First World War. All had ingredients peculiar to Ulster.

Suffragism and nationalism

Unionist suffragists were faced with a dilemma: which came first, extension of the franchise to women or resistance to Home Rule? The violent acts of suffragettes could play into the hands of Home Rulers; loyal support of the Union could mean failure to obtain the vote. Southern nationalist feminists had their own form of the dilemma: which was the prior cause, suffragism or nationalism?

When, though, it came to violent action, the nationalist could be less inhibited, for both causes made life difficult for the imperial Parliament. In these days of social unrest, Maeve was certainly in the ascendant, but it was usually left to nationalists to invoke her. Although the Ulster branch of the Women's Social and Political Union persuaded its membership that 'The Englishman's God is property' and adopted a policy of destruction, smashing windows, burning buildings (having made sure that properties were unoccupied before setting fire to them), and destroying pillar boxes with acid – the emphasis was not on reviving ancient heroines.

Nationalist feminists, however, did use Maeve, and other forceful female figures of the past as propaganda symbols. The process started gently, with *tableaux vivants*, a popular form of entertainment at the time. But the old heroines were more effective as strong ingredients of oratory. Women addressing public or closed meetings, anxious to rouse a sympathetic audience, or to convert a sceptical one, wished to show that they 'were worthy successors of Brigid, Maeve and Grainne Maol' (Doyle 1917, 4). The last-named was more clearly recognisable than those who had preceded her by many centuries. The product of Maeve's region, she first achieved fame as a pirate with three galleys and 200 fighting men at her command. The dominant partner in her marriages, she was an easily-used symbol for more than one cause. The Brehon Law, which still prevailed in her day, guaranteed to women certain rights which were denied to female citizens, North and South, throughout much of the twentieth century.

Visible propaganda

The outbreak of the First World War, in which propaganda became something of a science, saw words reinforced by powerful visual images. Allegorical portraits of women were to be seen on posters and postcards. One of the most graphic cards was published by William Strain and Son, of Belfast. A lone, young, black-haired female is carrying a rifle which she is able, but not eager, to handle. With an indeterminate tartan draped over her shoulders, she stands with her back to a stone wall. The Union flag forms a backdrop as it flies behind her. At the top of the picture: 'ULSTER 1914'; at the base: 'DESERTED! WELL – I CAN STAND ALONE'. Although this is Ulster personified, it gives a good insight into a shift of approach to womanhood in the part of the island soon to become Northern Ireland; it also heralds further changes which will be brought about by the need for women to perform countless tasks long restricted to men.

The idealism of nationalist images echoed the republican movement's reputation for lagging behind when it came to the recognition that women, too, were individuals with rights. Northern Ireland's unionist women have more often been depicted in realistic terms; one might possibly meet one and recognise her as an individual. Nationalist representations seem more generalised, anonymous symbols; and this appears to be as true today as it was in 1916, when the formless white of diaphanous drapes was relieved only by the green, white and gold of the tricolour which the figure waved. Other than the rare apt witticism, there has been little to commend the ubiquitous graffiti. It has to be agreed, though, that some aesthetic improvement can be observed in the Belfast murals.

There was definitely something to be said for the republican mural which appeared the day after the Downing Street Declaration was signed. A woman with long red hair swept back by the wind, sitting on a rock in open countryside, releases a dove. She is clothed all in green, and the otherwise sparse scenery is relieved by the presence of a cromlech, a massive horizontal rock associated with ancient burials; the huge picture is framed in conventional Gaelic decoration.

These overt pictorial representations of allegorical women serve to demonstrate the self-perpetuating factor in symbolism: an inclination leads to the birth of a symbol, the symbol gives encouragement to the development of the inclination. While not every woman in Northern Ireland is a rampant unionist or a militant nationalist in her daily thoughts or actions (nor an articulate feminist), the Troubles have served to focus the mind on political issues to an unusual extent. This is in large part caused by the concentration in small areas of quite large populations belonging to rival traditions. The ghettos have long been uniformly working-class and the violence which has come from the criminal element of sections of these communities has usually led to the production of graffiti and murals which define an area as nationalist or loyalist, and which are sometimes calculated to intimidate.

The province's survival as a political entity had been so long under threat that the vocabulary of symbolism was in danger of becoming stagnant. Feminists have, however, laboured in the conventional arena of legitimate art to use highly dramatic symbolism to put across their message. A powerful example of this may be seen in Belfast-born Rita Duffy's triptych in oils *Emerging from the Shamrock*. The artist's concerns may be summed up in her own words: 'The central picture turned into a sort of self-portrait: Irish women, disillusioned with Republican ideals and the macho heroes of nationalism, step into the twenty-first century. The tableaux left and right represent State and Church, with symbols of death, hypocrisy and empty-headedness' (Rita Duffy quoted in Sotscheck 1991). Her target may have been more south of the border than north of it, but her images have relevance for more than 26 counties, whether or not one agrees with her sentiments.

Feminist artists who create symbols to challenge what they perceive to be bourgeois stereotypes, might expect to find it not too difficult to gain sympathy within the working class context, where harsh circumstances may prevail. They might also hope to achieve, as happens in other modern societies, some sort of rapport with those members of the middle classes who are not so much the bourgeoisie as the intelligentsia. But, if they were not engaged in political activity, the working classes have tended to keep their heads down; and the middle classes have distanced themselves utterly, and understandably, from radical ideas which risk destabilising the province and destroying its right to self-determination. Traditional images and role models must not be discarded too lightly.

It is a different story for those who wish to change society, but they, too, instinctively hang on to old symbols. When Bernadette Devlin (now McAliskey) came to write an account of her early life, she paid tribute to her mother by choosing as her title one which Elizabeth Devlin had chosen for a book that she was never able to write: *The Price of My Soul*. The

Figure 15   *Rita Duffy 'Emerging from the Shamrock'.* R Duffy.

price was what 'we must all pay to preserve our own integrity' (Devlin 1969, Foreword). The title implied that Cathleen ni Uallacháin was the preferred model, and that Yeats was the source. In his play, *The Countess Kathleen,* (Yeats 1912), Yeats's portrayal of Ireland's most familiar symbol had had distinctly ethereal qualities. But Miss Devlin's style and methods were much more in keeping with more earth-bound exemplars of Gaelic womanhood. One would not go so far as to substitute Aife, a female chief described as the 'hardest woman warrior in the world' (Kinsella 1970, 32), but there is a considerable pantheon of strong-minded women from which to choose. The point is that her mother, and presumably she herself, felt it necessary to fit, however tenuously or unconsciously, into the symbolic scheme of things. Unlike Yeats's Kathleen, she neither sold her soul to save the peasants of Ireland, nor portrayed herself as a self-effacing figure. Her behaviour on the Bogside and in the House of Commons was reminiscent of heroines of another stamp. She, herself, became, for part of the community, a symbol of liberated, politically-aware womanhood.

A group, rather than an individual, may be chosen to illustrate female warriors who fight within the terms of the existing constitution in support of Northern Ireland's political integrity. The old stereotypes are not only of use to radicals; the same symbols can mean different things to different traditions, and can evoke distinct responses from people of contrasting backgrounds. The Greenfinches are not a token gesture to the female dimension of the British military presence in Northern Ireland; numbering about 700, they were formerly members of the Ulster Defence Regiment. Now part of the Royal Irish Regiment, they can boast that they were operationally integrated before all other women serving in the British Army. Most Greenfinches may not be aware of it, but they are one of the most potent symbols of womanhood in Northern Ireland today; they come from an ancient pedigree, and they exemplify equality, in most respects, of the sexes in one of the last surviving bastions of male exclusiveness.

The Greenfinches' commander-in-chief, Queen Elizabeth II, besides being Head of State and Defender of the (Protestant) Faith, fulfils more symbolic functions for Northern Ireland than any other person living today. Although at first sight a number of these might as easily be fulfilled by a man as by a woman, the history of female British monarchy, combined with Ulster's special and ancient traditions with regard to sovereignty, motherhood and other features peculiar to womanhood, give a female monarch certain built-in advantages.

Moreover, a remarkable number of those opposed to the British connection concede respect on various counts for the monarch as an individual. Her personal qualities could explain this, but the mystique of the monarchy seems to come into play when many nationalists are actually exposed to it. A woman head of state has an appeal, even when there is ideological opposition to the throne itself, or even to its occupant.

The day-to-day manifestations of tokens of monarchy – the queen's head on coins or stamps – are the petty reminders of the existence of the symbol; they might be called 'the symbols of the symbol', and they might be dismissed as lacking social significance. But they do not. The mere fact that some nationalists have made a point of sticking stamps on upside down shows that the image on the minute piece of paper can touch a nerve. These are the particular details which reinforce the universal potency of symbols. They also show symbolism in reverse mode, as it were. The symbols which really count are accumulations of the influences generated by a number of great characters or events. They are generalisations and, as such, may be dangerous – as Maeve was dangerous. But semantics demand that generalisations be used; without them communication comes to a halt. All one can do is avoid, as best one can, the crime of over-generalisation, particularly when dealing with race or gender.

While it has been said that much truth can go into the creation of a stereotype, and this has often happened, stereotypes remain a dangerous species of generalisation. Symbols of womanhood in Northern Ireland, or anywhere else, have a validity of their own. But, by definition, they carry with them the marks of sexism and racism, if for no other reason than that they are the products of sexual and racial tensions that have lasted for centuries.

The future

What of the future? To take one example, Kremer and Curry (1986) have investigated on a scientific basis the nature and causes of 'myths and out-dated assumptions about women's abilities and interests' ('myths' here meaning 'misconceptions'), the aim of such enquiries being the eradication of sex discrimination. The brief of the researchers was 'to determine the attitudes of the people of Northern Ireland to the rights and roles of women in society' (Kremer and Curry 1986, 1). As is usual with this sort of research, questionnaires were circulated to as broadly representative a sample as could be found; then the responses were analysed. Unfort-unately, though, there were preconceptions which lay behind the vocabu-lary of analysis, and these tended to undermine the conclusions. Symbolism was not part of the researcher's vocabulary, nor did they acknowledge the significance of ancient stereotypes to this sort of enquiry. And yet 'stereotypes' were discussed.

The trouble with ignoring powerful symbols of womanhood is that the meanings attached to terms like 'traditional' or liberal', when applied to society's attitudes to womanhood are entirely at the mercy of the authors of the report. What, for instance, is to be made of this conclusion: 'Religion clearly plays a part in determining attitudes to women, with those individ-uals professing no religious convictions being substantially more liberal than other groups ... Catholics also tend to be more liberal than Protestants'? (Kremer and Curry 1986, 27) 'Liberal', as is revealed else-where in the study, is taken to mean among other things preferring pursuit of a career to accepting obligations of motherhood; and most liberal of all in their attitudes are divorced and separated women.

Is one to believe that Brehon divorce, as demonstrated when Grania O'Malley cried 'I dismiss you' to Richard Burke (Chambers 1979, 77–8), is an example of liberal or of traditional behaviour? Celtic secular marriage persisted for centuries, and was the norm until 1603. If one were to carry this misuse of terminology into adjacent areas of human rights one would be faced with even more confusion of issues: surely pro-abortionists could claim to be liberal in their approach to mothers, anti-abortionists could make the same claim in the context of their approach to foetuses. Until terms are properly defined, argument leads nowhere, and symbols can be manipulated by anyone. One conclusion arrived at by analysing question-naire responses was that 'co-educational schools can actively encourage sex-role stereotypes'. Given present trends in educational practice, it is not surprising that the researchers end their report with an admission of their own disappointment that a Northern Irish woman's first commitment is to the family. They express the hope that 'Oscar Wilde was incorrect in his assertion that "All women become like their mothers ... No man does"'.

For a truer picture of traditional attitudes to womanhood, researchers would be well-advised to make a common-sense evaluation of the symbolism that actually affects attitudes today. Both the Catholic and Protestant faithful have symbols – signs and saints – which reflect strong commitment to the responsibilities of womanhood in general and motherhood in particular. To take an extreme example, terrorist women when interviewed cite the old personified symbols as sources of inspiration; by this means they seek to rationalise their behaviour. Law-abiding citizens have no need for rationalisation. Day-to-day life in Northern Ireland indicates that for most citizens the religious dimension is reinforced by secular imagery that emphasises a woman's role in the wider world where, provided that obligations to the family can be met, a woman may aspire to the highest positions in the land. That she should do so is in keeping with the oldest traditions of the land.

Contrary to the common impression, in Northern Ireland the mother/wife archetypal figure, according to popular rural and middle class conviction, is today largely seen in terms of a matriarch, somewhat mellowed by the passing of the centuries.

This generalisation is, however, challenged with increasing frequency: a familiar and understandable, feminist complaint is that too much satisfaction is expressed with the principle of women exercising power, or rather influence, from behind the throne. Such a complaint, though, may be said to ignore too many lessons of history. Much interpretation depends on whether one looks at society from a social or an individualistic point of view, or whether one tries to reconcile these approaches. To those wishing to change society symbolism, selectively employed, can be a useful tool. But its continuous effect is, almost by definition, to reinforce the status quo – which it helped to create in the first place.

Those who wish to preserve 'traditional values' tend to take symbolism for granted. All would probably agree, though, that the various women who have contributed to the history of Ulster and its relationship with the other provinces of Ireland were not only individuals; they were the products and producers of a many-faceted symbolism which continues to affect the condition and varied attitudes of those who share all, or part, of their cultural heritage. Old representations of womanhood are too deeply embedded in the folk-memory to be easily dislodged. Maeves and Deirdres are active today, as are female icons of Church and State; they can be most powerful when one is least aware of their presence.

References

Catholic Encyclopedia. London.
Chambers, A, 1979 *Granuaile: the life and times of Grace O'Malley.* Dublin, Wolfhound Press repr. 1983 and 1986.

Devlin, B, 1969 *The price of my soul.* London, Andre Deutsch.

Donovan, K, 1994 'A woman's place is a woman's choice'. *Baetyl, the Journal of Women's Literature.* Autumn, 1994.

Doyle, C, 1917 *Women in ancient and modern Ireland.* Dublin, Kilkenny Press.

Ferguson, S, 1897 *Lays of the Red Branch.* (New Irish Library), London, T Fisher Unwin; and Dublin, Sealy, Bryers and Walker.

Fitzpatrick, D, 1989 and 1991 'Ireland since 1870'. In (ed) R Foster, *The Oxford illustrated history of Ireland.* Oxford and New York, Oxford University Press.

Gregory, Lady, 1902 *Cuchulain of Muirthemne,* London, John Murray.

Gwynn, S, 1923 *The history of Ireland.* London, Macmillan; Dublin, Talbot Press.

Kinsella, T, (tr.), 1970 *The Táin,* translation of *Táin Bó Cuailnge,* Dublin and Oxford, Oxford University Press in association with Dolmen Press.

Kremer, J, and C Curry, 1986 *Attitudes towards women in Northern Ireland.* Belfast, Department of Psychology, Queen's University of Belfast, 1986.

Macalister, R A S (ed. and tr.), 1938–1956 *Lebor gabála erenn, The book of the taking of Ireland.* (5 vols), Dublin, The Irish Texts Society.

O'Maille, T, 1928 In *Zeitschrift für Celtische Philologie, Halle.* Max Niemeyer Verlag, 1928, XVII.

Raithbheartaigh T Ó (ed. and tr.) 1932 *Genealogical tracts.* Dublin, Irish Manuscripts Commission.

Rees, A and B Rees, (trs.), 1961 *Celtic heritage: ancient tradition in Ireland and Wales.* London, Thames and Hudson, repr.1994.

Rhys, J, 1901 *Celtic Folklore: Welsh and Manx.* (2 vols), Oxford, Oxford University Press; London, Wildwood House, 1980.

Sawyer, R, 1993 *'We are but women': women in Ireland's history.* London and New York, Routledge.

Stokes, G T, 1886 *Ireland and the Celtic Church.* London, Hodder and Stoughton.

Sotscheck, R, 1991 'Dublin as "European City of Culture"'. *The Guardian* 21 June.

Wilde, Lady, 1888 *Ancient legends, mystic charms, and superstitions of Ireland.* London, Ward and Downey.

Yeats, W B, 1912 *The Countess Kathleen.* London, T Fisher Unwin.

Author index

General index